OCR APPLIED BUSINESS for GCSE
DOUBLE AWARD

Finance
Business
Marketing

KAREN HOUGH
REBECCA BENTLEY
EDITOR: JANICE AUGUSTIN

HODDER EDUCATION
AN HACHETTE UK COMPANY

Orders: please contact Bookpoint Ltd, 130 Milton Park, Abingdon, Oxon OX14 4SB. Telephone: (44) 01235 827720. Fax: (44) 01235 400454. Lines are open from 9.00 – 5.00, Monday to Saturday, with a 24 hour message answering service. You can also order through our website www.hoddereducation.co.uk

If you have any comments to make about this, or any of our other titles, please send them to educationenquiries@hodder.co.uk

British Library Cataloguing in Publication Data
A catalogue record for this title is available from the British Library

ISBN: 978 0 340 98739 1

First Edition Published 2009
Impression numbe   10 9 8 7 6 5 4 3
Year   2013

Copyright © 2009 Karen Hough, Rebecca Bentley

All rights reserved. No part of this publication may be reproduced or transmitted in any form or by any means, electronic or mechanical, including photocopy, recording, or any information storage and retrieval system, without permission in writing from the publisher or under licence from the Copyright Licensing Agency Limited. Further details of such licences (for reprographic reproduction) may be obtained from the Copyright Licensing Agency Limited, Saffron House, 6-10 Kirby Street, London EC1N 8TS.

Hachette UK's policy is to use papers that are natural, renewable and recyclable products and made from wood grown in sustainable forests. The logging and manufacturing processes are expected to conform to the environmental regulations of the country of origin.

Artwork by Stephanie Strickland
Cover photo © Sirin Buse/iStockphoto.com
Typeset by Dorchester Typesetting
Printed and bound in Italy for Hodder Education, an Hachette UK Company, 338 Euston Road, London NW1 3BH

Contents

Preface v
Acknowledgements vii

UNIT 1 BUSINESS IN ACTION 1

1 Business type – forms of ownership 2
2 Business activity – why and how businesses start, succeed and/or fail 10
3 Business organisation – how businesses organise themselves 17
4 Framework for activity – aims, objectives and mission statements 22
5 Stakeholders – their differing interests 26
6 Employers/employees – how they operate in enterprising ways, develop their working relationship and meet their various rights and responsibilities 32
7 Changing use of ICT – in business and economic activities 37
8 Uncertainty – risk, reward and change 42
9 Business within society – ethics and sustainability 47
10 Use of relevant terms, concepts and methods – to understand business and economic behaviour 52

UNIT 2 MAKING YOUR MARK IN BUSINESS 59

11 Getting organised 61
12 Understanding the market 65
13 Customers and competitors 72
14 Presenting data effectively 89
15 The marketing mix 93
16 Costing implications 107
17 Reflection and review 112
18 Sourcing work 113

UNIT 3 WORKING IN BUSINESS 115

19 Business structures – how businesses organise themselves 117
20 Job roles – key activities and responsibilities 121
21 Forms of communication 127
22 Functional areas within businesses 137
23 Finance 140
24 Marketing and sales 170

25 Administration and ICT 175
26 Customer service 180
27 Production 184

UNIT 4 BUSINESS AND YOU 189

28 The human resources functional area 191
29 The recruitment process 196
30 The selection process 202
31 Induction 218
32 Promotion 222
33 Effective research 226

APPENDIX 1 Blank documents 227

Index

Preface

This book has been written specifically to meet the needs of the new Specification for OCR GCSE in Applied Business for first teaching in September 2009. It has been designed and written with GCSE candidates of all abilities in mind to allow them to develop a better understanding of the way in which the business world operates. One of the key focuses has been on the stretch and challenge now required for A* students.

The book is not intended to be a scheme of work, but a resource which both candidates and teachers can use in the process of preparing students for the coursework and examination in GCSE Applied Business. The effectiveness with which this resource is used will depend on the skill and professionalism of the teacher and the commitment and determination of students. Material in the book will need to be adapted and supplemented with clear explanations designed to suit the differing needs of candidates.

OCR GCSE in Applied Business Specification

The book covers both the single and double award. The new specification employs an analytical, evaluative and investigative approach to the study of Applied Business. This will require candidates to both understand the dynamic environment in which business operates and appreciate the many and varied factors which impact upon business activity and behaviour in the 21st century.

The unitised design of the specification enables candidates to be assessed in particular aspects of business activity and business behaviour. The specification is divided into four units of assessment. Two will be evidenced through the completion of a portfolio and two by external examination. Each unit is comprised of discrete sections which have been clearly broken down throughout the content of the book in order to help candidates structure both their portfolio development and revision.

Candidates may attempt the Units in any order.

About This Book

Whilst the material in the book has been written to support the OCR GCSE in Applied Business specification, large amounts of the material in the book will be relevant to other business specifications.

The content of the book is not intended to be a definitive work, beyond which examiners cannot go in seeking ways to assess the Assessment Objectives where candidates are expected to:

- recall, select and communicate their knowledge and understanding of concepts, issues and terminology
- apply skills, knowledge and understanding in a variety of contexts and in planning and carrying out investigations and tasks

- analyse and evaluate evidence, make reasoned judgements and present appropriate conclusions

The limiting factor to what an examiner may set as a question in an examination is the specification content. For this reason, teachers must plan their teaching around the specification content using the material in the book as a resource upon which to draw. It is the specification content which is being assessed and not the book content.

How to use this book

The book is organised into four units, which reflect the specification content. These units are then further broken down into chapters which match the sub-headings found within the specification.

Throughout each chapter there are small activities which will enable candidates to develop their depth and breadth of understanding of the topic being covered. At the end of each chapter there is a case study which will help reinforce the candidates learning and help prepare them for either the external examination or controlled assignment.

At the end of each of the chapters found in units 1 and 3 there are examination tips. Throughout the chapters found within units 2 and 4 there are activities that will help candidates to start structuring their coursework. These chapters also contain portfolio tips. These have been closely linked to the scenarios which OCR has released to be used in conjunction with units 2 and 4.

Acknowledgements

The authors and publishers would like to thank the following for permission to reproduce copyright illustrations:

p2 © Alex Segre/Alamy; p6 John Walton/EMPICS Sport/Press Association Images; p10 BBC Photo Library; p16 Gregory Wrona/Alamy; p45 Sigrid Dauth/Alamy; p50 Alex Segre/Alamy; p65 Chris Howes/Wild Places Photography/Alamy; p75 © Thomas Cook; p76 Alton Towers Resort, 2009; p78a © BMW AG; p78b Motoring Picture Library/Alamy; p78c Elizabeth Whiting & Associates/Alamy; p78d © Stockbyte/Getty Images; p79 Rob Walls/Alamy; p86 Patrick Eden/Alamy; p92 Justin Kase zsixz/Alamy; p95 © Mike Ehrmann/WireImage/Getty Images; p97a Keith Morris/Alamy; p97b Alex Segre/Alamy; p98 imagebroker/Alamy; p103 David R. Frazier Photolibrary, Inc./Alamy; p120 © iStockphoto.com/ Brasil2; p121 Comstock Images/Photolibrary Group Ltd; p127 Ingram Publishing; p138 E. M. Welch/ Rex Features; p177 © Imagestate Media; p178 Chris Howes/Wild Places Photography/Alamy; p181 Vehbi Koca/Alamy; p202 © www.fotoie.com/iStockphoto.com; p208 LH Images/Alamy; p211 Photofusion Picture Library/Alamy; p214 NICHOLAS BAILEY/Rex Features; p223 © Catherine Yeulet/ iStockphoto.com; p224 Image Source Black/Alamy.

The authors and publishers would like to thank the following for permission to use copyright material:

p9 Yeo Valley Organic; p19 Samworth Brothers; p25 Warden Park School; p41 Moonpig; p42 *The Independent*; p44 Free Press Release; p45 Cadbury; p70 London Dungeon; p73-74 National Readership Survey; p85 Datamonitor; p92 *Daily Mail*; p99 BARB; p101 Digital Cinema Media; p171-172 Advertising Standards Authority. Crown copyright material is reproduced with the permission of the Controller of HMSO and the Queen's Printer for Scotland.

Every effort has been made to trace and acknowledge ownership of copyright. The publishers will be glad to make suitable arrangements with any copyright holders whom it has not been possible to contact.

UNIT 1
BUSINESS IN ACTION

Chapter 1

Business type – forms of ownership

There are a range of different businesses currently trading on the high street

Activity

Make a list of businesses that you are familiar with in your area. Share your list with a partner. See how many different types of business you have thought of. Look at the business name: does it end with plc, Ltd, & sons, & daughter, or is it simply a person's name? This will give you a clue as to the form of ownership of the business.

Sole trader

A sole trader is someone who sets up and runs their own business. They may employ other people in order to help them cope with the workload, but often they are the only person working within the business.

One of the advantages of becoming a sole trader is the ease with which it can be set up. The only legal formality is to inform HM Revenue and Customs that the individual is now self employed and, as such, will be liable to pay their own income tax based on yearly profits.

In order to start up as a sole trader the owner will be required to raise the funds necessary to get the business 'off the ground'. This initial investment of funds is known as the start-up capital of the business. As the business is only owned by one person the amount of money available as initial capital could be quite limited. Lack of start-up capital might affect the viability and ultimate success of the business venture. If the sole trader has insufficient funds to start the business they will have to investigate the possibility of external borrowing. Banks do not always view sole traders as a safe risk and additional funds can often be hard to raise. On the positive side, if the business is successful the owner will reap all the financial rewards. On the negative side, if the business fails the owner will be liable for all the debts of the business. Being responsible for the debts of the business could mean that the owner not only loses all the money they have invested into the venture, but also their personal possessions. For example, the owner might have to sell their house in order to raise the funds to pay off the people the business owes money to. This risk is known as unlimited liability.

A sole trader is responsible for all the decisions that are made within the business. This can work to their advantage as they are able to make decisions very quickly, enabling the business to react to changes in the market rapidly.

There are a variety of statistics stating how many sole trader businesses fail within their first year and these range from between 1 in 9 and 50%. The two main reasons cited for this failure are: lack of initial capital, and an inability to manage and run the business.

Consider the following scenario to illustrate some of the advantages and disadvantages of starting up as a sole trader.

> **Activity**
>
> Lilly decided to start up as a sole trader running a mobile hairdressing service. She already has a number of clients who would be willing to use her services on a regular basis. Spend a few minutes jotting down all the skills that Lilly will need in order to run her business successfully.

The most obvious skill that Lilly is going to need is to be able to cut people's hair well. However, that is not the only skill that will be required to run this business and ensure its profitability. Lilly will need to consider how to price her services: does she simply charge the same as her competitors or should she work out how much it will actually cost her to deliver the service? This should include the costs associated with running her car, the cost of her materials and the rate of pay she expects to earn per hour. She also needs to include other business expenses such as her mobile telephone bill and advertising costs.

Having decided on a pricing structure she will have to gain the knowledge of how to keep her financial records to ensure that she is actually making a profit on a weekly basis. In order to expand her business she will need to consider how and when to advertise her business. You can see that in order to run a sole trader business Lilly will need a lot of different skills.

The other problem is what happens to Lilly's clients if she wants to take a week's holiday or is off sick for a few days? Will they wait to have their hair cut or will they take their business to another hairdresser?

> **Activity**
>
> Using the information above, describe the advantages and disadvantages of becoming a sole trader. Do you think the advantages outweigh the disadvantages? Justify your reasons.

Remember that running a business as a sole trader can be extremely hard work, it often involves long hours and is very risky, but the rewards can be high.

Partnership

In order to combat some of the disadvantages of becoming a sole trader an alternative could be to start up a business as a partnership. This means that the people who have invested money into the business have made a long term commitment to work together. Each person who contributes to the capital of the business is known as a partner. A partnership generally consists of between 2 and 20 partners, but there are some exceptions to this rule: there is no maximum number of partners for accountants, solicitors, Stock Exchange members, surveyors, auctioneers, estate agents, land agents, estate managers, or insurance brokers.

Partnerships also have unlimited liability. All partners are liable for the debts of the business regardless of how they were accrued. So if one partner runs up huge debts without the other partner(s) knowing, all partners are still liable for full repayment of the debts. It is possible for a partner to have limited liability within a partnership. The partner(s) would invest money into the business but take no part in the management or running of the business. These partners are often referred to as 'sleeping partners'. If the business did run into financial problems the sleeping partners would only lose their initial investment. Within all partnerships at least one partner must have unlimited liability.

A partnership brings a number of advantages: there are more people to contribute to the initial start-up capital of the business, which ultimately means that the business might find expansion easier than a sole trader.

When there is more than one person working within the business there is a greater chance for each individual to specialise. For example, in a firm of vets one partner might deal with the small domestic animals whilst the other works with the large animals which are usually visited off-site.

This is the beginning of the division of labour. Decisions can be shared amongst the partners so there is more support. The workload can also be shared, enabling each partner to have time away from the business. There is less risk of losing customers if one partner is off sick or takes a week's holiday.

The partnership will probably have a greater initial investment than a sole trader would, and external financial institutions may be more willing to lend the business funds for future expansion.

On the negative side, as soon as more than one person is involved in the decision-making vital decisions might take longer to make – this means that immediate opportunities that require instant decisions might be missed. There is also the possibility of arguments and disagreements that could sour the working relationship between the partners.

When starting a partnership the partners should consider drawing up a legal document which is known as a 'Deed of Partnership' or 'Partnership Agreement'.

This document will outline how the business should be run and how the profit will be split between the partners. The agreement will usually contain the following information:

- The capital to be contributed by each partner
- The ratio in which profits and losses are to be shared
- The rate of interest, if any, to be paid on capital before the profits are shared
- Salaries to be paid to partners
- The role of each partner within the business
- Arrangements for the admission of new partners
- Procedures to be carried out when a partner retires or dies

All partnerships are governed by the Partnership Act of 1890 which clearly states that in a disagreement, in the absence of a Private Partnership Agreement, the Act will overrule any verbal agreement. This means that any profit or losses made must be shared equally between the partners.

Activity

Working in groups of three or four, consider the type of business that you might all like to set up. Using the bullet points above create a Partnership Agreement for the new business venture.

Think about how your group made the different decisions. Was it easy/hard? Did you take a vote or did one person take charge and make all of the decisions? This is what running a partnership could be like.

Private limited companies (Ltds)

One of the major disadvantages of starting up as a sole trader or partnership is the fact that the business has unlimited liability. This could result in the owners losing not only the business, but personal possessions as well if the business runs into financial trouble and is unable to pay off its debts. A limited company has limited liability. This means that if the business faces financial problems the owners/shareholders would only lose their initial investment in the business.

In order start up in business as a private limited company, the business has to decide how many shares it is going to sell in order to raise its initial start-up capital. The potential owners then purchase shares from the newly formed business. The owners then become the shareholders of the business.

For example – let us assume that Paul, Peter, Yvonne and Estelle want to start up a business selling DVDs and CDs. They decide that the business will have a share issue of 40,000 £1 shares. Each of them will buy 10,000 shares. The four of them become the shareholders of the business. The total start-up capital amounts to

Business type – forms of ownership

£40,000. Limited liability means that should the business face financial problems each of the shareholders will only lose their initial investment of £10,000. Often the shareholders own and work within the business. They will receive payment for their endeavours in two ways: shareholders who work within the business will receive an agreed salary, which is deducted as an expense prior to the calculation of net profit, and the net profit is then shared out between the shareholders in the form of dividends. Using the above example, if the business had made a profit of £30,000 the dividend might be 50p per share. Each shareholder holds 10,000 shares and would therefore receive £5,000. Any remaining profit would be retained within the company in order to aid expansion.

Private limited companies are often small to medium sized businesses which are commonly started up by family members. One of the largest private limited companies currently operating is Virgin. Private limited companies are not allowed to advertise their shares and extra shares can only be sold with the full agreement of all the shareholders.

One of the major drawbacks to setting up a private limited company is the legal formalities that have to be fulfilled in order to start trading. The name of the company has to be registered with the Registrar of Companies by completing the memorandum of association and articles of association

The memorandum of association set out what the company is and the nature of its business. The articles of association set out how the business will be run internally – the rules and regulations that shareholders will be governed by. This can help resolve disputes that might arise in the future. Once these documents have been submitted to Companies House the business will receive a Certificate of Incorporation. The business now has a separate legal identity to its owners. If something goes wrong in the business it is the company that is sued and not the owners directly.

Public limited companies (plc)

Public limited companies are another form of 'limited company' and are identified by the fact that they have plc after their name. They are usually bigger than private limited companies. They are also owned by shareholders who all have the benefit of limited liability, exactly the same as the private limited company.

The difference is that the business has been floated on the Stock Exchange, enabling anybody to purchase shares in it. The business might have thousands of different owners, enabling it to raise large sums of money in order to develop and expand. Shares can be traded between different owners on a regular basis, thereby enabling the possibility of a takeover – one person could purchase sufficient shares to gain a controlling interest.

Obviously all of these different owners do not work in the business and, generally, they will not be involved in the day to day running of the venture. The shareholders have a right to attend an Annual General Meeting where they are able to vote on a board of directors. It is this board of directors who run the business on a day to day basis for the benefit of its shareholders.

One of the major disadvantages of public limited companies is the time it can take for decisions to be made. A plc is often a very large business, for example Tesco, and slow decision-making could allow a smaller business to react to changing customers trends much more quickly.

All limited companies (including Ltds) are required to submit their yearly financial accounts to the Registrar of Companies. This is a disadvantage as it means that the financial status of the company is available to the general pubic and competitors to view.

Private limited companies who want to expand into much larger businesses are often those who decide to float their business onto the

Case Study

Manchester United Football Club

Manchester United Football Club was a public limited company until 28th June 2005. Malcolm Glazer had shares in the club, but on 26th September 2003 it was noted that he was slowly increasing his shareholding. By 12th May 2005 he was gaining more shares and had managed to take his holding to 71.8%. On 16th May 2005 he had achieved 75% of the shareholding enabling him to end the club's plc status and de-list from the London Stock Exchange – this took place on 22nd June 2005. On 28th June 2005 he had gained sufficient shares for a compulsory buyout of the remaining shareholders. The club was now owned by one person.

Old Trafford is now back in private ownership

Stock Exchange, thereby enabling them to sell shares to a wide variety of potential shareholders. The paperwork to set up a plc is very similar to that of a private limited company, except a plc has to issue a prospectus – which is an advertisement or invitation to the public to purchase shares in the business.

Summary of advantages and disadvantages of limited companies

Advantages

- Shareholders have limited liability.
- It is easier to raise capital through share issues.
- It is often easier to raise finance from banks and other external financial institutions.
- It becomes possible to operate on a larger scale.
- Suppliers feel more confident dealing with legally established bodies.
- The company name is protected by law.

Disadvantages

- Formation and running costs can be expensive.
- Decisions can be slow and 'red tape' can be a problem.
- Companies can become too large and as such ineffective (dis-economies of scale).
- Employees and shareholders are distanced from one another.
- Affairs are public – accounts available to the general public.
- The running of the business is tightly regulated by the various Companies Acts.

Activity

Find out more about setting up a company. Go to: www.companieshouse.gov.uk to help you with your research.

Franchises

Franchises are not a type of business ownership in their own right. The business that buys the franchise will have to be a sole trader, partnership or limited company.

Franchising allows someone to buy into an already established business, which greatly reduces the risk associated with starting up a new venture. The person that buys into the business is known as the franchisee. They pay a business for the right to use their name and sell their products. The franchisor is the business that is selling the right to use their name.

The franchisee gains advantages by setting up a branch of an already established business. The franchisor will provide training and support to help the franchisee achieve success. The franchisee is not able to make as many decisions in the way a sole trader can because, to a certain extent, they have to do what the franchisor tells them.

The franchisee still has to work hard and put in long hours but it is not as risky as setting up independently. Franchises are very popular in the fast food industry, for example McDonald's and Pizza Hut.

Voluntary/charitable/ not-for-profit organisations

Most businesses run with the aim of making a profit. Organisations in this section operate with a 'not-for-profit' aim.

Voluntary organisations are run by people who are working on a voluntary basis (for free). They are usually run for a good cause. One example is VSO; 'it is the world's leading independent, international development organisation that works through volunteers to fight poverty in developing countries' (source: www.vso.org.uk). People from all walks of life volunteer with VSO, from students taking a gap year to senior managers in business who wish to put their skills to good use.

Charities are set up to raise funds for a particular cause or to help people. Any money they make is given to the people they have been set up to help. They keep the costs of running the charity low so that as much money as possible is given to the cause. The work of a charity is overseen by trustees. Charities have to register with the Charity Commission and produce accounts to show how

Activity

Visit the McDonald's website at www.mcdonalds.co.uk to research franchising. Use your findings to help you answer the following questions.

1   When McDonald's sells a franchise what rights does it sell to the franchisee?
2   What are the responsibilities of the franchisee?
3   How does McDonald's benefit by selling franchises?
4   What support does McDonald's provide to the franchisee?
5   What might happen if McDonald's did not support the franchisee?
6   What impact could this have on McDonald's?
7   What are the necessary characteristics to be a successful franchisee?
8   How do you think McDonald's decides whether or not to let someone buy a franchise?

much money they have received and what they have done with that money.

One of the disadvantages of a charity is that it may have been set up and subsequently run by people who do not have any prior business experience. The business may be inefficient and as such not able to take full advantage of business possibilities as and when they arise.

The table below shows that since 1999 the number of charities registered in England and Wales has nearly doubled, and the annual income from these charities has more than doubled. This money comes from donations as well as consumer spending in charity shops.

At 31st December	Total Number of charities	Annual income £bn	Number of large charities (annual income >£10 million)	Annual income £bn	Proportion of total income %
2007	169,297	44.55	679	22.41	50.3
2006	168,609	41.26	627	20.10	48.7
2005	167,466	37.86	570	17.59	46.5
2004	166,336	34.86	511	15.84	45.4
2003	164,781	31.62	460	14.19	44.9
2002	162,335	29.45	421	13.04	44.3
2001	160,778	26.71	372	11.42	42.7
2000	159,845	24.56	336	10.27	41.8
1999	163,355	23.74	307	10.19	42.9

Table 1.1 Register summary – recent history (1999 to 2007)

(Source: www.charity-commission.gov.uk)

Activity

1 Draw a plan of your local high street or shopping centre.
2 Indicate on your plan shops which are:
- run by a charity
- franchises
- sole traders
- partnerships
- public limited companies
- private limited companies.

Examination Tip

In your exam you will need to be able to identify the different forms of ownership covered in this chapter. You may also have to evaluate the advantages and disadvantages of each form of ownership. You could be given an example business and you will have to write about which form of ownership would be the most suitable by showing the advantages **and** disadvantages **and** drawing a conclusion.

Read the case study below and answer the questions that follow. Further research can be carried out at www.yeovalleyorganics.co.uk.

Case Study

Yeo Valley Organic is part of a family-owned farming and dairy business that is based in Somerset.

Its founders, Roger and Mary Mead, began making yogurts in 1974, using milk from their dairy herd and selling them to local shops.

'Production of organic yogurts was started in 1993, when we were approached by a handful of local farmers who were producing organic milk, but had difficulty finding a consistent demand for it.

The first organic product, a natural yogurt, was an instant success. This encouraged Yeo Valley to look at the possibility of additional products, and also ways to encourage more farmers to become organic, so that an increasing supply of organic milk would become available to cope with growing demand.'

(Source: www.yeovalleyorganic.co.uk)

1 What form of business ownership do you think Yeo Valley took when it first set up?
2 Outline the advantages and disadvantages of the form of ownership you have stated in question 1.
3 Yeo Valley is now a private limited company (Ltd). Why do you think it became a private limited company?
4 Evaluate whether being a private limited company is the most suitable form of business ownership.
5 Rachel's Organics is a competitor of Yeo Valley. Conduct research to find out who the owners of Rachel's Organics are.
6 Evaluate the advantages and disadvantages to Rachel Rowlands (the founder of Rachel's Organics) of the current form of business ownership of Rachel's Organics.

Summary

- Sole traders and partnerships have unlimited liability – they are responsible for the debts of the business.
- Partnerships – all partners are responsible for the debts of other partners.
- Sole traders and partnerships are usually small businesses that can react rapidly to changes in the market enabling them to seize opportunities. Size of business enables them to develop excellent customer relations.
- Limited companies have separate legal identity. If the business fails the shareholders only lose the money they have initially invested in the business – they will not lose personal possessions.
- Larger companies are unable to react to market changes quickly due to their size. This might cause them to lose market advantage.
- Franchises are not a type of organisation but a method of setting up a business using an already established business name and brand.
- Charitable organisations exist in order to provide services to other people and are run on a not for profit basis.

Chapter 2

Business activity – why and how businesses start, succeed and/or fail

The Dragons know how to take risks in order to achieve success

Some people have an innovative idea and they want to start their own business in order to develop this idea. James Dyson is a good example of such a person. Visit www.dyson.com to find out more about how James developed his ideas.

There might be a gap in the market and you want to start your own business to target this gap. For example you might think that, as people are becoming more health conscious, there is a need for a specialist organic food shop in your local town.

Activity

Go to www.bbc.co.uk/dragonsden and watch video clips of entrepreneurs looking for investment from the Dragons. Make a note of the reasons why the entrepreneurs started their businesses.

Activity

You want to open a shop in your local high street. You have decided to try and spot a gap in the market, something that consumers cannot already buy in your local high street. Conduct research to find out what your shop should sell to meet the needs of local consumers.

Reasons why a business starts

Businesses are started for many different reasons. Some people want to run their own business so that they can be their own boss. They are able to make all of the decisions about the running of the business. They may have had an ambition for a long time to run their own business. If the business makes any profit the owner will be able to keep the profits and so there can be a financial reason for wanting to start a business.

Types of activity a business may become involved in

There are three main types of activity that a business may become involved in. These are:

- Extractive (primary industry)
- Manufacturing and construction (secondary industry)
- Services (tertiary industry).

Business activity – why and how businesses start, succeed and/or fail

Case Study

Read the case study and answer the questions that follow.

After 12 months of struggling unsuccessfully to find work, Claire Foster (27) approached The Prince's Trust for help in achieving her ambition to run her own business. In late 2005 she set up Superjuice – a mobile juice and smoothie bar in Taunton with the help of a grant.

In just two years, Claire has boosted Superjuice's range to include hot juices, porridge and homemade soups. Her funky, bright green mobile unit has become a landmark in Taunton town centre and she is now looking for new locations so that she can expand the business. Claire said: 'Two years ago I was unemployed and the future looked bleak. Starting my own business has changed everything, all the hard work has been worthwhile. Success is sweet!'

(Source: www.princes-trust.org.uk)

1 Research The Prince's Trust. How can it help young people to set up in business?
2 Explain Claire's reasons for wanting to start her own business.
3 What evidence is there in the case that Claire's business is a success?
4 Why do you think Claire's business is a success?

Extractive industries deal with natural resources. Types of activity include farming, fishing, mining and oil drilling. Traditionally, a lot of sole traders or family run businesses would have been involved in the farming and fishing industries.

Manufacturing and construction uses raw materials to make and assemble products. These products are either known as consumer goods or capital goods. Consumer goods are bought by the general public for their own use, eg bread, computers and clothes. Capital goods are goods used by a business to produce other goods, eg machinery. This sector within the United Kingdom has decreased over the years as more of our goods are imported from foreign countries.

The service sector is a growing sector of the economy within the United Kingdom. It includes banking, leisure, retail, transport, education, health services and telecommunications.

Changes in the external environment that can impact business activities and their potential consequences

The external environment includes anything that the business cannot control. For example this would include interest rates, the rate of inflation, the amount of goods being imported from abroad, the strength of the pound against other currencies, new competitors entering the market and general trends in consumers' buying habits and tastes.

It is hard for businesses to control changes in the external environment but they do need to be able to react to them in order to limit the impact they have on the business. Hopefully changes in the external environment can be used to the business's advantage, help to increase their customer base and, hopefully, profits.

Activity

Study the table below showing the number of businesses in each industry sector in the UK in 2007.

Businesses	UK Industry Summary	
All industries		4,679,080
A, B	Agriculture, Hunting and Forestry, Fishing	168,495
C, E	Mining and Quarrying, Electricity, Gas and Water Supply	13,025
D	Manufacturing	348,250
F	Construction	978,065
G	Wholesale and Retail Trade, Repairs	562,030
H	Hotels and Restaurants	149,765
I	Transport, Storage and Communication	297,550
J	Financial Intermediation	67,275
K	Real Estate, Renting and Business Activities	1,130,890
M	Education	162,540
N	Health and Social work	273,570
O	Other Community, Social and Personal Service Activities	527,625

Table 2.1 (Source: www.berr.gov.uk)

1 Calculate the total number of businesses in the primary, secondary and tertiary sectors.
2 Draw a pie chart to show your findings.
3 Carry out research to see if the percentages have changed since 2007.
4 Why do you think there have been changes?
5 What effect would the changes have on someone wanting to set up a business?

Table 2.2 shows the findings of a survey where owners of small and medium enterprises were asked what they felt the biggest obstacle to their success was.

As you can see, the highest rated factors concern the external environment.

Changes in the external market – a new competitor enters the market

If a new competitor enters the market, the business needs to find out as much as it can about its competitor. They will need to find out exactly what products they are selling, how they are advertising, who their target market is and the selling price of the product/service. This will help them to compete successfully. Think about how you would find out about your competitors if you owned a restaurant.

Your business will need to gain a competitive edge. This could be achieved by having a prime location, offering lower prices or better value for money, selling a wider range of goods or providing a better service than your competitors. The focus could also be on improving current advertising in order to raise awareness of the business and encourage customers to visit.

Business activity – why and how businesses start, succeed and/or fail

Obstacle	Per cent
Competition in the market	15
Regulations	14
Taxation, VAT, PAYE, National Insurance, business rates	12
The economy	10
Cash flow	10
Recruiting staff	6
Shortage of skills generally	4
Availability/cost of suitable premises	4
Obtaining finance	3
No obstacles	2
Shortage of managerial skills/ expertise	1
No opinion	2

Table 2.2 Base: All SME employers (weighted data); unweighted N- 8949

(Source: www.berr.gov.uk)

Consequences of a new competitor entering the market

If a new competitor enters the market this gives some businesses the push they need to improve and perhaps find more customers, or new markets for their products. If the competitor is a much larger business and is able to offer lower prices, the original business may cease trading as they are unable to compete and make a loss.

Changes in the external market – changes in regulations and subsequent consequences

Regulations cover laws about employees, trading hours, what you can sell, who you can sell to etc. In 2005 the law changed so that pubs and clubs could apply for a 24 hour drinks licence. This could have a positive effect on your business if you wished to apply for the licence and it was granted. On the other hand, if your competitor was granted the licence and you were not then your business might suffer. Customers might go to the competitor because they could remain there longer.

Employers have to pay a legal minimum wage rate to employees. If the Government increases this rate, then employers have to pay this. Some businesses find it hard to pay the increase and struggle financially. This could result in employees being made redundant in order to reduce the wage bill. This would then mean that the remaining employees would be required to take on extra work in order to keep the business running efficiently.

The third biggest obstacle is taxation, VAT, PAYE, National Insurance and business rates. Once again these are factors that the business owner has no control over. If these rates increase then they have to pay the extra costs. If VAT increases all businesses are required to pass these extra costs on to the customer. The result of this is that people might start to reduce their expenditure, making trading conditions very difficult for the retail trade. If the cost of National Insurance rises employers could be required to make higher contributions for each employee. This might result in a reduction in the workforce as the business can no longer afford to employ so many staff. If PAYE income tax contributions rise employees will see a reduction in their income, which again could reduce spending and businesses selling non essential items could therefore see a decrease in their sales figures.

Business rates are the money that a business has to pay the Government on an annual basis. It is very similar to the Council Tax that is paid on domestic houses. The amount is calculated on the retail value of the property that the business owns. On 1st April 2009 business rates were due to increase by 5%. The increase was based on inflation rates that were relevant during September

Case Study

On 28 November 2008 the Chancellor reduced VAT from 17.5% to 15%. VAT will increase back to 17.5% on 1 January 2010.

The purpose of the reduction was to try and stimulate consumer demand – it would automatically reduce the price of consumer goods but would not impact on the retailer's profit. Let us see how this works: if we take a pair of jeans retailing at £85, the VAT element of this is calculated as follows:

> £85 divided by 117.5 x 100 = £72.34 this is the net value of the jeans before VAT was added. Therefore VAT = £85.00 – £72.34 = £12.66

If VAT is only 15% the retail price of the same pair of jeans would be calculated as follows:

> Take the net price of £72.34 divided by 100 x 15 = the VAT element equals £10.85. The retail price would therefore by £72.34 + 10.85 = £83.19.

This means that the consumer is saving £1.81.

It was felt that the reduction in the amount was too small to actually stimulate consumer spending and during the early part of 2009 some sections of the retail trade have seen a significant reduction in their sales.

2008. Due to the economic decline experienced during the latter part of 2008 and at the time of writing (March 2009), inflation has decreased and is expected to fall further. The rates to be charged are also based on the value of businesses' premises across two years. The 'credit crunch' has also seen property losing value. At the end of March 2009 the Government announced that it would bring forward regulations to enable businesses to defer payment of 60% of the increase in their 2009-10 business rate bills until 2010-11 and 2011-12. This was very good news for businesses that were struggling in the economic climate.

In a letter to Retail Week, Debenhams' chief executive Rob Templeman said: 'No retailer is happy with the 5% increase. It does not reflect where inflation is now and what's happening in the economy'.

Kingfisher boss Ian Cheshire said: 'Helping the retail sector in 2011 will be too little too late for many retailers that find the April rises pushes them under'.

Changes in the external market – the economy and subsequent consequences

The economy is the next factor. Changes in the national economy could involve a period of growth, when consumers have enough money to spend on goods and services, unemployment is low and generally businesses are successful. The opposite is a downturn or slowdown in the economy where consumer spending decreases and unemployment increases. Some businesses may close as a result of loss of sales.

A downturn in the economy means consumers have less money to spend. The economy is currently entering a time of decline. This has been referred to as the 'credit crunch', which was stimulated by the failure of some banks who had lent money that was unlikely to be repaid. These debts have become known as 'toxic loans'. At the time of writing the state of the economy is changing almost on a daily basis. Please refer to Chapter 10 for in-depth coverage.

Business activity – why and how businesses start, succeed and/or fail

Since October 2008 the Government has reduced the Bank of England base rate by 4% with the hope of stimulating the economy. They are trying to encourage banks to start lending to people again with the hope that this will stimulate the demand for goods and services within the retail trade, which in turn will hopefully support the manufacturing sector. These measures have not helped some large businesses who have already gone into liquidation, including Woolworths, Principals and MFI. Zavvi called in the administrators on 24th December 2008 with the reported loss of more than 3,000 jobs.

In these times of reduced spending on the high street it is not all doom and gloom. In August 2008 McDonald's announced it was going to create 4,000 new jobs in response to its strong sales.

This growth appears to have been maintained through the first quarter of 2009 as McDonald's has seen in an increase in sales as people move from eating out in restaurants to eating cheaper fast food. McDonald's will now have to ensure they are able to supply these new consumers with the products they want – perhaps by developing their healthy menu they will retain these customers as the economy climbs out of recession.

Due to the economic situation in Britain the value of the pound has been falling dramatically over the last few months. If the exchange rate continues to fall it means that British exports become more expensive abroad and there will be less demand. This could lead to loss of sales for manufacturing companies which might cause them to go out of business. It also means that foreign holidays become more expensive, and as such travel agents could suffer a loss in trade.

Examination Tip

In the exam you will have to identify reasons why businesses start. You will also have to identify the types of business activity a particular business might be involved in. You will have to explain possible changes in the external environment that can impact upon the activities of businesses. There could be a case study about a business and you may be asked to evaluate the consequences of changes in the external environment on that business. This would mean you should look at a range of consequences and then conclude by saying which you think is the most likely, giving your reasons.

Case Study

Downturn boosts Poundland sales

Poundland announced a rise in sales in December 2008 despite the UK being in an economic downturn. Same store sales had risen by 3.9% compared to December 2007 while sales including new store openings had risen by 24.3%.

Poundland planned to continue to grow in 2009, with plans to open 30 new stores and create 1,000 new jobs.

'We are well positioned to capitalise on the continuing strong customer trend to shop savvy and seek value for money', said chief executive Jim McCarthy.

(Source: adapted from www.bbc.co.uk)

Use the article above and your own research from www.poundland.com to answer the following questions.

1 What type of business activity is Poundland involved in?
2 What evidence is there in the article that Poundland has been successful?
3 Explain why you think Poundland has been successful.
4 State the competitors of Poundland.
5 Explain why consumers wanted to cut the amount of money they spend on their shopping.
6 Explain how Poundland is able to charge £1 for each of the items it sells.

Summary

- People start their own business for a number of different reasons. They wish to work for themselves which enables them to do what they want, when they want. Another reason is the entrepreneur has spotted a gap in the market and feels they have an innovative way of meeting this need.

- Primary industries consist of, for example, farming, fishing, mining and oil drilling.

- Secondary industries consist of manufacturing and construction.

- Tertiary industry consists of the service sector. Employment today is dominated by this sector.

Chapter 3

Business organisation – how businesses organise themselves

Introduction

Businesses will group key tasks together into departments/functional areas within their overall business structure. This enables a business to operate more efficiently and allows a business to develop discrete job roles that can be undertaken by specialist staff.

The functional areas that you will cover in this chapter are:

- Finance
- Human Resources
- Marketing
- Operations
- Administration/ICT

All businesses will carry out each of these functions but this may not be undertaken by a separate department in every business. You will find that large businesses will have specialist staff in each department. Some very large businesses operating in a number of different countries might, for example, have a finance department in each country. Whereas small businesses may have one or two people who undertake the roles of all the functional areas mentioned above.

The role of functional areas is also covered in the introductory sections of Chapters 4 and 8.

Finance

The finance functional area is all about money. One of its major roles is to monitor the performance of the business by monitoring all the money coming into and out of the business.

This might be money coming into the business from customers as either cash or credit sales. Credit sales are where customers are allowed to receive goods and make payment at a later date – they are known as debtors. The business needs to keep track of credit customers to ensure they are paying for their goods and services on a regular basis. This is known as credit control and is a very important role within the functional area.

Money will also be going out of the business to pay for purchases made. These people are known as suppliers or creditors. The functional area must ensure that the business pays its creditors on a regular basis and on time. If they do not they might get a poor reputation and find it difficult to find suppliers willing to supply products.

Another important part of monitoring financial performance is to monitor how much the

Activity

From the list of job roles below, decide which functional area you would work in if you had that job role:

Receptionist	Accounts clerk	Training manager
Payroll assistant	Production supervisor	ICT technician
Quality control manager	Market researcher	Sales manager

business is selling its goods and services for, and whether customers are increasing or decreasing.

If the business wants to buy new equipment or build new premises it will have to raise finance to do this. This functional area would have to prepare the financial figures to be presented to the bank to apply for a loan in order to fulfil their plans.

The final task of the finance department is to prepare the final year-end accounts of the business. This includes the profit and loss account. These financial statements take into account the total sales less the total expenditure of the business. The final figure is known as the net profit. The balance sheet shows external parties the value of the business by adding up all the assets of the business (those items it owns such as cars, machinery and stock) minus what the business owes to other people (creditors and loans). The second part of the balance sheet outlines how the business has been financed – ie the initial start-up capital.

Human resources

The role of the human resource department is covered in depth within Unit 4 Business and You and can be found on pages 191–195.

The human resources department deals with people. This department will be responsible for calculating the number of staff required in order to facilitate the smooth and efficient running of the business. This is known as human resource planning.

If there are job vacancies within the business, this department is in charge of recruiting and selecting candidates to fill the vacancies. Members of staff, whether new or existing, will be offered training during their time working for the business which will be arranged through the human resources functional area.

The human resources department puts in place schemes to motivate employees and encourage them to continue working for the business. These are then cascaded to all other functions so that the whole workforce can be motivated.

Health and safety at work is very important and this department is in charge of making sure employees work safely. The trade unions also link with human resources on many issues, including health and safety.

Marketing

The marketing department is in charge of decisions concerning what products consumers want and how they are then promoted. This department undertakes market research to find out what customers want. A product is then designed to meet the customers' needs.

The marketing department will help to decide on the price for the product. They have a lot of different methods they can use to decide on the price.

Next they are involved with promoting the product – letting the customer know about it. There are many different ways of promoting a product; the chosen method depends on a number of factors, including the type of product it is and who the customer is.

Decisions have to be made about how the business gets its product/services to the customer. See Chapter 15.

Operations

This department includes the production of the product. Production could take place on a very costly automated production line in a huge factory, or by hand in a small workshop.

As well as actually making the product this department is responsible for planning the number of products to be made, and looking to the future to see if production needs to increase to meet demand.

It is in charge of sourcing the raw materials that will be used to make the products. Quality control is vital in all aspects of the operations department, from the raw materials to the finished products.

This department also looks at efficiency – ie making sure that time is not wasted on the production line so that costs do not increase.

Administration/ICT

This functional area could be described as the backbone of the business. All of the other functions rely on administration and ICT to allow them to complete their work successfully.

The responsibilities of this department are very varied. The reception would come under the administration area. This is a vital role as it is usually the first contact point someone has with a business. Security and looking after the buildings are also roles within this function.

All general clerical work would be carried out by administration staff. There would be ICT support staff ensuring that the computer network throughout the business was always working correctly.

Consequences for a business if the functional areas do not operate efficiently

The various functional areas within any business have to be working towards the same overall goals. If this was not the case there could be conflict between the functions. For example, the marketing department might want to spend a large sum of money on promoting a new product but the finance department is aiming to reduce costs.

The human resources department wants to increase the amount of job training for all

Case Study

The following information is an introduction to Samworth Brothers. To find out more about this business, go to www.samworthbrothers.co.uk.

'Samworth Brothers is a family business producing quality food that we are proud to take home and share with our family and friends.

We make a wide range of chilled foods in well-invested sites that give our staff the facilities and environment to produce food to the highest quality and food safety standards.

We run each of our sites as autonomous businesses in order to respond as quickly as possible to our customers' needs, with each business linked by our common culture of 'People, Quality, Profit'. This allows the people closest to the customer to make important decisions speedily and accurately, so that all our people can directly influence the performance of their business.'

(Source: www.samworthbrothers.co.uk)

1 For each of the following functional areas describe key operational tasks that would be carried out at Samworth Brothers:
- Finance
- Human Resources
- Marketing
- Operations
- Administration/ICT

2 From your research, which do you think is the most important functional area for Samworth Brothers? Give reasons for your answer.

3 What do you think would be the consequences if the functional areas within Samworth Brothers did not work together effectively? Justify your answer.

production line employees. This could cause conflict with the production department which is aiming to increase production and so therefore needs all of its employees working. In the long term the training would probably make the employees more efficient, which would in turn increase productivity.

There needs to be good communication between all functional areas of the business so that all deadlines can be met and everyone is working for the same goal. Think about each department within your school – what would the consequences be if each department did not communicate with each other or work towards a common goal?

Which is worse, doing something twice or not doing something at all? Both of these are possible consequences for a business if the functional areas are not efficient.

Doing something twice, that is two functional areas completing the same task, means that the business will be wasting money. Functional areas need to work together on projects so that expertise from different departments can be used to produce the best solution for the business to meet its aims.

Not doing something at all means that the business could potentially lose customers and profit. It might give the competition a chance to get ahead and increase its market share. In order to avoid either situation, all functional areas need to work together.

Activity

For each of the scenarios below, complete the following tasks:

- Identify the functional areas that might be affected.
- Describe what actions need to take place.
- Describe the possible consequences if the functional areas you have identified did not work together.

Scenario 1:
The production department has decided that there needs to be a lot of overtime carried out by production line employees so that they can meet current orders.

Scenario 2:
The reception wants to install a new telephone system with more up-to-date facilities, the supplier says that it will have to change the internal phone numbers.

Scenario 3:
The marketing department wants to decrease the price of one of its products to keep in line with a competitor.

Scenario 4:
Due to a need to cut costs, the finance department announces that it will not be paying bonuses for this year.

Scenario 5:
The human resources department is allowing employees to work flexible hours if they wish.

Business organisation – how businesses organise themselves

Examination Tip

In the exam you will need to be able to write about what each of the functional areas does. You will need to understand the key operational tasks that are connected with each of the areas. You may be asked to write about the functional areas in a business you have studied, describing what happens in each department.

You need to be able to evaluate the consequences for a business if the functional areas do not operate efficiently. This means writing about a range of consequences (likely things to happen) and then writing a conclusion that says which of these things is most likely to happen and giving reasons for your answer. This could be about a case study business given in the exam or a business you have studied; the question will make it clear which you are to use.

Summary

- The finance department is responsible for monitoring the money coming into and out of the business.

- The marketing department is responsible for establishing the potential demand for a product/service and for creating customer awareness of the availability of the product.

- The operations department is responsible for the production of the product which will involve production scheduling, ordering raw materials in order to maintain production and ultimately the quality of the finished product.

- The administration department is responsible for the paperwork side of the business – which could include reception, management of incoming and outgoing post and compilation of documents. Establishment of the ICT policy falls under the remit of the ICT department. They will also be responsible for the delivery of ICT training and maintenance of all ICT equipment.

- If all these departments do not work together, the business will not run efficiently and jobs might get done twice whilst others are forgotten. It could also cause conflict within the working environment. Potentially, customer service provision will fall which could result in falling customer numbers.

Chapter 4

Framework for activity – aims, objectives and mission statements

> **Activity**
>
> Think about what you are trying to achieve over the next few years. It could be something to do with school, college, work or leisure activities. How are you going to be able to achieve this? In order to remain focused on your target it is best to break the activity down into a number of simple achievable steps.
>
> This is how businesses have to think all the time in order to be successful.

The main aims of businesses

When a sole trader sets up they may have some unstated aims or objectives – for example to survive for the first year. Other businesses may wish to state exactly what they are aiming to do, such as Amazon, the Internet CD and bookseller, who wants to 'make history and have fun'.

An aim is where the business wants to go in the future: its goals. It is a statement of purpose, eg we want to grow the business into Europe.

Making a profit – this is often the most common aim of all owners and shareholders of a business. Larger businesses might be aiming for profit maximization which is to make as much profit as possible. Smaller business owners might aim for enough profit to keep themselves comfortable.

Sales growth – this is where the business aims to increase the amount of goods it sells or services it provides. This might not necessarily be related to profit as to sell more goods or services the business might have to decrease its price.

Expansion – the business could be aiming to sell to new markets, possibly abroad, or if it is a local business it might simply mean aiming to sell to consumers in the neighbouring town. The business may also want to diversify and expand its product range.

Customer satisfaction – this is becoming increasingly important with the growth in Internet shopping. Consumers have a number of different places in which to shop: their local high street, an out of town shopping complex or the Internet. Businesses need to have customer satisfaction as an aim if they want to keep their customers' loyalty. This is dealt with in much greater depth in Chapter 13.

Being environmentally friendly – many business owners nowadays are seeing this as a very important aspect of the way that they run their business. Some consumers are looking at whether or not a business acts in an environmentally friendly way before deciding whether to buy from that business.

Being ethically and socially responsible – previously these aims would be set by businesses like the Co-op or the Body Shop, but more and more businesses are setting aims of this nature (see Chapter 9).

The importance of business aims

Businesses may have problems helping all employees understand and work effectively for the benefit of not only the business but the security of their own positions. One way to do this is to create aims and objectives that can be broken down into separate targets for functional areas, teams and individuals. This structure helps everyone within the company to fully understand what they are required to do within the framework to achieve the business's overall aims.

If the overall aim is to increase profit this can then be broken down into specific aims and objectives for different functional areas. For example, the production department might be required to investigate ways of reducing wastage in order to cut the cost of producing each item; the marketing department might be asked to run an advertising campaign in order to increase awareness of the product which will hopefully result in increased sales.

Businesses might have more than one aim. For example, a business could aim for growth but also social responsibility – it needs to make sure that all decisions about how the business should grow also meet the aim of being socially responsible. If a plot of land was available to purchase where the business could build new premises, the business might reject that particular site if it was going to cause undue pollution to the local community. An alternative approach that still meets both aims could be to plant trees around the site to reduce the effects of pollution.

Business objectives

The objectives of the business are the stated, measurable targets of how to achieve its aims. For example, the aim might be growth, and the way the business is going to achieve this (its objective) could be sales of £10 million in European markets in 2010. This objective would then be further broken down for each individual department. In breaking the objective down the department and employees within the department know exactly what they are required to do in order to achieve this overall target of achieving sales of £10 million in European Markets in 2010.

As you can see from the example above, objectives give the business a clearly defined target. In order to be effective, business objectives should meet the following criteria:

S – Specific – objectives are aimed at what the business does; eg a restaurant might have an objective of having the restaurant 50% full each night during October – an objective specific to that business.

M – Measurable – the business can put a value to the objective, eg £10,000 in sales in the next half year of trading. The business can easily measure whether or not this has been achieved.

A – Achievable – are the objectives the business has set achievable and attainable? Setting objectives that are not achievable could de-motivate employees and managers.

R – Realistic – can the business realistically achieve the objectives with the resources available? As with achievable, if objectives are set that are not realistic, employees and managers could be de-motivated.

T – Time specific – there is a time limit as to when the objective should be achieved, eg by the end of the year. This will push people to try to meet the deadline rather than just saying the business wants to increase sales.

A business may find that some of their objectives conflict with one another.

Growth versus profit – a business might want to achieve higher sales in the short term. One way to do this would be by cutting prices but this could reduce short-term profit.

Short-term versus long-term – businesses with shareholders might try to create happy investors by paying them a large dividend each time, whereas the business really needs long-term investment in order to continue to perform well.

The importance of business objectives

As we have seen, objectives show how the business is trying to meet its aims. They are stepping stones in achieving an overall goal. When objectives are written everyone within the business has a clearer idea of what they are trying to achieve. Each department within the business has to set its own objectives. They must refer back to the business's overall aim to ensure that the objectives they set are in line with this aim.

Setting objectives can motivate the employees as they know what they are trying to achieve. Some businesses offer a bonus payment to employees if their own or departmental objectives are achieved.

The business as a whole can measure its progress towards the stated aims. It can see whether departments are under or over-performing and take action as necessary.

A business may change its objectives over time. This could be because it has achieved its first objective. For example, survival in the first year may lead to an objective of increasing profit in the second year.

The competitive environment might change, eg with the launch of new products from competitors. It is important at this stage that the business looks at its own objectives again to make sure they will stay competitive.

The importance of a mission statement

As the business sets its aims and objectives it writes a mission statement to show its vision and values. This allows all stakeholders in the business (see Chapter 5) to understand the way that the business is trying to operate. Possible stakeholders include: employees, managers, customers, financiers and suppliers.

It is important for a business to have a mission statement that is inspirational and gives the business something to aspire to. However, it will lack specific detail needed for planning. To plan properly the business will use the mission statement to structure the initial aims and then objectives of the business. In this way all three stages are connected and achievement is easily monitored.

If you were looking to apply for a job in a business, looking at the mission statement would give you an idea of the vision and values of that business. It might help you to decide whether or not it would be a good business to work for.

Below are four examples of mission statements from different businesses all trying to attract customers and keep them loyal to the business.

At Domino's Pizza, our mission is to be the best pizza delivery company in the world. Our culture is best summed up in a chant that's sung in our stores: 'Sell More Pizza, Have More Fun!'.

(Source: www.dominos.uk.com)

At Sainsbury's we will deliver an ever-improving quality shopping experience for our customers with great products at fair prices. We aim to exceed customer expectations for healthy, safe, fresh and tasty food, making their lives easier everyday.

(Source: www.j-sainsbury.co.uk)

Tesco

Our core purpose is to create value for customers to earn their lifetime loyalty.

(Source: www.tescoplc.com)

Tarmac

Our vision, mission and values

To be the first choice for building materials and services that meet the essential needs for the sustainable development of the world in which we live.

(Source: www.tarmac.co.uk)

Activity

Take two of the above mission statements and write out two aims. Break down each of your aims into two different objectives that are SMART.

Framework for activity – aims, objectives and mission statements

Examination Tip

In your exam you will have to identify the aims and objectives of a business. You might be given a case study from which to identify these aims and objectives or you may be asked to write about the aims and objectives of a business you have studied. You will need to be able to explain the importance of mission statements, aims, and objectives. You might have to do this, in theory, for a business you have studied or from a case study provided.

Activity

Many schools and colleges now have mission statements. Below is one such example:

Warden Park School is an ambitious, well-established 11–16 comprehensive school with an excellent reputation. Warden Park's maxim, *The Best from All* sums up our mission to encourage students to make the most of the many opportunities here.

(Source: www.wardenpark.w-sussex.sch.uk)

1. Find out if your school/college has a mission statement.
2. Why is it important for schools/colleges to have mission statements?
3. If your school/college does not have a mission statement can you suggest one?
4. Do you think mission statements are better short or long?

Summary

- Business aims (increasing profit, expansion and growth) are what the business wants to achieve within a set period of time.

- Objectives are how a business intends to achieve its stated aims. For example, the aim could be to increase profit by 3%. The marketing objective might be to run a sales campaign for two months in order to increase awareness of the product. The production department might have been given the objective to decrease wastage levels by 3% over the next six months.

- A mission statement outlines the business's vision – what it wants to stand for and achieve in the future.

Chapter 5

Stakeholders – their Differing Interests

Activity

When you go shopping what are your expectations as a customer? Consider a fairly large purchase you have recently made and jot down how you expected to be treated, what information you required to know prior to purchase, the payment options that were offered to you and finally how did you feel once you had left the shop having made the purchase. Would you make another purchase from that shop?

Identification of stakeholder groups in business

Stakeholders are groups of people who take an interest in the decision-making process of a business. They are similar to the groups you identified for your school/college. Stakeholders can be internal, inside the business, such as employees and employers, or they can be external, outside the business, such as customers and suppliers.

Differing interests of stakeholder groups

Customers

Every time you make a purchase from a shop you are a customer. Therefore people who buy goods and/or services from a business are their customers. Without customers a business would not survive very long. It is therefore very important that businesses ensure they are able to respond to their differing customers' interests.

Different customers will have a variety of different interests depending on the product or service being purchased. The main interests are outlined below:

- The quality of the product or service
- The range and choice of products
- Customer service received from staff
- After sales service and guarantees – especially important with electrical goods
- The price of the product – is it good value for money?
- The methods of payment available
- Availability of the product – especially important with Internet sales
- Reputation of the business

The successful business will ensure that all these interests are met in the hope that each customer becomes a regular repeat customer.

Suppliers

Businesses can also trade amongst themselves. If Business A buys goods from Business B they become a customer of Business B. However, Business B also becomes known as a supplier of goods to Business A.

Suppliers are therefore people who sell goods and services to other businesses. Let us now consider what interests Business B will have in Business A as their supplier.

- Is Business A able to pay for the products purchased?
- Will they pay for the goods within the specified time period or will they keep Business B waiting for payment, which could cause cash-flow problems? (This area will be covered in Chapter 23 in greater detail.)
- Will they become a regular customer and place even larger orders?
- Is there the potential for Business A to expand and therefore increase the value of products being purchased?
- Does the business trade ethically and have a sound reputation?

Employees

These are the people who work for the business. Pay is probably one of the biggest areas of interest for a new employee – how much will I receive for doing this job? However, after starting the job an employee's interest will start to move towards their working conditions: is their environment pleasant, warm in the winter and cool in the summer? Is there a kitchen where they can fix themselves a drink and have lunch? As the employee settles into the job they might become interested in further training so that they can gain promotion and additional benefits.

Employees who are well looked after by the business tend to work harder and do their job well. This is very important to the business. If the working conditions do not meet the employees' needs they may not work as efficiently and the business could suffer.

Employers

These are the owners of the business who are responsible for the decisions made within it. The owner has become an employer as they have decided to employ somebody to work within their business.

The main interest of an employer is to maintain or increase profits. In order to do this an employer will have to pay particular interest to the income and expenditure of the business. This could involve researching market trends in order to remain competitive within the market-place.

In order to retain profitability the employer will be interested in keeping employees' pay stable, and will probably not be that willing to offer big pay rises which could reduce overall profits.

The employer will also be interested in the amount being paid to suppliers – could cheaper suppliers be found which would not impact on the products being purchased?

An employer who wants to maintain his workforce will pay attention to their wants and needs. Taking an interest in staff will greatly help increase motivation and often efficiency, which will help with the smooth running of the business.

Shareholders

These are owners of public limited companies and private limited companies (see Chapter 1). Shareholders have invested their money into the business generally for two reasons. The first is that they hope to receive a good dividend payment at the end of the financial year. They will therefore be interested in the profitability of the business. They want to know about the future plans of the business. Does the business have expansion plans which might reduce dividend payments one year but create the potential for bigger dividend payments in the future? The second reason is that they were able to purchase the shares at a low price, with the hope that their resale value will increase so that they can be sold on again at a profit. Shareholders' main interest in business is current and future profitability.

The local community

Think about how having a factory or a supermarket near to your house could affect you. There could be positive effects; for example, you could obtain a job there when you are older or the business might sponsor a local event. There could also be negative effects, for example noise pollution and congestion on the surrounding roads.

Small businesses in the local community could also be affected by a new supermarket opening in the area. They will lose some of their customers as the new supermarket will have more choice and will probably be able to charge less as they can buy in bulk and gain discounts. This could result in small businesses closing down.

The residents of the local area need to be consulted when the business is making decisions that could affect them. They are more likely to agree to something if they have full details from the business in advance.

Pressure groups

These are organisations that try to affect the way the business is run. Employees have their own pressure groups: these are called trade unions.

Trade unions protect the rights of their members, the employees. Their main aim is to make sure that the employees have the best possible working conditions. This could include:

- better pay
- training
- health and safety
- shorter working hours
- involvement in decision-making.

If a business wanted to expand, a pressure group might be formed by people who did not want the expansion to go ahead. They might campaign to show the disadvantages of this expansion on the local area.

Activity

Think of any well-known pressure groups that you have heard of. What do they campaign about? How could they affect a business?

The Government

All businesses have to act within the law. The Government is a stakeholder as they are the body that creates the legislation (laws) that businesses have to work within. The Government also collects taxes from businesses. Businesses have to pay tax on profits made, so the Government will have an interest in how much profit has been made by the business. It is illegal for a business to pay its employees less than the minimum wage – the Government would take action on behalf of the employees if this was found to be happening.

The Government also ensures that businesses are complying with the Health and Safety at Work Act. To do this they arrange health and safety inspections of premises to ensure that no employee's health or life is being put at risk due to the negligence of their employer.

Financiers

These are the people who lend money to businesses. They will charge interest on the money they lend. This could include bank loans or raising external finance through leasing agreements.

The financier's major interest is going to focus on the business's ability to repay the loan. Do they have sufficient funds and cash-flow to make regular repayments? Having established that the business is able to repay the debt they might also be interested in how the finance is going to be used. If the usage was considered unethical the financier could withdraw from the agreement.

Stakeholders – their differing interests

> ### Examination Tip
>
> In your OCR examination you may be asked to give examples of stakeholder groups in businesses that you have studied. You need to be prepared to answer questions explaining the different interests these groups have in a business you have studied.
>
> The examination could use a case study of a business and you might have to identify possible stakeholder groups. Be careful – if the business is not a company (plc or Ltd) it will not have shareholders. Read the case study very carefully for clues. Once again, the questions could be about the interests of these groups.

> ### Activity
>
> 1. Sali Evans is a sole trader who owns a hairdressing salon. List four possible stakeholders for this business.
> 2. Helsor Ltd owns a number of hotels. Describe the main interest of their shareholders.
> 3. You have been working at Helsor Ltd for a number of years. The business wants to change your working conditions. Name a stakeholder group that might negotiate with Helsor Ltd on your behalf.
> 4. For a business you have studied, explain the interests of two different stakeholder groups.

Possible conflict between different stakeholder groups

As we have seen, the various stakeholder groups have different interests. This can lead to conflict between them. Conflict can also occur when someone is part of more than one stakeholder group.

An employee of a business could live nearby and so be part of the local community. That person could also be a shareholder. Each group wants something different. As an employee you would want good working conditions. Living in the local community you want the area to be free from pollution and congestion. As a shareholder you want the business to make high profits so that you gain a large dividend. As you can imagine, these three 'wants' do not go together.

Conflict can exist between the supplier and the business. The supplier wants to sell their raw materials at a high price but the business wants to buy them at a low price.

Employees may ask for a pay increase. The employers do not want to pay this as it will increase expenditure and reduce profit. If agreement cannot be reached employees may then seek the help of their trade union to negotiate with the employers.

The employers may wish to use any profits to expand the business. If it is a company that has shareholders, they may want all of the profits in the form of dividends. This conflict could greatly affect the future of the business.

> ### Examination Tip
>
> In your OCR examination you may be asked to discuss a conflict that has occurred between two different stakeholder groups. This could be from a business you have studied or there could be a case study in the examination that you have to use.
>
> To help you to practise, think of possible conflicts in your chosen business. You could draw a flow chart to help you to work out all of the consequences. Here is an example to get you started.

```
┌─────────────────────────────────────────┐
│ The suppliers are putting up the price  │
│           of raw materials              │
└─────────────────────────────────────────┘
                    ↓
┌─────────────────────────────────────────┐
│  The business does not want to lose     │
│                profit                   │
└─────────────────────────────────────────┘
                    ↓
┌─────────────────────────────────────────┐
│ Increase the price charged to its       │
│              customers                  │
└─────────────────────────────────────────┘
                    ↓
┌─────────────────────────────────────────┐
│         OR Find a new supplier          │
└─────────────────────────────────────────┘
```

Consequences to businesses of not listening to stakeholder groups

The various stakeholder groups that have already been discussed try to influence the decision-making process of the business. If the business ignores these stakeholders there can be consequences.

Employees may go on strike if negotiations over pay have broken down. The business will therefore not be producing any goods or providing a service, and will have nothing to sell to its customers. If employees feel their working conditions are poor they may become de-motivated and productivity will drop.

If employers do not take notice of their employees they are likely to either lose them or suffer from their inefficiency, caused by their unhappiness in the work environment. For example, if employees are demanding improved heating as they are always cold, failure to do so could breach health and safety legislation but would also de-motivate the workforce – this would cause a drop in productivity and efficiency. If the employees were those dealing directly with the public they might become moody and unhelpful with customers.

If pressure groups are demonstrating outside the business, customers may be put off from using the business, and there could be bad publicity.

Suppliers might be warning that better quality raw materials are needed in order to ensure products meet new health and safety legislation. Ignoring this could cause the products to be faulty and in breach of new safety laws. This could lead to the business being prosecuted for failure to conform to new legislation.

If shareholders want an increase in their dividends and the business does not fulfil this desire they may sell their shares. This could lead to the shares falling in value and rumours that the business is in trouble.

If the business ignores the Government, legal action can be taken. This could be expensive, both financially and in terms of negative media coverage.

These consequences potentially all have a negative impact on the business. In some cases there could be a positive outcome to not listening to the stakeholders. For example, money is saved because the employees' request for a wage increase was ignored. The business was able to expand as profit was retained for investment and not all given back to the shareholders as dividends – the shareholders might even receive better dividends in the future due to this expansion.

A business needs to think carefully about the consequences of any action it takes or ignores.

Activity

For a business you have studied, evaluate the consequences of them asking an employee to sign a declaration saying that they do not mind working more than 48 hours per week. Try to use at least three different stakeholder groups in your answer.

Stakeholders – their differing interests

Examination Tip

In the OCR examination you could be asked to answer questions about the consequences to a business of not listening to stakeholder groups. You may be asked to write your answer about a business you have studied or there may be a case study that you have to use.

When you are answering, you need to think about the positive and negative effects on the business.

To practise, think about something your chosen business is trying to do that some stakeholders do not agree with. Write down all the things that could happen if your business does not listen to its stakeholders. For example:

Action – close shop in town centre and open out of town.

Possible consequences of carrying on regardless of stakeholders:

1 It could be hard to attract employees as they have to travel further.
2 Congestion on roads could lead to pressure groups campaigning.
3 Customers do not agree with the move and refuse to shop there.
4 The business could see an increase in customers as there is a lot of free parking.
5 Business has a bad reputation.

Activity

1 The business that supplies Sali Evans hairdressers with shampoos is increasing its prices. What should Sali do? Explain any conflict that could arise between different stakeholder groups included in your answer.
2 Your local supermarket is looking to expand at its current location. Discuss the possible conflicts between the local community and the shareholders.
3 For a business you have studied, discuss any possible conflicts between the employers and the employees.
4 You have seen television reports that your favourite high street clothes shop is paying very low wages to people overseas who are making the clothes. As a stakeholder, explain the actions you could take to show you do not approve.

Summary

- Stakeholders are anybody who has an interest or will be affected by the business. They can be internal (inside the business) or external (outside the business).
- Internal stakeholders include employees, owners/shareholders.
- External stakeholders include suppliers, the local community, pressure groups, the Government and financiers.
- Each stakeholder will have different interests within the business which might bring them into conflict.

Chapter 6

Employers/employees – how they operate in enterprising ways, develop their working relationship and meet their various rights and responsibilities

Activity

Think of ways that you, as a pupil, could help your school be successful. It's not just about working harder, but perhaps working in a different way and doing different things.

How businesses can be seen to operate in enterprising ways

In order to stay ahead of the competition a business needs to be a bit different. It needs to come up with ideas that will make it stand out in order to attract and keep customers. The business could do this by taking risks or being innovative in the way that it operates.

The risk could be introducing a new product or service; this could be costly to do and it is not known whether or not the customers will want to buy the product. The product itself could be innovative: that is something completely different.

The products invented by James Dyson have always been innovative and when they have been introduced there has been a possible risk to the business as a lot of money had been invested to develop these products. His G Force Dual Cyclone Dyson vacuum cleaner took five years to develop and 5,127 prototypes before it became a marketable product.

The business also needs to be innovative in the way it operates; that could be in terms of commerce or working practices. The business needs to look at how its customers are aware of the products it sells. There is an increasing use of the Internet for shopping and this is something the business needs to consider to keep up with its competitors. If your competitor has a website they are able to reach their customers 24 hours a day, 7 days a week. If you don't respond to this your customers might start purchasing online and will fail to return to your premises.

Retaining excellent employees is vital to the success of any business and there are now many flexible working practices that can be used to help employees to keep their work life balance suitable. With the ever increasing use of technology people can work from home – they are able to link to their office through the use of internet and intranet connections. Office workers are also given the opportunity to work flexi-time. This means they have to be in the office for core hours, perhaps 10-12 am and 2-4 pm. They are able to make up the remainder of their hours any time around these. For example one employee might like to start at 7 am in the morning and then go home at 4 pm. Another might like to start at 9.30 am but work until 5.30 pm in the evening. If the employee works more than their allotted hours they are able to build up a reserve and take half and full days off in lieu.

The business may also look at the way it is run. If it is currently a partnership, perhaps becoming a private limited company might allow the business to expand and increase its profits at the same time as reducing the risk for its investors (see Chapter 3).

How employees can assist businesses operating in an enterprising way

It is not just up to the business to operate in an enterprising way, employees have a role in assisting the business to run in such a way. Suggestion schemes encourage employees to put forward ideas that would improve the overall efficiency of the business. Often an employee who does a job repeatedly can come up with excellent ideas concerning how current working practices could be improved. A good way to encourage participation is to offer rewards for ideas that help the business become more efficient and ultimately save money or increase profitability.

Employees should be encouraged to take part in any new projects that are running within the business. The employer needs to communicate the new ideas in such a way as to encourage employees to want to be part of this project. A lot of people find change threatening and disconcerting. If employees can be part of the decision-making process concerning new ideas and projects they are more likely to want to participate and feel less threatened by the suggested changes. Employees will also need to be supported and encouraged throughout the changes in order to overcome any potential problems with the new working practices.

A flexible workforce is always much more useful to an employer than one that is unwilling to tackle different jobs willingly. One way to deal with this is to ensure that all employees are trained in a number of different job roles. This is known as job rotation. This ultimately has two benefits. The first is that the employee is less likely to become bored and de-motivated doing the same job day in day out – after all a little bit of variety is the spice of life! It also means that if another employee leaves or is unwell their work can be covered easily and efficiently by other members of the team.

Benefits to businesses of operating in an enterprising way

There are many possible benefits to the business of operating in an enterprising way. These are both internal (within the business) and external (outside the business).

If the employees feel that they are an important part of the business and that their opinions are taken into account then they will be more motivated and will work harder for the business.

The business should have an improved reputation. This could be from customers because they know that the products are good quality and up-to-date. It could also be from potential employees who think that the business sounds like the sort of place where they would like to work.

The business could experience increased sales and/or profits. If the products made are innovative, this could have a positive effect on sales. If the business changes its working practices to introduce Internet shopping, sales and profits could also increase.

Being innovative in some aspect of the design of the product or packaging could see the business gain an increased market share as customers are attracted to their product.

Activity

Working in small groups, consider how your school could operate in a more enterprising way. Don't forget that you do still have to come every day and learn!

What employees expect from employers

This area is also covered in detail in Chapter 30 The Selection Process – legislation that has to be adhered to during the selection process (pages 211–214), and Chapter 30 Human Resources Legislation (pages 208–214).

When you start work, you will have a range of factors that you expect from your employer, these include:

- Suitable working conditions – this covers many aspects of the job, including: the hours, holiday entitlement, any flexible working arrangements.
- Contract of employment – this will include details of the rate of pay. A written contract has to be issued within two months of starting work.
- Equal opportunities – there are laws that cover equal opportunities at work; these are covered later.
- Safe working environment – you expect your health and safety to be looked after, meaning that you are provided with any protective clothing that you may need and training in how to use equipment.

What employers expect from employees

When you start a new job your employer will expect things from you in the way that you work. You will be expected to adhere to the terms and conditions of your contract of employment. The main points will include:

- Punctuality – this means that you turn up to work on time, or if something has happened that means you will be late you let your employer know.
- Adherence to procedures – there will be many rules and regulations in the workplace and you must make sure you stick to them.
- Fulfilment of job role – this is actually completing the job you are being paid to do.
- Complying with health and safety procedures – as we have already seen, you expect your workplace to be safe but your employer expects you to work in a safe manner – for example, if protective clothes are provided then you wear them.

Employee/employer expectations are a two-way process. If both sides fulfil their requirements then the business will run more smoothly.

Activity

1 Research health and safety law – go to www.direct.gov.uk to help you. Design a poster to be displayed in a factory explaining the employees' and employer's role in adhering to the law regarding health and safety.

2 Design a contract of employment for a part-time member of staff working as a cashier in a bank.

3 Research flexible working conditions. Complete the online questionnaire at http://direct.gov.uk/en/Diol1/EmploymentInteractiveTools/DG_10028030. This will tell you if flexible working would suit you. Give five examples of flexible working arrangements that might suit you.

4 Go to http://direct.gov.uk/en/Diol1/EmploymentInteractiveTools/DG_10028510. Complete the online questionnaire to see what rights you would have when you go to work.

Legal framework that employees/employers must operate within

Businesses have to operate within the law at all times. Below is a brief summary of the four main Acts that you will need to know for the exam. If

> ### Examination Tip
>
> You will need to be able to answer questions on all parts of the theory that has been covered in this chapter. You may be given a case study in the exam and asked questions about the employee/employer relationship in this case study. Alternatively you may be asked to use examples from a business you have already studied.
>
> The question could ask you to evaluate how a good working relationship has been developed between the employees and the employer of a business you have studied or a case study business given in the exam. You would need to write about how the features of the business have helped to develop this relationship.

you wish to research these Acts further or find other Acts that affect the employee/employer relationship go to www.direct.gov.uk.

- The Employment Rights Act (1996) – covered in Chapter 30 (pages 208–210).
- The Sex Discrimination Act (1975)
- The Race Relations Act (1976)
- The Disability Discrimination Act (1995) – The three Acts above are covered in detail in Chapter 30 (pages 211–214).

How employees and employers develop a good working relationship

It is very important to the overall success of the business that there is a good working relationship between employees and employers. A happier workforce, where good relationships are in place, is a more productive workforce. It is important that the business has a culture of cooperation where everyone is working towards shared aims and objectives.

The employer needs to remember that each employee is unique and will have different needs and objectives. They must communicate with the employees to build a relationship. Holding meetings can improve communication within a business: the employees must feel that their contributions are welcome and important.

Another way to build the relationship is to recognise the successes of the employees. This can be done through reward schemes such as employee of the month. The appraisal system can also let employees know formally that their work is valued. An appraisal is where the manager and the employee discuss the employee's work. They look at successes and areas that need further work. A training programme may be developed as a result of the appraisal. This can also help to build the relationship.

The environment that people work in can have a positive or negative impact on the working relationship. A modern building that is well lit and heated, where the employee has space to work should have a positive impact. The business can also provide extra facilities, such as a canteen, sports facilities and rest areas.

It is vital for the employer to be aware of his or her employees, to know them and to communicate with them. This can be more difficult in a larger organisation, but may be more important so that employees feel that they are valued.

Summary

- An enterprising business will see and take opportunities when they arise in order to hold market share and grow.

- Enterprise can involve being inventive – launching new products, developing new working practices to help employees create a work life balance, considering the management structure of the business.

- An enterprising business will see many benefits. Employees will become more motivated and business reputation could improve which in turn could increase sales and profit.

- Employees are expected to arrive punctually at work ready to undertake their daily duties to their full ability. They must follow all procedures including complying with health and safety legislation.

- Employers are expected to provide employees with a contract of employment, safe and suitable working conditions and treat all members of staff equally.

- A good working relationship between employer and employee is established through trust, communication, and rewards for success.

Case Study

The extract below has been written by the human resources department of Virgin Atlantic. Its aim is to explain the culture of Virgin Atlantic to people who want to apply for a job within the business. Read the extract and answer the questions that follow. To undertake further research go to www.virgin-atlantic.com/en/gb/index.jsp.

> 'It's not easy to sum up our culture in just a few words. For starters, we're such a fast-moving, complex business that change is a constant feature of our operation. Every one of our people has to have the intelligence to think on their feet and respond to any new developments that come their way. All the while, of course, they'll be working hard to deliver the unique brand of service for which we are renowned.
>
> This, in turn, creates a lively, collaborative environment where everyone knows what's expected of them and works together to achieve it. In fact, we pride ourselves on being as honest and unpretentious as we are inspired and professional. Everyone has a chance to voice their opinions and no one's too proud to ask questions, which only serves to increase the inclusive nature of our culture.
>
> Similarly, we embrace innovation, wherever it comes from. So if someone – be they employee or customer – has a brainwave, we'll listen. And if we like it, we'll do it. It's another way in which our people are the driving force behind our success.
>
> Of course, it takes a certain sort of person to flourish in such a fast-paced, free-thinking environment. Talented, self-motivated, enthusiastic, you'll have to share in our passion for providing only the very best. Put people like this together, and you create a winning performance culture that thrives on inspirational leadership, positive attitudes and commercial flair'.

(Source: www.virgin-atlantic.com/en/gb/index.jsp)

1. How do employees at Virgin Atlantic assist the business to operate in an enterprising way?
2. What evidence is there that Virgin Atlantic operates in an enterprising way?
3. What are the possible benefits to Virgin Atlantic of operating in an enterprising way?
4. What does Virgin Atlantic expect from its employees?
5. What can employees expect from Virgin Atlantic?
6. Evaluate whether or not a good working relationship is developed at Virgin Atlantic.

Chapter 7

Changing use of ICT – in business and economic activities

> **Activity**
>
> Write a list of all the different types of ICT you use. Then think about what you use ICT for. You will probably find that businesses uses similar types of ICT and for similar reasons.

Different types of ICT

There are many different types of ICT that are used in business activities. The list below contains the main ones that you will come across.

Personal computer (PC) – this is a computer that is designed to be used mainly by one person at a time. You probably have a standalone computer at home which your family all share. You might even be lucky enough to have your own laptop.

Network – a network is as basic as two computers being connected together. Computers are linked together in order for them to share and exchange data with each other. The computers you use at school are probably all networked together. This enables you to access a wide range of programs and reload your work from computers in different parts of the school. You will probably have your own network space in which all your work is saved.

Spreadsheet – this is a piece of software which is used to carry out calculations. They are very common in business, as they are excellent for handling data such as sales, engineering or financial data.

Word processing – this is a piece of software used to display written materials. Letters, reports etc can be typed and then either emailed or sent by post. Word processing makes it very easy to change mistakes made within work, recall it at a later date and print off as many copies as required. Each printed copy retains the same quality as the first edition.

Database – this is a piece of software that enables data to be stored in a logical and structured way. A database is an excellent way to record customer details, which could be used to help target a marketing campaign.

PowerPoint – this is a presentation application; it allows you to produce slides for presentation to an audience. Each slide can include text, images, animations, video or sound. It could be used to present plans to financiers or to show business customers the new range of products available.

Desktop publishing – this is software that allows you to lay out pages yourself on the computer monitor. It achieves a more professional look than that available with a word processor. A business could produce leaflets and posters using this application.

Internet – this is a computer network that connects computers worldwide. The Internet is used for many things such as email, online chat, news services and websites.

E-commerce – is short for 'Electronic Commerce'. It means to buy and sell by means of the Internet.

Email – is short for 'Electronic Mail'. It is a form of communication where text based messages are exchanged by using computers attached to a network. Email is covered in depth in Chapter 21 (pages 134–135).

The purpose of ICT in business activities

ICT is now frequently used by all businesses as a method of communication. Letters, reports and memorandums can all be created using word-processing programmes. The use of email has increased dramatically as a method of communication. With the simple click of a button information can be sent all over the world. An email can be a quick communication passing on simple information or it could contain a large report as a separate attachment. The main advantage is the speed and cost of communication using this method.

Businesses need to keep a check on their stock levels and a spreadsheet can be used for this purposed. It will calculate how many items have been sold, how many are left in stock and will let you know when you need to re-order. This helps the business so that they don't have too much stock, costing them money and taking up space, or too little stock so that they are unable to meet customer orders. In large businesses, such as superstores, the till is connected to a computer program that will automatically re-order stock when the minimum levels of stock have been reached.

Databases can record information. This could be used by the human resources department to keep a record of employee details. There could also be a database of customer details. In some service industries it is important to keep a record of the services a customer has received. For example a hairdresser might record the treatments clients have had on a database. This enables them to make reference back to recent colours used, or if the client had a poor reaction to certain chemicals. Information kept on the database is easy to access and can be securely stored through the use of passwords and restricted access to the computer.

The use of ICT in economic activities

The main use of ICT in economic activities is e-commerce for online sales. There are different kinds of e-commerce.

- Business-to-Business – this is where companies buy and sell goods to each other.
- Business-to-Individual – this is where you buy from an e-commerce shop such as iTunes.
- Individual-to-Individual – this is where people buy and sell from each other, eg eBay.

Some customers have been concerned about using their credit card to make payments over the Internet. There are now 'Payment Gateway' firms that will handle all the credit card payments for you, eg WorldPay and Paypal. These are more secure for the business and the customer.

More shoppers online at Christmas

IMRG, an online retail group, predicted that more than five million people would use the internet for online shopping on Christmas Day 2008. They estimated that more than £100 million would be spent online, compared to £84 million in 2007.

Some of the major high street stores began sales on their websites early to meet the demand. Marks & Spencer launched its online sale on Christmas Day with savings of up to 50% on some products.

Debenhams announced that their sale would begin on Boxing Day morning with price cuts of up to 70%

(Source: adapted from www.bbc.co.uk)

The article on the previous page details the dramatic increase seen in online shopping during Christmas 2008.

> **Activity**
>
> List all the websites that you have used to purchase goods from. Compare your list with a partner – how many of them are the same? Investigate two of the websites you have identified. Explain how and why they appealed to you – why did you buy from them rather than an alternative site? Try and find two competitors to your selected websites – explain how these websites differ. Are they more colourful, easier to use etc?

Potential benefits/ drawbacks of upgrading ICT provision to a business

Businesses need to evaluate their ICT provision. This is the hardware (including monitors, keyboards, printers, hard disk, wiring, central processing unit) and the software (this includes all computer applications and operating systems used with computers).

The decision to upgrade the technology used to run the business needs careful consideration. Any decisions the business makes may have benefits and drawbacks for the business, the employees and the customers. If it is successful, the business will run smoothly. On the other hand, the business could end up with PCs that will not talk to each other, a printer that will not print, email that works intermittently and frustrated staff.

Labour saving benefits

The general assumption in society is that increasing the use of ICT within a business will actually make it more efficient. Unfortunately this is not always the case. Some businesses have run extremely efficiently for many years without the use of complex ICT. For example many hairdressing salons run a manual diary with appointments being written in pencil. The system stops stylists becoming over booked and also cancellations can be easily erased. A computerised diary is not really going to improve the efficiency of the hairdressers. The introduction or updating of ICT systems will initially cause disruption usually due to teething problems. Staff will have to learn how to use the new software and then adjust to how this will affect their daily working lives and routines. When this initial settling in phase has been worked through efficiency might increase.

Having decided to update the ICT facility there may be some benefits to be gained in terms of general labour efficiency. For example, a till that can also control stock will save time compared to undertaking manual stock controls. This type of system could also ensure that there is always sufficient stock available to meet customers' needs.

Today's modern garages have all had to embrace new technology in order to diagnose faults in new cars. This technology will need to be continually updated as new and more complex cars roll off the production lines. Without this technology the diagnosis and cure of some mechanical faults might be impossible.

Cost saving benefits

It is a decision not just based on the cost of the equipment. The business needs to look at the support available to install and maintain new equipment and software. The more complex the system is, the greater the technical skills required to support the system. This could involve employing specialists to work within the ICT department – something that was not previously required.

The possible benefits are that money could be saved if the new system is more efficient. A quicker system could also save time, or mean that more work can be achieved in the same period of time, thereby increasing the overall efficiency of the workforce.

Paperless Office

As computers slowly began to dominate most of our working lives it was always presumed that they would create the 'paperless' office. In fact if you look around most office desks they are still piled high with paper. Although communications such as email are used regularly many people still print out important emails as evidence they were sent or received, and also so they can be referred to later. It appears that most people still like to see information in hard copy, and as such it appears the 'paperless' office is a long way from fruition.

Growth of e-commerce

As you can see from the extracts below, if a business does not join this increasing trend they are likely to lose out on potential customers.

A business will also have to consider the costs involved with such a development, they will need to design and maintain a website, pay a website host and then deal with the orders. This could impact on the way the business currently works and, if initial orders are not large, greatly increase the costs of the business.

In 2008, 16 million households in Great Britain (65 per cent) had Internet access. This is an increase of just over 1 million households (7 per cent) over the last year and 5 million households (46 per cent) since 2002.

E-Commerce has also increased among business enterprises across the European Union (EU). In 2006, the UK had the second highest proportion of enterprises receiving orders over the Internet or non-Internet information and communication technology (ICT) in the EU, at 30 per cent. Denmark had the highest proportion, at 34 per cent, which was well above the EU-25 average of 14 per cent.

Extracts taken from www.statistics.gov.uk.

Examination Tip

You will need to be able to write about the different types of ICT. You will have to explain the purpose of ICT in business activities and also explain how businesses use ICT in economic activities. You may be given a case study business in the exam that you will have to answer questions about, or you may be asked to write about a business that you have studied.

You will need to be able to evaluate the case for an upgrade in ICT provision. Evaluate means write about the good things (benefits) for the business in upgrading, and the bad things (drawback) for the business in upgrading. You then have to write a conclusion saying whether or not the business should upgrade, giving reasons for your answer. You might be given a case study business to write about or be asked to write about a business you have studied.

Do not forget this is an applied business exam and not an ICT or computer studies one. You will not be required to go into a lot of detail about the technical aspects of ICT: this exam is more about what a business uses ICT for and the decisions a business may have to make about its ICT provision.

Changing use of ICT – in business and economic activities 41

Activity

'Moonpig cards offer a totally new concept in buying greeting cards. You can order most of the best selling greeting card designs you see in the high street but we allow you to personalise the caption to create a completely unique card.

We produce all of the cards in our own hi-tech production facility in Guernsey and send them back to you or directly to your recipient by Guernsey Post and Royal Mail. Any card orders received before 2pm Mon-Fri will be posted the same day.

The Moonpig website was launched in July 2000 and since then we have been striving to improve the selection of cards we offer. We are here to offer you a better service so if you have any suggestions or comments please contact us.'

(Source: www.moonpig.com)

1 What type of business activity is Moonpig involved in?
2 List five different types of ICT that could be used by Moonpig.
3 Give examples to show that Moonpig has acted in an enterprising way.
4 Explain how the Internet has allowed Moonpig to do business.

Summary

- The different types of ICT that you will need to have a basic working knowledge of are: personal computer; network; spreadsheet; word-processing; database; PowerPoint; desktop publishing; internet; e-commerce; email.

- ICT is used in business to aid communication which could involve the creation of letters to the management of stock and customer databases.

- Benefits of using ICT mainly focus on the speed of this type of communication, which could ultimately save labour hours.

- Drawbacks include the initial cost of implementation and potential need to regularly upgrade the system. The need to offer staff training has to be considered. A computer system is only ever as efficient as the staff that operates it.

Chapter 8

Uncertainty – risk, reward and change

Activity

Write a list of the things you think will happen today. Next to each item on your list, write down whether it is certain to happen or uncertain. You will probably have a mixture of certain and uncertain. This is the situation businesses find themselves in. They have to react to the uncertain things on their list in order to be successful.

Reasons why the business environment is uncertain

The business environment is uncertain, challenging and dynamic. This means that it is always changing. In order to continue to be successful a business needs to react to these changes. They might have to take risks to be rewarded in the long term.

There are a number of different reasons why the business environment changes. The business cannot do anything about the change itself, but it needs to act so that the change does not have a negative impact on the business.

There could be changes in the economy that mean the business environment is uncertain (this is dealt with in more detail in Chapter 10). The changes could leave consumers with less money, leading to a decrease in their spending, particularly on luxury goods. On the other hand, consumers could have greater disposable income and there could be an increase in demand for goods and services. Businesses need to be aware of any potential changes to the economy and have plans in place so that they can react quickly.

The environment might change because of changing customer demands. This could be that taste and fashions have changed and consumers are demanding products with greater technology. The mobile phone industry has to constantly update its products to keep ahead of competitors and satisfy consumer demand.

Activity

2008 saw television campaigns that caused changes to customer demand. Hugh Fearnley-Whittingstall and Jamie Oliver launched a high-profile campaign on Channel 4 to show the life of battery chickens. The article below shows the impact that their campaign had. Read the article and answer the questions that follow.

Case Study

The campaign that changed the eating habits of a nation

Boycott of battery chickens forces supermarkets to think ethically.

Sales of factory-farmed chickens have slumped since a high-profile campaign raised awareness of the cruelty at the heart of the poultry industry and implored consumers to pay more to improve the animals' welfare.

Sales of free-range poultry shot up by 35% last month compared with January 2007, while sales of standard indoor birds fell by

Uncertainty – risk, reward and change

7%, according to a survey of 25,000 shoppers by the market research company TNS.

Supermarkets have been stripped of free-range birds, prompting complaints from frustrated shoppers keen to embrace the movement away from intensive farming.

The rise in sales would have been even higher if poultry producers had been able to keep up with demand. Many suppliers in the £2bn-a-year poultry industry are now expected to convert cramped chicken sheds into more spacious accommodation.

Tesco, the country's biggest retailer, has doubled its order for higher-welfare chickens while Sainsbury's has been flabbergasted by the 'unprecedented' spurt in demand and forced to import free-range birds from France.

'If the growing consumer demand for free-range, organic and higher-welfare chicken continues, availability in store could certainly become an important barrier to consumer choice, at least in the short term', said Maria Carrol, ACNielsen's consumer insight manager.

'I just hope the British retailers and the industry are talking to each other, making sure that new free-range farms are built and new RSPCA Freedom Food farms are built to cater for a growing demand for high welfare chicken', said Hugh Fearnley-Whittingstall.

(Source: Martin Hickman, The Independent, 28th February 2008 © The Independent)

1 Carry out research into the current trends in chicken buying.
2 Research the views of three major supermarkets about sales of chickens.
3 Explain why there was an increased demand for free-range chicken.
4 Describe the problems faced by supermarkets after the campaign was launched.
5 What could supermarkets have done differently to ensure that consumer demand was met?
6 What do farmers need to do in order to meet demand?
7 Could farmers have predicted the increase in demand for free-range chickens?

Ways in which businesses can change existing business practices in order to be successful

As we saw in the example above, the farmers and supermarkets had to change their business practices in order to continue to be successful. If both stakeholder groups do not react to these changes they could lose out on potential income as consumer demand changed very quickly. To follow this up during February 2009 consumers had also increased their consumption of eggs due to the credit crunch. Eggs are a relatively cheap method of providing a healthy meal which is high in protein. Health concerns have also been dispelled as reported by the British Egg Council in Farmers Weekly (www.fwi.co.uk/Articles/2009/03/12/114697/egg-sales-reveal-the-best-increase-for-many-years.htm). Free range egg producers will have to increase production in order to meet a further increase in demand.

Some businesses find a change of ownership allows them to be successful. A sole trader could become a partnership as other investors are included in the business. This will bring new finance into the business but also expertise. It is quite often the expertise that is required in order to help the business keep up with the dynamic nature of the business environment. Have another look at the entrepreneurs that go into the Dragon's Den (www.bbc.co.uk/dragonsden/).

When the 'dragons' offer to invest money in the entrepreneurs business they include their own expertise as part of the deal.

Small businesses are sometimes bought out by bigger businesses and continue to trade using the original name. This can be seen with Rachel's Organics. The company is owned by Dean Foods, whose funds Rachel has utilised to finance new product launches and marketing campaigns. This has allowed Rachel's Organics to compete with Yeo Valley Organic (see case study in Chapter 1).

The business might look to change its activity in order to be successful. A business that is involved in the primary sector might decide to expand and include elements of the secondary and tertiary sectors as well. For example, a farmer that grows his/her own produce might decide to cook it in some way as a secondary activity. It could then be sold in their own farm shop as a tertiary activity. There is currently an increasing trend for farm shops and changing the business in this way can help it to remain successful.

Tesco was having a lot of success as a food retailer. It had food outlets of all sizes and a website where customers could buy food and related goods and have them delivered home. In 2006 it launched Tesco Direct to rival Argos. It would sell over 8,000 non food products from a catalogue and its website. This shows that Tesco changed its activity in order to be more successful.

Andrew Higginson, Tesco Finance and Strategy Director said: Our customers have told us they not only want easier access to our non-food products, but they would love to see a bigger range too.

He continued, Convenience is increasingly important to our customers and we believe that offering new ways to order and a wider range of products will be really popular with our customers.

Currently only around a quarter of UK shoppers are able to get to a Tesco Extra (www.tesco.com) store easily so Tesco Direct will make our non-food products more accessible than ever before. Tesco Direct will have more breadth and depth and all at the great value prices that our customers have come to expect from us.

The launch of Tesco Direct will mean that shopping for non-food items will be easier than ever before – combining easy access to a great product range and more choices on when and how to shop. Andrew Higginson added: We have invested £30 million in the start up costs of Tesco Direct. Over time we believe Tesco Direct will become a substantial on-line and catalogue-based non-food business.

(Source: adapted from www.free-press-release.com)

Consequences to businesses of not making changes/ taking risks

Some businesses might be happy to continue as they have for many years. They will not take risks or make changes and because of this will probably not increase their profits or expand as a business. There could be more negative consequences than just 'standing still'. The business could be left behind by competitors and risk losing market share.

As we have seen, Rachel's Organics was bought by Deans Foods. This has allowed the brand of Rachel's Organics to compete within the United Kingdom and it is currently the second biggest seller in the adult organic yoghurt sector, behind Yeo Valley Organic. Without finance from Deans Foods the business would probably still be a small-scale business, not the main competitor of the number one business in that sector of the industry.

Uncertainty – risk, reward and change

Businesses can lose market share if they do not take risks. If their competitor has a new product available then consumers will probably go to the competitor to purchase. It might mean a lot of finance has to be invested to purchase stock but that is where the reward comes in if the risk was worth taking. The business has to weigh up both sides and make their decision.

When the economy is in a downturn it is tempting for businesses not to take any risks, but they do still need to in order to attract customers who now have less money to spend. As we have already seen some businesses do well in an economic downturn because the goods that they offer meet the needs of the customers.

With the launch of 3G technology all mobile phone businesses had to design and build phones that were able to use this new technology. There are many customers who demanded this technology and if their regular mobile phone business was not making phones to this specification they would simply go to a competitor. This shows the importance of taking risks in order to keep up with competitors.

Examination Tip

You will need to answer questions about risk, reward and change. You may be asked to give an example of a business you have studied and then have to explain how that business has changed its existing business practices to be more successful.

You might then have to evaluate the consequences to your business of not having made these changes. That means suggesting alternatives that could have happened to the business if it did not make the changes, and then drawing a conclusion saying which would have been most likely to happen – giving reasons for your answer.

Below is an extract from www.cadbury.com. It explains the strategy for the business until 2011. Read the extract and answer the questions that follow.

Case Study

We believe that the business still has significant untapped potential – both in terms of top line growth and returns. By exploiting the strength of our leadership positions to continue to grow our market share and significantly increase our margins and returns, we aim to achieve our vision of becoming the biggest and best confectionery company in the world.

Our Vision into Action (VIA) plan for 2008 to 2011 aligns the energies and efforts of our teams around the world behind a number of priorities which will make the most impact on our revenue and margin performance.

In order to generate superior returns for our shareowners, our VIA will deliver a range of financial targets. These are set out in our financial performance scorecard below:

- Organic revenue growth of 4%–6% every year
- Total confectionery share gain
- Mid-teens trading margins by 2011
- Strong dividend growth
- An efficient balance sheet growth in Return on Invested Capital (ROIC)

To achieve these financial goals, we have a growth and efficiency strategy which aligns behind our focus on fewer, faster, bigger and better. This focus is being applied to all aspects of our business.

(Extract reproduced under authority and with the kind permission of Cadbury. All rights reserved.)

1 Conduct research into Cadbury. Find out about the brands that it sells and which countries it sells to.
2 What is Cadbury doing to ensure that it remains successful?
3 Describe the ways that Cadbury changed existing business practices in order to be successful.
4 Were these strategies successful?
5 Explain what Cadbury means by 'fewer, faster, bigger and better'.
6 What would be the consequences to Cadbury of not taking any risks?
7 Recommend to Cadbury what it should do next.

Summary

- We live in an economic environment that is always changing. In order to retain market share a business must be prepared to take risks.

- Failure to take risks could mean the business does not see opportunities as and when they arise and as such allows their competitors to gain more customers, increasing their market share.

- Taking risks that pay off could enable a business to reap large rewards.

Chapter 9

Business within society – ethics and sustainability

> **Activity**
>
> Brainstorm a list of things that businesses can do to make themselves 'look good'. When you have completed this chapter see how many items on your list are to do with ethics and sustainability.

Meaning of ethics

Ethics are a written and unwritten code of principles and moral values. Business ethics refer to the actions of individuals within a business, as well as the business as a whole. It is about knowing the difference between right and wrong, and choosing to do what is right. Ethical values can be subject to different interpretations by individuals as well as businesses. These different interpretations can be influenced by the person's or business's religious, social and cultural background.

Something that is unethical might not be illegal but it would not be seen as the right thing to do, for example exploiting child labour.

Ways in which businesses can be seen to be operating in an ethical manner

Businesses need to show all of their stakeholders that they act in an ethical manner. They must be seen to act ethically in all areas of their operation.

Goods that are produced need to be fit for purpose – that is they need to be able to do the job they were designed to do. By producing poor-quality goods the business may not be treating its customers ethically, as the goods may not last long or be fit for the intended purpose.

When a business is sourcing raw materials or outsourcing production, it needs to look at the conditions in the factory where the goods are to be produced. It is not sufficient to have good employee/employer relationships in your own business; these must also exist with the suppliers.

Some businesses have been in the news because they outsourced production to less economically developed countries, such as India, where children were exploited and made to work in sweatshops. Gap Inc. was one such business that has since worked hard to improve its image. The following is a quote on ethical trading from www.gapinc.com:

> At Gap Inc., we believe we should go beyond the basics of ethical business practices and embrace our responsibility to people and to the planet. We believe this brings sustained, collective value to our shareholders, our employees, our customers and society.
>
> 'Acting in an ethical way is not only the right thing to do – it also unlocks new ways for us to do business better', Dan Henkle, SVP, Social Responsibility.

According to the Ethical Trading Initiative there are a number of things a business needs to address if it wants to trade ethically. A business must be committed to ethical trading by investing money and staff. There need to be checks in place to make sure that the working conditions of all employees and outsourced employees are up to standard. If a problem is found then there needs to be agreement about how conditions can be improved, and there also needs to be follow-up checks to ensure that the improvements have been made. Employees and suppliers need adequate training and support in order to help the business meet its ethical obligations.

The business needs to ensure that ethical principles are established in all areas of its decision-making, for example in the prices it pays its suppliers, and the lead times given to them to complete orders. Businesses need to work together, and with trade unions, to ensure that ethical business practices are introduced and maintained.

To conduct further research go to www.ethicaltrade.org.

Consequences to businesses of not operating in an ethical manner

Customers are placing ethical reasons higher up on their list of things to look for when considering a purchase. For this reason alone, before we consider whether or not 'it is the right thing to do', businesses must ensure that they act ethically and are seen to do so.

Customers want to see an end to sweatshops and child labour and so the business must not associate itself with these. It can be very bad for the reputation of the business if it is seen to be trading unethically. This could lead to customers deciding to shop elsewhere. The effect of this could be a decrease in profits. Suppliers might not want to supply to the business as they might feel that having their name associated with unethical practices will have a negative effect on their own business.

Poor ethical trading can result in bad publicity and this is not helpful to any business. It is better to be associated with good ethical trading and have your name publicised by organisations such as the Ethical Trading Initiative.

Meaning of sustainability

A common and internationally accepted definition of sustainability is: 'development which meets the needs of the present without compromising the ability of future generations to meet their own needs'.

As the world has developed over the last 200 years we have become a major threat to the environment in which we live. We create air pollution through the use of transport; we consume natural resources that are being replaced at a much slower pace than our consumption; and have harmed wildlife through the destruction of their habitats.

Sustainability requires us to manage the pollution we create, which will include how we make energy, review our methods of transport and the amount of waste that has to be disposed of. We can all help. We can walk and cycle rather than use the car; we can turn off lights; and lower the temperature of our central heating systems. We must consider the packaging that we use when purchasing goods.

The UK Sustainable Development Strategy 2005 recognised that everybody has the right to a healthy, clean and safe environment. The UK has four main priorities:

- Sustainable consumption and production
- Climate change and energy
- Natural resource protection and environmental enhancement
- Sustainable communities.

Activity

Is your school a sustainable school? What does this mean to you? How does it affect your daily life at school?

Business within society – ethics and sustainability

> **Did you know?**
>
> Consumers currently produce approximately 28 million tons of domestic rubbish each year. That is equivalent to 500 kilograms for every person in the country. Most of this goes to landfill sites which are the second highest producers of the greenhouse gas, methane. The Government is hoping to increase recycling to 33% by the year 2015.

Ways in which a business may act in order to achieve sustainability

Businesses need to look at all aspects of the way they are run in order to find ways to achieve sustainability. Our carbon footprint is a buzzword at the moment and there are organisations in existence that aim to calculate a business's carbon footprint and try and offer ways to reduce it. Carbonfund.org is one such organisation. To find out more about its work go to www.carbonfund.org.

Business link (www.businesslink.gov.uk) has produced a list of top 10 tips for reducing waste and saving energy. These have been summarised below.

1. Turn off all office equipment when you are not using it – overnight, at weekends and during bank holidays. A single computer and monitor left on for 24 hours a day will cost over £50 a year in electricity costs.

2. Turn off lights in empty rooms and replace bulbs with energy saving ones. Lighting costs can be cut by as much as 15% by simply turning off lights in rooms and corridors that are not being used.

3. Reduce water consumption by turning of taps fully and fixing any drips. A constantly dripping tap can waste 500,000 litres of water per year. This could cost a business £400 per year.

4. Examine waste disposal costs and consider partnering with a nearby business to recycle your waste. Could your waste be turned into other businesses' raw materials?

5. Keep heating at a constant level and ensure doors and windows are shut when using heating and air conditioning. Heating costs rise by 8% every time the temperature is increased by just one degree.

6. Ask your suppliers about take-back schemes for unused products. This could reduce wastage and storage costs. You might not get all of your money back but it might be better than destroying old stock or sending it to landfill sites.

7. Minimise the need for travel, and drive efficiently when travel is necessary. A business with five company cars could save £5,300 per year through more efficient driving, leading to a reduction in fuel consumption and mileage repayment costs. Efficient driving could focus on routes taken and the speed and acceleration used by drivers.

8. Invest in efficient equipment to help cut your energy, transport and water costs.

9. Use email where possible, set your PC to print double-sided; and use refillable printer, fax and photocopier cartridges. You can fill inkjet cartridges for about half the price of a new one.

10. Let your customers and suppliers know you are committed to reducing your environmental impact, and promote it through your marketing.

Activity

Use the above information and further research the work of Carbonfund. Write a letter to a local business person explaining to him or her how they could become more sustainable.

Include in your letter possible benefits to the business if they carry out this work.

Did you know

The cost of wasted resources to UK manufacturing is equivalent to 7% of profit. Basic energy efficiency improvements could save £12 billion annually across the UK.

Examination Tip

You will need to understand what ethics and sustainability mean. You may be asked to give examples of ways that businesses can act in an ethical or sustainable manner.

You might have to evaluate how a particular business can be seen to be operating in an ethical manner. This could be a case study business given in the exam or you may be asked to write about a business you have studied. Evaluate means give evidence about the way the business operates and then draw a conclusion as to whether or not you think it is acting in an ethical manner. You may need to evaluate the consequences to your chosen business of not behaving in an ethical manner.

Activity

Below is an introduction to Plan A from M&S. Go to http:// corporate.marksandspencer.com/howwedobusiness to find out more about Plan A and then answer the questions that follow.

Plan A

Plan A is our five-year, 100-point 'eco' plan to tackle some of the biggest challenges facing our business and our world. It will see us working with our customers and our suppliers to combat climate change, reduce waste, safeguard natural resources, trade ethically and build a healthier nation.

We're doing this because it's what you want us to do. It's also the right thing to do. We're calling it Plan A because we believe it's now the only way to do business.

There is no Plan B.

(Source: http://corporate.marksandspencer.com/howwedobusiness)

Business within society – ethics and sustainability

By 2012 M&S aims to:

- Become carbon neutral
- Send no waste to landfill
- Extend sustainable sourcing
- Help improve the lives of people in our supply chain
- Help customers and employees live a healthier life-style.

1 Why is it important to M&S to act in a sustainable and ethical way?

2 Evaluate whether or not M&S is acting in an ethical way.

3 Evaluate the possible consequences to M&S of not acting in an ethical way.

Summary

- Ethics are a written and unwritten code of principles and moral values.

- Ethics are the way people expect a business to trade – fairly and without endangering anyone or anything. This could include their employees, suppliers, wildlife, wild animals and the environment.

- If a business is seen to operate in a non ethical manner it will attract bad publicity, which ultimately might decrease sales and hence profits.

- Sustainability is 'development which meets the needs of the present without compromising the ability of future generations to meet their own needs'.

Chapter 10

Use of relevant terms, concepts and methods – to understand business and economic behaviour

> **Activity**
>
> Write a list of the things you think will happen today. Next to each item on your list, write down whether or not you have any control over the item. You will probably find you have a mixture of things you have control over and things you do not have control over. This is the situation businesses find themselves in: they have to react to the things they have no control over.

Economic factors

You have identified things that you have no control over; the things that businesses have no control over are known as economic factors. Examples of these factors are: inflation, interest rates and exchange rates.

Inflation

This is the increase in the price of goods and services measured over a set period of time. As inflation rises the money you have buys you fewer goods and services than a year ago.

There are two measures of inflation – the retail price index (RPI) and the consumer price index (CPI). The Government uses the consumer price index to measure inflation. In order to calculate these indexes the Government compares the cost of an average basket of shopping from one month to the next. When calculating the average basket of goods the CPI does not include mortgage and housing costs which are included in the calculation for the retail price index. The percentage increase or decrease in the index is a reflection of the rate of inflation. The Government's aim is to maintain inflation at 2%. On 24th March 2009 the Office of National Statistics announced that the inflation had unexpectedly risen from 3% in January 2009 to 3.2% in February 2009. One of the reasons for the rise was the increase in petrol costs and the weakening of the pound. A breakdown of the figures showed food prices had risen by 12.5% in the year to February 2009.

The RPI is a broader measure of inflation as it does take into account mortgage repayments and the cost of housing. This measure slipped to an annual rate of 0% during February 2009. Economists think that the RPI may drop as low as –4% during 2009 as tumbling interest rates and mortgage costs and a reduction in energy prices filter through to the consumer.

The RPI illustrates that the average household, when housing and mortgage costs are considered, are currently not worse off than they were last year. Their disposable income will still purchase the same amount of goods as last year. However, if housing and mortgage costs are removed (CPI) they would be able to purchase 3.2% less goods and services than they could a year ago.

Impact of inflation on business behaviour and possible reactions

When inflation is increasing the price of products the business needs to use in production will increase in price. The business could also be

Use of relevant terms, concepts and methods – to understand business and economic behaviour

experiencing increasing expenses; for example energy prices might be rising. This will leave the business with a number of possible options:

- They can pass these price increases on to customers through higher prices. This might cause a reduction in sales as people can no longer afford the product or service.

- They can absorb these costs which will reduce their profitability. It could mean that sales will remain stable or possibly increase if competitors raise their prices.

- The business could look at possible ways of reducing costs. Could raw materials be purchased from a cheaper supplier? Could energy be saved through a reduction in heating, turning lights off etc?

Sales of products might fall even if the business does not raise its own prices. This is especially true with luxury goods and services. If inflation is rising rapidly consumers will have less money to spend and will therefore have to make cutbacks in expenditure. This could result in them taking less holidays, eating out less, and going to the cinema once a month rather than weekly.

If the prices of goods produced in the United Kingdom increase too much then people and businesses may start to import more goods from abroad because they are cheaper. This can make the situation worse for United Kingdom businesses which may be forced to reduce prices in order to compete.

If inflation goes into negative figures consumers will be able to purchase more for their money – goods and services will become cheaper. If this is the case businesses may see a surge in demand as consumer money will go further and they can now afford items which were once beyond their expenditure limits.

Exchange rates

This is the price at which one currency is bought and sold for another. In the United Kingdom, businesses that trade within Europe have to exchange the pound sterling for the euro. Most countries within the European Union also have the euro as their currency and this makes trading between those countries in the eurozone easier and without the risk element of the currencies changing. The graph below shows the value of the euro against sterling.

VALUE OF THE EURO AGAINST STERLING

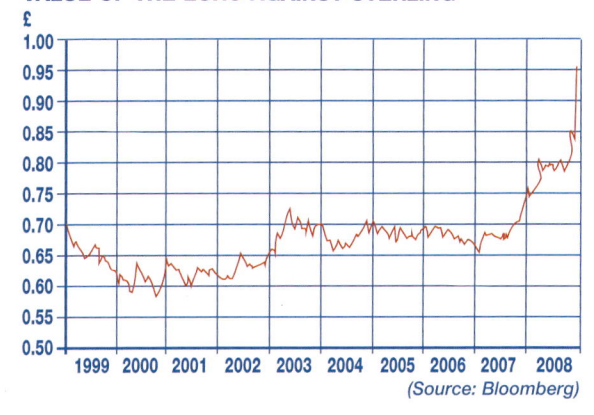

(Source: Bloomberg)

While the euro initially fell against the pound it has soared over the past few months, primarily on the perception that the UK may suffer a worse recession than the eurozone. It has risen to be worth as much as 98 pence on the foreign exchange markets, with many analysts predicting it is on the way to being worth more than £1 (source: www.bbc.co.uk).

Impact of changes in exchange rates on business behaviour and possible reactions

On 25th March 2009 you could get 0.9258 euros for one pound sterling. One pound sterling was also able to purchase 1.47 US dollars. Sterling has seen an overall 28% loss in value since January 2007. This has had the impact of making imported goods more expensive in our shops if retailers wish to maintain their profit margins. This has helped fuel inflation.

Let us consider this: if a firm imported jeans from America for $35 when the exchange rate was $1.75 dollars to the pound the cost of the jeans would have been: $35 divided by 1.75 = £20 sterling. If the shop sold them for £45 their gross profit would have been £45 – £20 = £25.00.

So what happens when the exchange rate falls? Let us use the same example with the exchange rate falling to $1.45 to the pound:

$35 divided by 1.45 = £24.14. If the retailer still sells the jeans at £45 their gross profit has fallen to £45 – £24.14 = £20.86.

Let us now consider what happens when the exchange rate rises. We will use the same example but consider the exchange rate has risen to $1.95 to the pound

$35 divided by 1.95 = £17.95. This time gross profit has increased if the sales price was to remain constant at £45. £45 – £17.95 = £27.05.

As you can see from the above example the higher the exchange rate the greater the potential profit a business can earn through importing goods. Currently exchange rates have been falling which means that profit margins on imported goods have also been shrinking. Businesses will have to decide whether to increase the price of the goods in order to retain profit margins or to continue selling at the same price and sustaining smaller profit margins. If the prices of goods are increased customers may stop purchasing them and try cheaper alternatives or another supplier.

The above example considered a business who imported goods from the USA. We now need to consider how changes in exchange rates can impact on businesses that export goods.

Let us consider Wicker Seats Ltd who exports wicker furniture to France. Currently wicker chairs are exported for 100 euros each. The current exchange rate is 0.9258 euros for one pound sterling.

The business will receive 100 divided by 0.9258 = £108.

If the exchange rate falls to 0.75 euros per one pound sterling the business would receive 100 divided by 0.75 = £133.

If the exchange rate rises to 0.98 euros per one pound sterling the business would receive 100 divided by 0.98 = £102.

In the above example we did the calculations based on a sales price being agreed in euros. In reality the exporting business might negotiate their sales price in pounds sterling. The fluctuations in exchange rates would have the same effect on profits.

For example, if Wicker Seats Ltd set a sales price of £20 for a wicker foot rest what happens when exchange rates go up and down? We will consider the same three rates again – 0.9285, 0.75 and 0.98 euros per one pound sterling.

£20 divided by 0.9258 = £21.60

£20 divided by 0.75 = £26.67

£20 divided by 0.98 = £20.41

As you can see from the above examples the higher the exchange rate the less money the exporting business receives for its goods and services. As the exchange rate fluctuates on a daily basis this makes it very difficult for businesses to be able to accurately calculate their potential profits. When businesses export within the eurozone this could be an argument for adopting the euro.

Changes in exchange rates might make the business want to stop importing and exporting and only deal with suppliers and customers from within the United Kingdom. The business might also decide to lobby the Government in order to encourage them to adopt the euro if this would make it easier for them to do business with most of the countries in mainland Europe.

Interest rates

This is the price or cost of borrowing money. If a bank lends a business money the rate of interest charged is the bank's reward for taking the risk. Interest payments are one source of income for banks.

Let us illustrate this concept through the use of an example.

Use of relevant terms, concepts and methods – to understand business and economic behaviour

Brown Brothers Ltd wants to borrow £25,000 in order to invest in some new equipment. They would like to take the loan out over five years. Brown Brothers Ltd has approached two different banks. The first quoted an interest rate of 5.6% and the second 6.2%. Let us consider the repayments that would be required.

The amount borrowed is known as the capital repayment. This is the £25,000. As the loan has been taken over five years it means that each year the capital repayment will be £25,000 divided by 5 = £5,000.

For bank one interest rate is 5.6%. The calculation for this would be:

£25,000 divided by 100 x 5.6 (interest rate) = £1,400.

Total payments on the loan for year one from bank one would be £5,000 (capital repayment) plus £1,400 (interest due) = £6,400.

For bank two the interest rate was 6.2%. The calculation for this would be:

£25,000 divided by 100 x 6.2 (interest rate) = £1,550.

Total payments on the loan for year one from bank two would be £5,000 (capital repayment) plus £1,550 (interest due) = £6,550.

As you can see the higher the interest rate the more expensive the loan becomes.

From the above examples you can see that in the first year bank one would earn £1,400 from the loan and bank two would earn £1,550.

Every month he Monetary Policy Committee (MPC) of the Bank of England reviews the bank base rate. This is the rate at which the Bank of England lends money to the commercial banking institutions. The lower the Bank of England base rates the cheaper loans and mortgages become, and the reverse is also true. If the MPC increases the base rate then the cost of mortgages and loans will increase. Currently (March 2009) the Bank of England has been dramatically reducing its base rate in an attempt to encourage banks to start lending money to people again in order to encourage consumer spending. Below is a table which illustrates how interest rates have fallen over the last 15 months.

Year	Month	Base Rate %	Change
2009	5th March	0.50	–0.50
	5th February	1.00	–0.50
	8th January	1.50	–0.50
2008	4th December	2.00	–1.00
	6th November	3.00	–1.50
	8th October	4.50	–0.50
	10th April	5.00	–0.25
	7th February	5.25	–0.25

Table 10.1

Below is a graph which illustrates the Bank of England's base rate since 1951. You can see that it reached a peak during the late 1970s. It is currently at its lowest rate since records began.

BANK OF ENGLAND'S OFFICIAL BANK RATE SINCE 1951

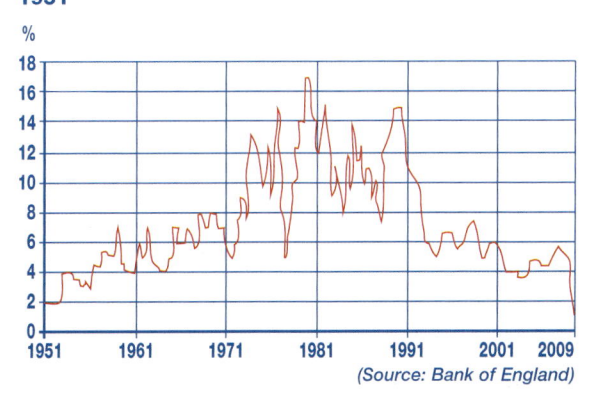

(Source: Bank of England)

Impact of changes in interest rates on business behaviour and possible reactions

There is a direct link between interest rates and inflation. If the Government feels that inflation is rising above their target of 2% they will increase interest rates in order to curb consumer spending. For consumers this means that the cost of their external borrowing increases. Loans and mortgages become more expensive, leaving the family with less money to spend on other items. This will mean that some businesses may find that consumer demand drops and the only way to maintain sales is to decrease the price of goods and services. Not all consumption will be hit; for example people will need to still buy staple food such as bread but they could cut down on cakes and biscuits.

Businesses that have external loans will also find that their expenditure has risen. If sales are falling and the costs of loans have increased this could push some businesses into liquidation. This simply means they have insufficient income to meet the costs of running the business.

In order to combat the increased cost of loans a business may decide to raise its prices. This will only work if the target market who purchases the items can still afford the higher price or the competition is using the same strategies. This type of strategy will further fuel inflation as prices are increasing.

If a business was planning an expansion or a move to alternative premises this would have required an increase in borrowing; these ideas might now be put on hold until interest rates are lower.

When interest rates rise people or businesses that have money in savings accounts will benefit. Their investments will provide a better return and this could encourage consumers to save rather than spend their money. If this happens businesses could experience a fall in demand.

The MPC lowers interest rates when it wants to stimulate the economy. The idea is that by reducing the cost of borrowing and mortgages people will start to spend money which in turn creates employment and wealth.

Let us consider this on a number of levels. If consumers already have loans and mortgages a decrease in interest rates will mean payments will be reduced. They will have a greater amount of money available each month to spend on 'other' things. This could be a holiday abroad, days out, excursions to nice restaurants. Businesses will see an increase in trade and the number of price reduction sales could be reduced as consumers are returning to the high street.

If consumers do not currently have loans they might consider taking one out as the cost has been greatly reduced. For example they might want to purchase a new car and a lower rate of interest would mean they could now afford the repayments. This would stimulate demand within the car industry.

The housing market plays a major role in the British economy. If mortgages become hard to obtain, or too expensive, people stop entering the market which then brings the whole process to a grinding halt. If interest rates reduce first-time buyers are more likely to be able to afford a mortgage which stimulates the housing market. When people move house they need removal services and they often buy new furniture. All of these businesses should see an increase in demand, which will keep them in business and might even allow them to expand.

When interest rates fall businesses will also see a decrease in their expenses if they have external loans. This will help them maintain healthy profit margins as their expenditure has decreased. The money being saved through a reduction in loan payments can be channelled elsewhere in the business.

If a fall in interest rates stimulates increased demand a business may wish to expand. The price of borrowing is likely to play a major part in this decision.

When interest rates fall consumers who save money will see their returns decreasing and might then decide to spend their money rather than save it. This will fuel consumer demand, again stimulating the economy.

Use of relevant terms, concepts and methods – to understand business and economic behaviour

Currently (March 2009) the country has a CPI of 3.2% which is 1.2% over the Governments target for inflation. The general feeling is that inflation will fall within the next few months because inflation earlier in the year had been driven by increasing food prices, rising energy prices and surging oil prices. These factors are no longer occurring. The MPC has cut the base rate to its lowest ever rate of 0.5% in order to help stimulate the economy as it moves into a deeper recession than originally expected. VAT has been cut to 15% and other measures have been proposed in order to support businesses through these difficult and turbulent times.

The case study below shows how a downturn in the economy is having a positive effect on United Kingdom tourist businesses. Read the case study and answer the questions that follow.

Examination Tip

You might be asked to identify and describe different economic factors in the exam. You will need to be able to evaluate the possible impact of changes in these factors on business behaviour. You may be given a case study business and you will have to write about the impact of changes and then say which change is most likely to happen, giving reasons for your answer.

You will need to be able to assess how businesses can react to changes in economic factors. There may be a case study business given and you will have to say how that business might react to, for example, an increase in interest rates.

Case Study

Booking figures treble as UK-tion sweeps the nation

Hoburne Holiday Parks has revealed a 200 per cent increase in advance booking figures as a growing number of families choose a UK-tion – a holiday in the UK – over a break abroad next year.

Bosses at the company's Dorset head office are talking about inflation of a different kind than has dominated the headlines to date – the meteoric rise in reservations for the 2009 season, which has seen advance bookings increase from £200,000 by November 2007 to £600,000 so far this year.

The bookings boost at Hoburne follows a rise in the popularity of UK-tions last summer, when the combined force of the credit crunch, the strength of the euro and fuel increases pushing up the price of long haul flights convinced many families to explore breaks closer to home.

Managing Director of Hoburne Holiday Parks, James Lapage, said:

'A lot of people are naturally concerned about what is around the corner, but they look forward to their family holiday. We have frozen many of our 2008 prices to help ensure families tightening their purse strings can still enjoy precious time away together.

Recent research carried out by insurance company Towergate Bakers has revealed that two thirds of people are planning a holiday in the UK next year. Some 20 per cent of parents intend to take their children on a caravan holiday, inspired by happy memories of UK breaks when they were young, and almost a quarter are planning a British seaside holiday'.

(Source: www.hoburne.com)

1 Identify and describe the economic factors mentioned in the article.
2 Explain why more people want to holiday in the United Kingdom.
3 What can businesses, like Hoburne, do to ensure that they see an increase in bookings?

4 Evaluate the possible impact of changes in economic factors on Hoburne.
5 Will customers see the effects of inflation if they book a holiday with Hoburne? Explain your answer.
6 On 1st January 2010 VAT will revert back to 17.5%. How will this affect Hoburne?
7 What action should Hoburne take to ensure they have high bookings in future years?
8 Research the current rate of exchange between the pound and the euro. Based on your findings, do you think Hoburne will see an increase in customers from Europe or a decrease? Explain your answer.

Summary

- Inflation – the percentage goods increase in price each year. As inflation rises the money you have buys you fewer goods and services than a year ago.

- Exchange rates are the price at which one currency is bought and sold for another. In the UK businesses that trade within Europe have to exchange the pound sterling for the euro.

- Impact of economic factors on business – see table below:

Economic factor	Possible impact	Possible reaction
Inflation rises	Purchase of raw materials to manufacture goods becomes more expensive.	Manufacturer might raise selling price. Manufacturer may seek alternative cheaper supplies which could lower quality of product.
	Sales may be lost as people are able to buy less goods because goods cost more.	Business may offer sales and special deals in order to retain customers.
	Some goods may see an increase in purchase – lower price goods.	
Exchange rates	If the exchange rate is strong you are able to get more of another currency for your pound sterling. This means buying goods abroad becomes cheaper.	Could encourage businesses to import goods from abroad. Exports abroad become less attractive.
	A weak exchange rate means that you are able to get less of another currency for your pound sterling.	Exports could rise but imported goods would become less attractive to customers in the UK.
Interest rates	This has been covered in Chapter 2.	

MAKING YOUR MARK IN BUSINESS

UNIT 2

Introduction

Businesses will only be able to survive and grow within the current competitive market-place if they are able to stay one step ahead of the competition, paying particular attention to the demands of their target market.

In order to complete the controlled assessment for this unit, you will need to develop knowledge and understanding of the following areas:

- Action planning and subsequent review.
- The importance of primary (field) research and secondary (desk) research, and how to conduct such research.
- The role of two key stakeholders, customers and competitors, and their impact on business.
- How businesses identify and respond to the needs of their target market.
- How the marketing mix can be used to respond to the needs of the target market, enabling a business to gain a competitive advantage over its rivals.

Throughout the unit you will find 'Portfolio Tips', which should help you to work through the controlled assessment produced by OCR.

Chapter 11
› Getting organised

> **Activity**
>
> Working in groups of two or three, consider the following questions and discuss your answers.
>
> 1 Why do you think it is important to plan ahead?
> 2 What happens if you do not make plans?
> 3 Think of an occasion when you have been very busy and needed to consider what to do first. How did you decide to prioritise your tasks?

Action planning

There is an old saying, 'If you want a job done, look for the busiest person'. Consider this statement for a few moments. Why do you think that this is so?

The answer may be that very busy people are used to structuring their time effectively, in order to fit in as many jobs as possible into their busy lives.

Being able to structure your time effectively is a key component when considering the value of action planning. Action planning is the ability to break down large tasks into smaller sections, decide how and by whom they should be tackled, and set realistic dates for their completion. Action plans should be used as a tool for planning and scheduling workload, so that the creator can meet deadlines. Action planning also allows the creator to prioritise their workload, giving them a clear idea of what to complete first.

If an employee has a well-planned day, it will probably enable them to become more productive. It is also less stressful for them, as they are aware of exactly what is required. However, it must be remembered that not all well-laid plans come to fruition. Things can suddenly change and emergency situations arise, which may mean that the employee is unable to meet the targets set within the original plan. If this is the case, the plan should be revisited and realistic alterations made to the targets. The main point to remember here is that an action plan is an 'active tool'. It is not a static document, but one which is revisited, updated and revised.

Action planning can be broken down into three main sections:

- identification of actions
- explanation of how actions will be completed and by whom
- time allocation for completion of actions.

Portfolio Tip

The first task within the controlled assessment requires you to create an action plan. In task five of the assignment you are required to reflect on your learning experience. You will only be able to do this if you regularly revisit your action plan – making notes on progress, updating it and making alterations as required.

Gaining the skills required to create an action plan successfully will help you to structure your own workload. The action plan should help you to structure your lesson and homework time, so that you can meet all deadlines. You may even find you have more free time available to pursue your hobbies or just relax, because you have become more focused and productive.

Identification of actions

This is probably one of the most crucial stages. Each task needs to be accurately broken down into smaller sections/actions. It is important that care is taken throughout this stage to ensure that no part of the task is missed out. The creator also needs to consider the exact order in which tasks need to be completed. For example, if you were making your breakfast, you could be boiling the kettle at the same time as putting the bread into the toaster.

This activity illustrates how hard it can be to break down tasks accurately, making sure that no part is forgotten.

Even making a cup of tea has many tasks to be broken down

Activity

In pairs, identify the different stages involved in making a cup of tea. Compare your answers with other members of the class.
- How many stages did you finally identify?
- Did everyone do the task in the same order?
- How many different methods did the class finally have?
- Would all the different methods achieve the same end result (a cup of tea)?

Explanation of how actions will be completed and by whom

Having decided exactly what needs to be done in order to complete a set task, the next stage is to explain how each action should be tackled. This is only possible if the creator of the action plan has an excellent understanding of the requirements of the task, in order to break it down into a range of actions. When considering how an action should be completed, the creator must consider the resources that are available and the skills of the people who are going to be allocated each action. An action plan is only going to be effective if the actions allocated to people are achievable. People will invariably delay tackling an activity if they are unsure of what they are supposed to be doing or do not have the necessary skills.

Portfolio Tip

Make sure that you fully understand the task you are being set within the controlled assessment, prior to completing your action plan. If you are unsure about anything, ask your teacher.

Time allocation for completion of actions

It is very difficult to calculate exactly how long a particular action will take. It is unwise to allocate too little time, but on the other hand allocating too much time can result in loss of productivity. If the time allocation has been too generous, a business's employees could be sitting around with no work to complete.

If you underestimate the time needed to finish each action, you will always be missing your internal deadlines. This can be quite depressing and may cause you to rush and hand in work that is not to your highest standard. You must therefore think very carefully about how much time you have available, and realistically estimate how much you can complete in the allocated time space.

What does an action plan look like?

There are many different designs and methods of writing/organising an action plan. The first step is to consider the type of information that is required in order to design a robust action plan:

- What will the actions be?
- Prioritisation of actions – what needs to be completed first?
- How will the action be addressed? How will you achieve it?
- How will you know when it has been completed successfully?
- How will you monitor and review progress?
- How many hours will the action take to complete?

Examples of action plan headings

The Health and Safety Executive recommend the use of the following headings to assess management standards for tackling work-related stress (adapted from www.hseni.gov.uk).

Standard area	Desired state	Current state	Practical solution	Who will take the work forward	When	How will staff receive feedback	Action completed

The following headings have been adapted from www.southampton.gov.uk and are used by Southampton City Council for their DDA (LA1) Action Plan.

Target	Actions	Person responsible	Cost/resources	Deadline	Success criteria

The following headings have been adapted from the website www.everyactioncounts.org.uk. Every Action Counts have recommended their members use the following template.

Our chosen actions are	When will it be done?			What are the things we need to do to make this happen?	Who is going to be responsible for making sure these things happen?
	Now	Sooner	Later		
Action one					

From the three examples we can see that there are some similarities; for example, they all consider who will do what. The main problem with the three examples selected is that they do not have a column which allows progress to be monitored.

Taking some of these ideas, here is an action plan that could be used for your controlled assessment.

Name of student:							
Action plan: Controlled assessment A242 – Making your mark in business							
Description of chosen actions	Control dates			What are the things I/we need to make this happen?	Who will take the work forward?	Resources required	Monitoring/ review – what is happening/ has happened?
	Set	To be completed by	Completed				
Action One							

Activity

Complete an action plan for the following task, using either the sample action plan or your own action plan.

Working in pairs, you have been asked to research your fellow students' opinions on the quality and range of food currently being served within the school. You need to present your findings to the headteacher in three weeks' time. Consider the following points:

- How are you going to break down the task into smaller actions – what needs to be done?
- Who will carry out which actions?
- Time allowed for each action.
- What do you need to find out?
- How are you going to gather this information? What techniques will you use?
- How will you analyse the information you have collected?
- How will you present the data to your head teacher – written report, discussion, PowerPoint presentation?

Summary

- Action planning is the ability to break down large tasks into smaller sections in order to decide what needs to be done, by when and by whom.
- Good organisation allows employees to use their time effectively and productively.
- A well organised individual is less likely to miss deadlines and suffer stress.

Chapter 12
Understanding the market

> **Activity**
>
> Identify four different ways of conducting research.
> Describe a time when you have been asked to complete a questionnaire – what type of information were you being asked? Why do you think the business needed to find out this information?

Market researchers are a common sight in shopping centres

Market research

All businesses need to undertake market research in order to analyse the trends that are happening within their market. For example, fashion boutiques need to observe the famous fashion shows in Paris and London, and talk to their customers to find out what is likely to sell next season. If a business fails to consider trends within their own market, they are likely to lose sales to their competitors who have listened to what customers want.

Market research is broken down into two different types:

- primary (field) research
- secondary (desk) research.

Primary (field) research

In a busy shopping centre, you may have seen people trying to encourage the general public to answer questions. These people are market researchers and are employed by various organisations to collect information on behalf of different businesses.

Primary research involves the collection of data which a business will use for its own specific purposes. This type of research is very time-consuming and often expensive as it generally involves talking directly to different sections of the population. In order to ensure that the results are accurate and not biased, questionnaires have to be carefully designed and analysed. To achieve results that represent the whole country, a large number of people need to be included in the survey.

The collection of primary research can take many forms.

- The business may design a questionnaire where people are interviewed on a one-to-one basis and asked a range of different questions.
- A questionnaire may be handed to people to complete on their own and hand back at a later date.
- A market researcher may gather a number of people together in order to hold a 'focus group'. The group will be able to offer their opinions on a range of different questions.
- Observation of how people (especially customers) behave: by watching customers'

shopping behaviour, a retail outlet could gain ideas on how best to lay out the store, and learn about the buying patterns of different types of customers.

- Some businesses run surveys – this could involve asking members of the public to try out their products and give their opinions on performance, reliability and value for money.

Portfolio Tip ✔

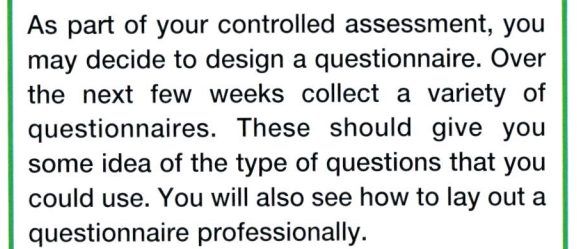

As part of your controlled assessment, you may decide to design a questionnaire. Over the next few weeks collect a variety of questionnaires. These should give you some idea of the type of questions that you could use. You will also see how to lay out a questionnaire professionally.

Which ride made you scream the loudest?

Secondary (desk) research

This is research that has been collected either by another organisation or within the business for other reasons. Internal information could include past sales figures, which can then be used to estimate future sales trends. It could also include visitor numbers so that busy times of the year can be identified, enabling the business to employ extra staff as required.

The Government is responsible for the collection of a variety of different statistics, such as the labour force survey, population and employment statistics, and the ten-year census. These statistics are found on www.ons.gov.uk. Another good website for information on your local area is www.upmystreet.com.

National and local newspapers can also contain information that might be useful in the development of business strategy. For example, if a florist wanted to open up a shop in a new area, the local paper could help the owner to identify competition and find suitable premises and employees. National newspapers report national and international events which could influence the progress of a business.

The Internet is an extensive source of information which has made secondary research available at the touch of a button. However, it must be treated with some caution. Make sure that you only use reliable websites. All information taken from websites must be clearly referenced within your work; if you do not acknowledge your sources, you will have committed plagiarism.

Other forms of secondary research include trade journals, periodicals, trade associations and organisations that specialise in the collection of data, for example Mintel and Key Note.

Target market

If market research is going to be informative and aid decision-making, a business must first decide who to talk to. It would be a waste of money asking people aged over 40 about their opinions on a new holiday experience aimed at 18–30-year-olds!

Activity

In pairs, discuss whom the following products are aimed at:

- Mars bar
- lawnmower
- country and western CD
- Adidas trainers.

The above exercise should have illustrated that all of those products could appeal to a wide range of customers. It would be very difficult to state categorically the type of people who consume Mars bars. This might also be different to the people who actually buy Mars bars. Parents may actually buy them, but for their children to eat.

There are many ways in which different markets can be split into market segments. This will depend on the type of product or service being offered by the business.

Activity

- Name a product or service that is mainly targeted at women.
- Identify a product or service that is mainly targeted at men.
- Describe a product that would be purchased mainly by people aged 14–16 years.

Markets can be broken down by gender, age, occupations or income. Businesses may look at the different stages of family life, breaking the groups down into single people, married couples without children, married couples with children, married couples whose children have left home, and pensioners. This topic will be dealt with in greater depth in Chapter 13.

Portfolio Tip

In order to conduct your own primary and secondary research for your assignment, you will need to consider the type of people to whom your selected business is aiming to sell its goods or services. Think carefully about who you think would use the products or service. Is the group easily segmented, or is it a product that could be aimed at a wide range of the population? If the target market is wide, you will need to ensure that each part of that market is represented in your primary and secondary research.

Sampling methods

When undertaking market research, it is important that the sample of people you choose is representative of the whole population. In order to do this, there are a number of different sampling methods to choose from:

- non-probability sampling, or
- random sampling.

Non-probability sampling involves choosing the sample randomly; there is no way of knowing who will be included. It would involve questioning a person either because they were available at the time or were prepared to be interviewed.

Random sampling can be further broken down into a further three sections.

Simple random sampling

This method is used when the product or service being researched can be used by every member of the population, for example a bar of soap. When conducting this type of sampling, every member of the population has an equal chance of being included within the survey.

Systematic sampling

This method of sampling is used when the product or service is targeted at a particular section of society. Using this method the business will question every 'nth' person who fits into the target market. For example, if your school wanted to know your opinions on the sports facilities available within the school, it could print out an alphabetical list of all the pupils' names and interview every 20th pupil on the list.

Stratified random sampling

This is where the population is broken down into groups. This could be by gender, age or income. Each one of these groups is randomly sampled. This method would be used where the product is targeted at the whole population and the business wants to ensure that they talk to a fair representation from each sector. For example, if Cadbury's wanted to find out people's opinions on a new chocolate bar, they could divide the population up into age groups and then randomly sample each age group.

Activity

You have been asked to find out what pupils/students currently think about the food that is available at your school/college.

- Identify your target audience.
- Describe the type of sampling method that you could use to gain this information.
- Identify the most important topics.
- Draft some questions that would provide the required information.

Questionnaire design

This is a much harder task than most people imagine. In order to ensure that you collect the correct information, you must first consider exactly what information you are trying to discover. This must always be your starting point.

You will need to read your selected scenario carefully and then decide what you are being asked to investigate through primary research. Make a list of the information on which you need to gain people's opinions. You will then be able to use this list to formulate your questions.

Having decided on the information that you need to find out, the next stage is to establish how you are going to formulate each question. There are two different types of questions – open and closed.

Open questions

Open questions allow people to express their opinions; for example, 'What do you consider about … '. This is known as qualitative data.

These types of questions will provide a wealth of information, but it often becomes very difficult to draw sound conclusions. If you stood outside your local leisure centre and asked 50 people what they thought about the temperature of the swimming pool, some might say it was fine, others too cold or too hot. This range of answers makes it almost impossible to draw solid conclusions.

Closed questions

Closed questions are those which direct the respondent to set answers – for example, 'yes' or 'no'. Closed questions enable respondents to answer quickly, and are much easier to analyse and draw conclusions from. Within closed questions, ranges of answers could be offered. If you asked respondents how much they would be prepared to pay for an item, you could give them a range of options; see Figure 12.1.

How much would you be prepared to pay for an adult entrance ticket to the attraction?
£4.00 – £4.99 ☐
£5.00 – £5.99 ☐
£6.00 – £6.99 ☐

Figure 12.1 Example of a closed question

Likert scales

Within your questionnaire you may need to establish your respondent's feelings or opinions on a subject. To do this, you could use Likert scales. This allows your respondent to say how strongly they agree or disagree with a statement; see Figure 12.2.

Do you agree that our staff made your visit more enjoyable?	
Strongly agree ☐	Agree ☐
No opinion ☐	Disagree ☐
Strongly disagree ☐	

Figure 12.2 Example of Likert scale

Rank order scales

Another type of closed question might ask respondents to rank statements in order of importance. If you are going to use this type of question, it is important that you explain to the respondent how the ranking system works; see Figure 12.3.

Rank the following statements 1–5 in relation to your enjoyment of the attraction (number 1 is the most important; number 5 the least important).	
Length of queue	_____
Good value for money	_____
Entertainment value	_____
Attitude and helpfulness of staff	_____
Photography	_____

Figure 12.3 Example of rank order scale

Intention to buy scales

The final type of question you might like to ask your respondents is if they intend to purchase your product or service; see Figure 12.4.

If the attraction were to produce a brochure which supports the different features of the attraction, would you:	
Definitely buy	**Probably buy**
1 ☐	2 ☐
Probably not buy	**Definitely not buy**
3 ☐	4 ☐

Figure 12.4 Example of 'intention to buy' scales

Activity

Using the Internet, investigate the London Dungeon's website (http://www.the dungeons.com) to familiarise yourself with what the attraction offers its customers. Outlined below are some questions taken from their visitor survey. Using the scenario questions below and information gained from the website, try to answer the questions that follow.

Q18 We'd like to know the ages of the people in your party. Please write in the boxes below the number of people in your party who are in that particular age range.

0–5	6–10	11–14	15–24	25–35	36–44	45–64	65+
☐	☐	☐	☐	☐	☐	☐	☐

Figure 12.5 Questions from the London Dungeon website

1. Why do you think the London Dungeon asked this question? What were they trying to find out?
2. How could they use this information?
3. The span of ages is not the same for each category. Why do you think this is?
4. What type of question is this?

Q3 Would you recommend a visit to your friends and family?   Yes ☐   No ☐

---

1. Describe this type of question.
2. Why would the business want to know this information?
3. Design another question that could be added if the respondent said 'no' to recommending the attraction to their family/friends. What type of question would this have to be?

Q1 How did you hear about the London Dungeon before your visit today? Please tick as many boxes as apply.

Website	☐	Radio	☐	Holiday guide	☐
National newspaper	☐	Road sign	☐	Local newspaper	☐
Television commercial	☐	Promotional offer	☐	Television news	☐
London underground posters	☐	Sightseeing bus	☐	Posters elsewhere	☐
Recommendation from	☐	Tube station barriers	☐	Friend/family	☐
Other	☐				

---

1. Describe this type of question.
2. Why would the London Dungeon want to know this information? How could they use the results?

Q10 Please tell us the most and least enjoyable part of your visit:

Most enjoyable _____

Least enjoyable _____

1 Describe this type of question.
2 The respondent was not given much space to write their answer. Why do you think this was?
3 How useful would this type of question be to the attraction?

Summary

- Primary (field) research involves the collection of data which a business will collect and use for its own specific needs.

- Secondary (desk) research has been collected by another organisation or within the business for a different use – eg sales figures. Secondary research could involve using statistics compiled by the Government.

- Target market defines the type of people a business wants to sell its goods or services to. Will the product appeal to the very young, men rather than women, people with older children?

- Open questions are those that require a descriptive response. It allows the person answering the question to discuss their opinions. For example 'What did you think of the film?'

- Closed questions are those that direct the respondent to a set answer – this could be 'yes' or 'no'. For example 'Would you go to see the film again?'

- Linkert scales ask the respondent to state how they feel about a matter – the possible answers often include 'strongly agree', 'agree' etc.

- Intention to buy scales ask the respondent to state if they would 'definitely buy', 'probably buy', 'probably not buy', 'definitely buy'.

Chapter 13
Customers and competitors

Activity
What do you remember?
- Define the term stakeholder, and use examples to illustrate your answer.
- Identify five different stakeholders.
- Select two stakeholders from your list of five above and explain their differing interest in a business. If possible, use real-life business examples to support your explanation.
- Describe the possible conflict that could occur between the stakeholder customer and the business owner.

In what kind of segments could we group these people?

Market segmentation

Within Chapter 12 we started to consider different target markets and how these could be broken down into sub-groups known as segments. Using this type of categorisation, businesses are able to analyse customers' and potential customers' buying habits. When it works well, segmentation is a very powerful tool for any business and is essential if it wants to market a new product or service successfully. Markets can be segmented using a number of different characteristics:

- age
- gender
- socio-economic group
- frequency of use
- lifestyle
- family circumstances
- geography.

Age
Segmenting a section of society according to their age is relatively easy and often very successful. The travel company Saga target all their products to people aged over 50. However, targeting by age is not always relevant for products that appeal to a wide variety of people, for example different chocolate bars.

Activity
Working in small groups, compile a list of products or services that would be targeted to the following categories of people:
- school children, aged 11–16
- 17–25-year-olds
- middle-aged people, aged 40–60
- elderly people, aged 65+.

Compare your list with other groups. Do you agree with the categorisation of the other groups? Discuss the differences.

Gender

This is one of the most important segments, with many products and services aimed particularly at women or men; for example, football boots are generally aimed at men while mascara adverts are targeted at women. However, men's aftershave is often purchased by women for men, and therefore promotions are targeted at both men and women.

Socio-economic group

This method of segmentation considers the type of occupation of people and then categorises them into a social class. This method assumes that people within a particular social class have similar tastes and habits; for example, it is assumed that people on low incomes will purchase 'own brand label' food, whereas people who have high incomes will purchase 'premium food ranges'. Businesses use these assumptions when targeting advertising and promotional material.

The most commonly used social classification is the National Readership Survey (NRS). This is shown below in Table 13.1. Table 13.2 gives estimates of the population of Great Britain by social grade between January and December 2008.

> **Activity**
>
> Working in pairs, write down a range of products which you think are exclusively aimed at men, exclusively aimed at women and aimed at both genders.

Social grade	Social status	Occupation
A	Upper middle class	Higher managerial, administrative or professional
B	Middle class	Intermediate managerial, administrative or professional
C1	Lower middle class	Supervisory or clerical, junior managerial, administrative or professional
C2	Skilled working class	Skilled manual workers
D	Working class	Semi- and unskilled manual workers
E	Those at lowest level of subsistence	State pensioners, widows (no other earner), casual or lowest grade workers

Table 13.1 Social classification

(Source: National Readership Survey)

Social grade		All UK adults (aged 15+)	Men	Women
Totals	Estimated 000s	49,700	23,875	25,202
	% profile	100	100	100
Social grade A	Estimated 000s	1,961	1,053	908
	% profile	4.00	4.4	3.6
Social grade B	Estimated 000s	11,177	5,638	5,539
	% profile	22.8	23.6	22.0

Social grade C1	Estimated 000s	74,123	6,494	7,629
	% profile	28.8	27.2	30.3
Social grade C2	Estimated 000s	10,303	5,541	4,762
	% profile	21.0	23.2	18.9
Social grade D	Estimated 000s	7,555	3,589	3,966
	% profile	15.4	15.0	15.7
Social grade E	Estimated 000s	3,957	1,561	2,397
	% profile	8.1	6.5	9.5

Table13.2 National Readership Survey estimate of population of Great Britain by social grade, January–December 2008
(Source: NRS, 2008)

Frequency of use

This type of segmentation can be broken down into three categories:

- customers who use the product/service frequently
- customers who use the product/service occasionally
- potential customers (people who have never before used the product/service).

It is vitally important for businesses to maintain their regular customers, as it is much harder to gain new customers than to retain your original customer base. Advertising and promotions must therefore appeal to the frequent users and also help encourage the occasional customer to become a regular customer. Specific and targeted promotions may need to be undertaken separately in order to encourage potential customers to try the product/service for the first time, so that they become regular customers. Businesses often report that 20 per cent of customers account for 80 per cent of sales. This is known as the Pareto effect or Pareto's law: a small proportion of causes produce a large proportion of results. A vital few customers may account for a very large percentage of sales. When launching a new product or service, it is important for a business to identify their 20 per cent of regular customers and target them specifically.

Lifestyle

Some products are aimed at people who have a particular lifestyle, for example working mothers with young children, or young professional people who are either still single or yet to start a family. Lifestyle choices can also be linked to religious or ethnic backgrounds, which may influence the products and services that each group purchases.

Family circumstances

Some businesses aim their products or services according to customers' stage in the family cycle. The travel and tourism industry is one area where holidays are targeted at different segments found within the following classification.

- child
- young adult
- young couple
- young couple with a baby or young children
- couple with a growing family (aged 5–18 years)
- empty-nesters (retired couple whose children have recently left home)
- elderly couple
- single elderly person.

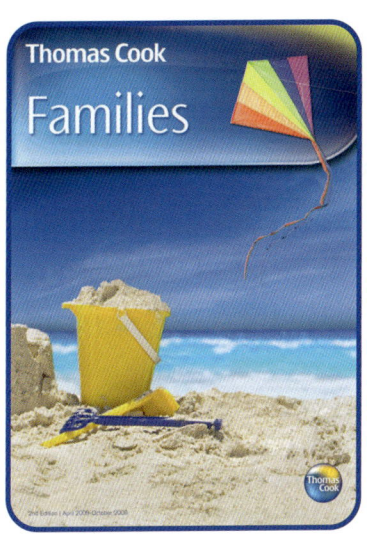

Holiday brochures are aimed at particular groups of people

Activity

Use the Internet to research a range of different holidays. Describe which family circumstance each holiday is aiming for, and give reasons for your choices.

Geography

A business may target customers in different regions of the country due to particular tastes and fashions. Another business may target both domestic and overseas sales. Businesses can also organise themselves into different areas of the country; for example, one section of the business may deal with the south-east of the country while another deals with the south-west. This enables the business to obtain specialist knowledge about the customers and their particular needs within their own area.

Conclusion: market segmentation

It is important to remember that identifying market segments is not a precise science, and can only provide general information. However, increasingly sophisticated market research is allowing the definition of market segments to increase in accuracy. Breaking down customers into market segments helps businesses to formulate effective marketing strategies. This allows them to target their marketing mix correctly, delivering the right product to the right people at the right time. A business can therefore ensure that all promotional activity ultimately increases demand for the product or service and avoids wasting both time and money.

Portfolio Tip

During the controlled assessment, you will be required to identify the target market of your selected business. This should be partly outlined in the scenario that you have selected to work with. Having identified the target market, you are then required to consider the needs of the target market.

Customer needs

What are customer needs? Having decided to purchase a product or service, the customer will have a range of thoughts and expectations of what they want to gain from the buying experience. This will include the availability of the product, the knowledge and helpfulness of staff, methods of payment on offer, what the product or service will be like, and finally any after-sales service. These are known as preconceived ideas. If the customer's expectations are not met, they will probably be unhappy either with the product or buying experience. It is therefore important that the business identifies and understands the needs of each market segment for their product or service. Businesses must have some idea of what to offer its customers, but will then conduct primary research in order to establish exactly what a customer wants from the product/service. Businesses will also observe what their competitors are offering customers to see if it appeals to the customer and whether they could improve on the competitors' offers.

In order to establish what the customer requires from their buying experience, the business has to segment the market. Who do they actually expect to purchase the product/service? This initial identification of customer type will help the business establish the range of services they need to offer in order to meet their customers' needs.

Example: Alton Towers

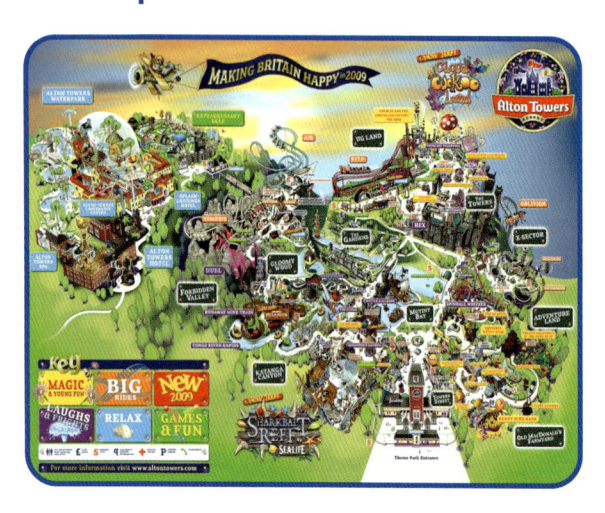

Let us use the example of Alton Towers to help illustrate the above points.

1. The first stage is to consider how the target market could be segmented. You could use age, geography (generally visitors have a two-hour drivetime) or family circumstances (probably the most suitable).

2. The next step is to identify who within that segmentation would probably come to Alton Towers.

3. The last stage is to identify what their customer needs would be when they arrived.

Some possible ideas are outlined in Table 13.3.

> **Activity**
>
> Looking at Table 13.3, can you think of any other needs that these different target groups might want and expect?

Once a business has established their customers' needs, it needs to decide how it can best meet these needs to ensure that customers remain loyal to their business.

Customer power

Without customers, a business would not survive. Very few businesses manufacture and sell goods that are totally exclusive (not available through any other outlet). Most businesses are in competition with a wide range of other

Target group	Customer needs of target group
Young adult (would probably come as part of a group – social educational)	Accessible transport – may not yet be able to drive Affordability of entrance fee Different payment methods Fast food Big, fast, thrill-seeking rides – roller coaster No queues Themed night – fright night Toilet facilities
Young couple (could also be part of a bigger group)	Directions Easy parking Affordability of entrance fee

Customers and competitors

	Different payment methods Special nights – fright night No queues Range of food Big, fast, thrill-seeking rides – roller coaster Range of alternative entertainment – not solely focused on fast rides
Couple with a growing family (5–18 years)	Directions Easy parking Range of payment methods Family tickets Family eating areas – to eat purchased and non-purchased food Range of different rides – some suitable for younger children Range of alternative entertainment – not solely focused on fast rides Health and safety of environment No queues Clean and accessible toilets Disabled facilities

Table 13.3 Customer needs

Activity

Using the Alton Towers website (http://www.altontowers.com), research how Alton Towers currently meets the customer needs identified in Table 13.3. Draw up a new table and insert a third column; see the example in Table 13.4.

Target market	Customer needs	How Alton Towers meets these customer needs
Couple with children	Directions Easy parking	http://www.altontowers.com/pages/search-results/keywords/Directions/page/1 – this gives clear instructions on how to arrive at the park. It also describes the car parking facilities available.

Table 13.4 Sample table

businesses who are selling identical or similar goods. As a customer, you have the power to decide where and when you will make your purchases. Businesses have to persuade you to purchase from them and not a competitor.

There are a variety of different ways that businesses try to stand out from the competition. They could decide to compete in terms of price, quality, customer service, or after-sales service. It is unlikely that a single customer will be able to influence the behaviour of a large business. Just think if you and your family decided not to shop at your local supermarket; it is unlikely to have a great impact on the sales of that business, and therefore in isolation your influence is limited. However, if all the pupils in your school decided to boycott the canteen because the canteen refused to use free-range eggs for a week, this is likely to have a huge impact on the catering company. It is very likely that the catering company would have to listen to the pupils and start using free-range eggs. In a large group, customers can influence the decisions of businesses, but individually it is much harder.

The next stage is to look at how businesses try to win customers and the different ways in which they can influence customers when deciding to make a purchase from a particular business.

What are the differences between these two cars?

Price and quality

There is an old saying, 'you get what you pay for'. This makes the assumption that the higher the price, the better the quality of the product or service; for example, clothes from Marks and Spencer have an image of higher quality than clothes from Matalan. What the purchaser has to consider is: what do they actually want from the product; how long do they want it to last; and therefore is it better to pay for the superior quality item that would probably last longer, or the cheaper item?

Some businesses have a strong image of producing and selling superior high-quality goods, for which they can command a high price. Consider the image portrayed by BMW against Citroen. BMW is promoting a high-value car which conveys the image of wealth and quality. Citroen is producing cars suitable for a larger proportion of the population with a greater emphasis on affordability and practicality. Branded goods are often more expensive to purchase than non-branded goods, but are they actually better quality?

Which one is the best quality?

Activity

Are the sports products sold through Nike or Adidas actually better quality than non-branded sports goods? Or is it the image of the brand that actually increases the price of the goods? Discuss this issue in pairs and then share your ideas with the rest of your class.

Value for money

In order to attract and retain customers, businesses have to ensure that the products they offer are perceived to be good value for money. This means that organisations need to be aware of customers' expectations of price and standards, and meet these expectations. The concept of value for money is closely related to the price and quality of the product/service. The concept does not mean that items are cheap, but rather that the customer is satisfied that the product is worth the money paid for it.

Services are offered at different levels; for example, on an aeroplane you can buy a business-class ticket which provides a more spacious seat and access to superior facilities. People are often prepared to pay considerably more for this kind of ticket because of the increased levels of service that it includes.

Obviously there are items that we have to purchase in order to survive on a daily basis, that we might not consider to be value for money. During the second quarter of 2008, petrol prices increased sharply because of the rising cost of oil on the wholesale market. Prices for unleaded petrol rose to over £1.25 per litre. During the third quarter of 2008, the cost of a barrel of oil fell dramatically, and prices at the petrol pumps fell to below £1.00 per litre. This 25p drop per litre encouraged customers to feel that they were getting greater value for money. However, the price was still nearly 10p a litre more expensive than it had been at the beginning of 2008.

Petrol prices have risen and fallen dramatically

Pre- and after-sales service

Some people dislike being approached by a shop assistant when browsing around a shop; on the other hand, it can be infuriating when you need help or guidance from a shop assistant but there is no one available.

Pre-sales service
The whole concept of customer service and meeting customer needs starts as soon as a customer decides to purchase a product. The service you receive from a business prior to deciding to purchase an item is very important.

Excellent service at this point encourages you to return to the store and make recommendations to other people. The salesperson needs to be able to present the product to you; they should be knowledgeable and able to answer all your questions. Advice should include:

- information about a product
- the benefits of owning the product
- discussion of the different payment methods available
- when and how you can receive the product.

Advice should be impartial and customers should not be encouraged to buy goods that are unsuitable and ultimately would not meet their needs.

Activity

Discuss with a partner your own personal shopping experiences. Do you like being helped to choose items, or would you rather be left alone? Describe one occasion when you have received some excellent help and guidance. Describe one occasion when you wanted some help but could not find an assistant, or the assistant was unhelpful. How did this make you feel? Would you recommend or re-use the shop?

With the increase in internet sales, businesses have to make sure that their websites contain all the information a customer might need prior to making a purchase. It has been stated that on average a customer decides whether to use a website within eight seconds. It is therefore vital that all the information which a customer wishes to access is readily available.

After-sales service
Customer service does not stop when the customer decides to purchase the product and hands over their money. After-sales service is the demonstration to the customer that the business actually cares and values their custom. It can include guarantees, which are especially

important for electrical and technological equipment. Part of the service could also include maintenance agreements where an engineer would be available to repair equipment when required over a set period of time. Telephone and internet helplines could also form part of the services offered by the business.

On a simpler note, it could involve members of staff asking the customer if they have enjoyed their visit to a leisure attraction. The after-sales service which a customer receives is often the reason they become regular customers. It is important to remember the maxim, 'once a customer, always a customer'.

Activity

The manufacturer Hoover has its own dedicated website which outlines all the after-sales services it offers. The website is easy to navigate and covers all the appliances that it currently sells. It advises customers on what to do if their appliance is out of guarantee or still in guarantee. It allows the customer to purchase extended guarantees. Take a look at the website (http://service.hoover.co.uk/) and answer the following questions.

1 What benefits do you think Hoover gain from creating the website?

2 What services do they offer on the website?

3 Identify the appliances listed under 'Problem Solving Guide'.

4 Click on 'Repair and Service'. How many options are there? Describe them.

5 Describe the two different warranties on offer under the category 'Extended warranties'.

6 Do you think the availability of the site would encourage potential customers to purchase Hoover products? Give reasons for your answers.

7 Analyse how helpful the site is.

Legislation

The section on pre-sales services discussed the advice that customers often seek prior to making a purchase. In order to ensure that customers do not receive misleading and inaccurate information, there are a number of laws to protect them. These include:

- the Trade Descriptions Act 1968
- the Sale of Goods Act 1979 (as amended).

The Trade Descriptions Act 1968

This Act states that any descriptions of goods and services given by a person acting in the course of business should be accurate and not misleading. The description of the product could have been given verbally, in writing (advertisement, brochure), or through illustrations on packaging. The Act makes it an offence to:

- apply a false or misleading description to goods; for example, stating that a coat is totally waterproof when in fact it is only shower-proof.

- supply or offer to supply goods to which a false or misleading trade description is applied. A person offering goods for supply (such as in a shop) or having them in their possession for supply (such as in a storeroom) is deemed to offer to supply them for the purposes of the Act.

A seller will only have committed an offence if the description misleads the purchaser so that it affects their ability to enjoy and/or use the goods/services, or has a large impact on the value of the item. The Act is not designed to cover very small inaccuracies that would not affect the purchaser's enjoyment or use of the product and have no impact on its value.

The following descriptions of goods are affected by the Trade Descriptions Act:

- The quantity, size or gauge – this includes length, width, height, area volume, capacity and weight (eg 17-inch television screen).

- The method of manufacture – this covers most of the aspects concerning the work done in the processing or repairing of goods (eg hand-finished).

- Composition – what the goods are made of (eg solid oak table).

- Fitness for purpose – strength, performance, behaviour or accuracy (eg immaculate condition, unbreakable).

- Any physical characteristics not included above (eg fitted with power steering).

- Testing by any person and results thereof (eg a statement that a car has been independently checked for safety).

- Approval by any person or conformity with a type approved by any person (eg a statement saying that the goods have obtained a British Standard).

- Place or date of manufacture, production, processing or reconditioning (eg a statement that goods have been 'made in England').

- Person by whom the product is manufactured, produced, processed or reconditioned (for example, misuse of brand names on items, stating an article is genuine when in fact it is only a copy).

- Other history, including previous ownership or use (eg clearly stating the number of previous owners of a car).

The Sale of Goods Act 1979 (as amended)

The 'as amended' part of this Act is important because it refers to laws which have been extended since the original Act in 1979 was introduced. Related legislation includes Supply of Goods and Services Act 1982, Sale and Supply of Goods Act 1994 and The Sale and Supply of Goods to Consumers Regulations 2002.

Activity

You run a second-hand car showroom. Three new cars have just arrived which are described below.

1 Peugeot 206 (1998), two careful lady owners, no service history, approximately 103,000 miles, three months' MOT and road fund tax.
2 Citroen C3 (2003), one owner, full service history, guaranteed 34,000 miles, ten months' road fund tax and MOT.
3 Ford Focus (2007), used as a fleet car, high mileage, full service history.

Write an advertisement for each of the above cars. Design two advertisements that would breach the Trade Descriptions Act 1968, and one that would conform to the legislation.

The Sale of Goods Act states several conditions that all goods sold by a trader must meet. The goods must be:

- as described
- of satisfactory quality
- fit for purpose.

'As described'

This refers to the description that has been provided about the product or service. This could be through an advertisement, other promotional material or verbally by the trader.

'Of satisfactory quality'

This means that the goods are expected to last a reasonable period of time. It covers minor and cosmetic defects as well as any substantial problems experienced by the buyer. If faults and defects are pointed out to the buyer at point of sale, the buyer has waived these rights as far as those faults are concerned.

'Fit for purpose'

This implies that the product must be able to fulfil the purpose for which it was sold. It will also cover any purpose that was implied by the trader.

The seller, not the manufacturer, is responsible if goods are not as described, of satisfactory quality or fit for purpose. Under the Act, if you buy something that does not meet these conditions, you have the potential right to return it and receive a full refund and compensation if it will cost you more to buy similar goods elsewhere.

The right to reject goods and receive a full refund lasts for a relatively short period of time. After this period the buyer is deemed to have 'accepted the goods'. As a purchaser you do still have a legal case against the seller, but you may not be entitled to a full refund. You may have to have the item repaired or accept a replacement.

The Act covers second-hand sales. If you buy privately, you can only claim your money back if the goods are not 'as described'.

If a customer wishes to make a claim, it is down to them to prove that they have a case. This will obviously prove more difficult, the longer the item has been owned. A consumer has six years from the time of purchase in which to make a claim. In order to claim your rights, you do not have to have the receipt of purchase. However, you may be required to show some proof of purchase, such as a cheque book stub, bank statement or credit card statement.

Monitoring customer satisfaction

Throughout this chapter you have been looking at the very important role which customers play in the potential success of a business. Businesses spend a lot of time identifying their customers and finding out how they can meet their individual needs in order for them to become regular customers. Businesses need to have systems in place that will allow them to assess whether or not they are successfully meeting their customers' needs.

Surveys

One way to find out if your customers are happy is to ask them. Surveys can be carried out in a number of different ways.

- A business could talk to its customers on a one-to-one basis. This would provide a lot of detailed qualitative data which the business could use either to enhance current services or introduce new ones. The drawback with face-to-face discussions is that they are time-consuming, and the business could base future decisions on the opinions of just a few people.

- Surveys can be left for customers to fill in whenever they please. Hotels and restaurants often leave comment cards in rooms or on tables. The disadvantage of this method is that a low percentage of people will complete the surveys.

- Businesses may offer incentives to customers who complete a survey for them. This could include entry into a prize draw. The airline Flybe asks their passengers to complete a survey during their flight. This ensures that the company receives a high response rate.

- Conducting surveys via websites is becoming an increasingly popular method of finding out what customers think of businesses' services. The internet service provider AOL has used this method to find out what their customers currently think of their services.

Mystery shoppers

This involves somebody coming into a store or restaurant as a customer. The staff members working in the selected business do not know that the shopper is assessing the customer-service skills of staff. The mystery shopper will use an agreed criterion to assess the business; this could include the cleanliness of the shop, speed of service, advice offered by staff and the general experience of the customer. After the visit, the mystery shopper will prepare a report to the business which clearly outlines areas of excellence and areas that could be improved upon.

> ## Case Study
>
> ### Pizza Hut
>
> Pizza Hut uses the CHAMPS checklist to monitor and assess their levels of customer service:
>
> - C – stands for cleanliness
> - H – hospitality
> - A – attitude
> - M – manners
> - P – product
> - S – service.
>
> Each category is further broken down into sections, and every restaurant has to meet these set criteria. Mystery shoppers visit different branches on a regular basis. The mystery shopper will grade the standards within the restaurant against this criterion. After each visit, the restaurant receives a report which clearly outlines areas where the customer-service criteria have not been met. If the restaurant fails the visit, it might then have another surprise visit to ensure that measures have been put in place to raise customer-care standards.
>
> 1 What are the benefits to the customers of this system?
>
> 2 How does this system help the restaurant meet the needs of its customers?

Repeat customers

One way to measure customer satisfaction is to calculate how many customers are returning regularly. This is easy for a small business as they will be able to recognise their customers and build up a relationship with them, but this is more difficult for larger businesses.

Customer and sales records may indicate customers returning to the business. For examples, hotels/conference centres such as the Aston Business School will make a record of your name, address, telephone number and email address so that this information can be recorded on the database. If you make a second booking, your name and address will be recognised by the computer.

Large businesses such as superstores that have thousands of visitors on a daily basis would not be able to record this type of information. They tend to issue loyalty cards to record repeat business. Each time the customer returns, they will use their loyalty card, and this information can be used to calculate repeat business.

Monitoring sales levels are another way to assess increased business, which usually indicates that customers are returning regularly.

> ## Activity
>
> Working in pairs, describe an incidence of poor customer service that you or a member of your family has experienced. Consider the following questions:
>
> - What went wrong?
> - What were you expecting to happen that did not happen?
> - How did this make you or your family feel?
> - What should the business have done to rectify the situation?
> - Did you tell anyone else about this?
> - Would you use the business again? If not, why not? If you would – why?

The impact of poor customer service

What happens when businesses fail to provide good customer service? When a person experiences poor customer service, they are unlikely to use the business again. On average, they are likely to share their experience with 15 people, whereas if they have received excellent customer service, they are likely to tell just three people. How a business deals with a customer's complaint and dissatisfaction is also important. Research has shown that 82 per cent of customers are likely to return to the business if their complaint is dealt with satisfactorily.

Good and bad customer service is very much interlinked. If excellent customer service is provided, customers will become repeat customers, and the reverse is true if a customer receives poor customer service. If customers are satisfied and they become repeat customers, profits are likely to increase. If customers are leaving a business due to being poorly treated, profits will ultimately fall.

The market share of a business will increase if a business continually gains new customers, or will shrink if it fails to meet customer needs and loses customers to competitors. Ultimately a business will not survive if it continually fails to meet its customers' needs. The business world is very competitive and customers are able to choose from a wide range of organisations to purchase their goods and services.

Competition

Successful businesses never take their eye off the competition. They must be aware of what they are doing and at the same time how successful are any new initiatives which they have. So the question is, how does the business do this? The first thing a business needs to establish is its market share.

Market share

Ultimately all markets have a total expenditure which is fought over by the different businesses who supply goods to that market. For example, if we consider the food market, there are three main players: Tesco, Asda and Sainsbury's. In order to work out total market share, the value of the market has to be known. This is then recorded and a percentage is calculated by looking at the sales of each of the individual businesses. Tesco currently hold the greatest market share of all the supermarkets; see Table 13.6 and Figure 13.12.

Supermarket	Percentage of market share
Tesco	30.6
Asda	16.6
Sainsbury's	16.3
Morrisons	11.1
Somerfield	5.4
Waitrose	3.7
Iceland	1.8
Other	14.5

Table 13.6 Market share of supermarkets
(Source: TNS, February 2006)

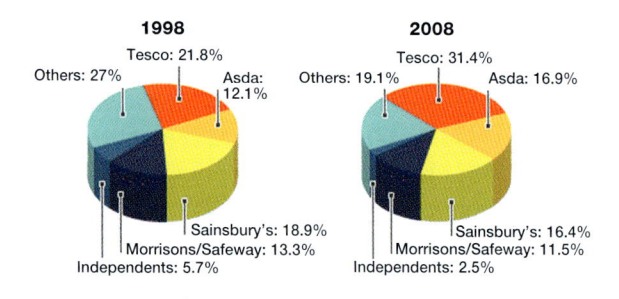

1998
Tesco: 21.8%
Others: 27%
Asda: 12.1%
Sainsbury's: 18.9%
Morrisons/Safeway: 13.3%
Independents: 5.7%

2008
Tesco: 31.4%
Others: 19.1%
Asda: 16.9%
Sainsbury's: 16.4%
Morrisons/Safeway: 11.5%
Independents: 2.5%

Figure 13.12 Comparing the grocery market
(Source: TNS Worldpanel)

In 2007, Verdict estimated that Tesco, Asda, Sainsbury and Morrisons accounted for 65.4 per cent of the £118.2bn market, up from 63.6 per cent in 2006, and grew their sales (excluding fuel) by a combined £3.3bn during the year. In order to retain their lead in the grocery market, Tesco continually create a wider range of products to supply to their customers. They also develop the services they offer to their customers in order to encourage them to remain loyal and return on a weekly basis.

Table 1 UK Grocers' market shares 2007	
	%
Tesco	27.6
Asda	14.1
Sainsbury's	13.8
Morrison	9.9
Somerfield	3.9
Co-op Group	3.8
M&S	3.8
Waitrose	3.3
Iceland	1.5
Aldi	1.5
Lidl	1.3
Netto	0.6
Sub total	**85.1**
Others	14.9
Total	**100.0**

(Source: Verdict Research, a Datamonitor company)

Market data

Once a business is aware of how much market share they currently hold, they need to consider ways to increase this percentage, or at least hold their current position. One way to do this is to look at data indicating trends within the market caused by external influences.

Prices of goods

One of the recent trends has been the increase in the price of food. In order to respond to this trend, supermarkets have been reducing the price of the essential items that people have to buy on a regular basis. The largest of the supermarkets have been investing heavily in promotion in order to inform the general public of their response to this situation.

Ethical concerns

Another trend recently has been healthy eating and the concern over the welfare of animals and suppliers. Good animal welfare was heavily promoted by celebrity chef Jamie Oliver in the summer of 2008, through his television programmes on welfare standards in the poultry industry. There was an immediate increase in the purchase of corn-fed chicken and free-range eggs. Due to consumer pressure, Colman, the mayonnaise manufacturer, stopped using battery eggs in their mayonnaise. However, due to the high increases in food prices during the autumn of 2008, the sales of organic products have fallen heavily because of their increase in price. This has meant that advertising during September and October 2008 focused on the price of food rather than ethics of its production.

Another recent trend has been the fluctuating price of petrol and concerns over global warming. This has led car manufacturers to research into the possibility of developing hybrid cars that will run on both electric and petrol.

Changing demographics

Market data also highlights other changes that are happening within the demographics of the country. The current birth rate and increasing life expectancy of the UK population means that it is an aging population, which by 2015 will have a higher percentage of people over the age of 65 than under 16. This means that the demand for products will change. A higher demand for products to suit elderly people will have greater demand than perhaps toys for the younger generation.

Changes to the economy

At the end of October 2008, the UK officially entered into a recession with the country showing no economic growth over the last quarter. This has resulted in increased unemployment which will affect people's buying patterns; they will have less money to spend on products and services, and will have to choose which items are luxuries and which are necessities. The businesses that supply these goods and services will also start to see sharp declines in their potential markets.

For example, thousands of workers at the manufacturing firm JCB voted in October 2008 to accept a pay cut of £50 a week to prevent the loss of 350 jobs. 2,500 employees from seven JCB plants in England and Wales agreed to work a four-day week for the following 13 weeks to help the company through the recession. The company's sales have declined because of the recent downturn in property sales and construction.

JCB has suffered in the downturn in property sales and construction

Activity

Working in pairs, make a list of all the goods and services that you purchase in a week. Now put your list into two columns:

- Essential items – you need these in order to survive
- Non-essential items – those items you buy because you like them but do not really need them.

Now consider what will happen to those businesses if people stop buying their goods or services. What could they do to respond to these changes?

Surveys

If the external environment starts to impact on the sales of a business, it might decide to conduct a survey in order to discover which trends are going to make an impact. The questions could focus on what customers actually want from the business, and how it could improve customer service in order to retain or attract customers. The business might also discover adaptations that customers want to see to products or services in order to make them more useful or attractive to the customer.

Lulworth Cove in Dorset is privately owned, although it provides access to the Heritage Coast at Portland. In order to establish the services that customers want when visiting the area, the business conducts an annual visitor survey. One purpose of this survey is to discover who actually visits the area. This information helps them develop the facilities within the area in order to satisfy their target market.

Monitoring competitors' actions

Competition can be either direct or indirect. A cinema's direct competition would be other cinemas in the area that can deliver the same goods in similar circumstances. Indirect competition would be any other business that offers indoor entertainment, for example a bowling alley, ice rink or theatre. A business must ensure that it keeps up not only with the direct competition, but also the indirect competition.

Let us consider the scenario of the cinema. If the bowling alley puts on special offers for students over the age of 16 on a Friday and Saturday night, it might encourage young people to go bowling rather than a trip to the cinema. The cinema may need to consider a similar promotional offer in order to retain their customer numbers over the weekend. The cinema must consider that as soon as they offer a special price, their profits will start to fall although they may have retained customer numbers. The cinema must therefore consider if it would be more profitable to drop the price or accept lower attendance numbers while the competitor is offering its special deal. There is also the consideration that the target market may not want to go bowling on a regular basis, and will therefore soon decide to come back to the cinema. Another consideration would be the popularity of the film that the cinema is currently showing. It may have been that the bowling alley put on a special offer as a Harry Potter film was due to be released. This would probably have had very little impact on the number of people who wanted to see the new film.

This scenario shows that a business must consider a wide range of different variables when deciding how to react to competitor activity.

How businesses remain competitive

It is very important for businesses to remain highly competitive. There are a number of different ways of achieving this.

Pricing strategies

Earlier in the chapter we looked at the idea of where to place a product in terms of quality and price. Where a business decides to place its products or services will have an influence on the pricing strategy that they choose to use.

One way to compete in a competitive market is to offer lower prices than competitors. The prices cannot however be too low, as the business will not be able to make a profit. If a business sells multiple products, they might be able to sell one at a loss as other items are being sold at a profit. These items are known as 'loss leaders'.

A common pricing strategy is to offer special offers to customers, such as 'buy one, get one free', 25 per cent extra free, or products at reduced price for a set period of time.

Some businesses prefer to offer their goods and services at a premium price which reflects the quality of the products being sold. It makes the goods appear exclusive and available only to a small minority of the population.

Actual pricing strategies will be covered in greater detail under Chapter 15, the marketing mix.

Promotional activities

Businesses need to keep customers aware of the products and services they have on offer, especially in a highly competitive market-place. One way to do this is to use promotional activities. This could include a wide variety of advertisements or promotional displays at the point of sale. Promotional activities are often used to bring customers' attention to special offers. Promotional activities will be covered in greater detail under Chapter 15, The marketing mix.

Place (where products are sold)

Customers will not be interested in a business's goods and services if they do not know where they are actually being sold. Businesses need to ensure that customers' buying experiences are easy. If they are not, customers are likely to take their business to the competition. When selling on the Internet, it is important that the 'shopping trolley' or 'checkout' pages are easy to follow and secure.

The next step is to ensure that the customer receives the goods by the stated delivery times. If customers have to wait to receive their goods, they are unlikely to use the business again. Place and distribution channels will be covered in greater detail under Chapter 15, The marketing mix.

Innovation and creativity

Businesses need to update their products or range of services often, in order to keep up with the competition. Products soon become outdated and in order to encourage customers to make repeat purchases, new models have to be developed.

Ben and Jerry's Ice Cream continually develop new types of ice cream in order to remain competitive in the luxury ice cream market. The following are some of the ice creams which have been taken out of production and replaced with new flavours in order to attract repeat and new customers:

- Chocolate Therapy (2008)
- Oh My Apple Pie (2007)
- Minter Wonderland (2006)
- Dublin Mudslide (2007).

(Source: www.benjerry.co.uk/flavourgraveyard)

> **Activity**
>
> Log on to www.benjerry.co.uk/ and find out which new flavours have replaced these old ones. Research other luxury ice cream manufacturers – what flavours of ice cream do they produce in order to compete with Ben and Jerry's?

The consequences of ignoring competitor activity

If a business fails to notice what its competitors are doing, they are likely to lose customers and market share, and ultimately profits. If the situation was to continue, the business could ultimately fail.

In the early 2000s Marks and Spencer failed to notice what their competitors were doing, and did not meet their customers' needs. This led to dramatic falls in sales. It has taken a number of years for the business to re-establish itself back in the market. Luckily it was a sufficiently large company to weather the storm, and is still trading. For a much smaller business, this decrease in sales could have signalled the end of the business.

Summary

- Market segmentation breaks society down into smaller groups that have similar tastes and buying habits.
- Markets can be segmented using a number of different characteristics: age, gender, socio-economic group, frequency of use, lifestyle, family circumstances, geography.
- If a business fails to meet the needs of its customers they are likely to lose repeat custom.
- Customers can purchase their products from a variety of different outlets so it is important that businesses stand out from the competition.
- Price, quality and value for money are closely linked.
- Pre-sales service is the information and help a customer receives prior to buying a product. After sales service are the services on offer after the purchase of the product.
- Trade Description Act 1968 – goods must be described accurately and not mislead the customer in any way.
- Sale of Goods Act 1979 – All goods sold must be as described, of satisfactory quality and fit for the purpose they were sold.
- It is much easier to retain current customers than find new ones. Businesses must monitor customer satisfaction.
- Successful businesses never take their eye off the competition in order to try and keep 'one jump ahead'. Businesses need to review the price being charged and the promotional methods of competitors. Businesses that ignore their competitors do so at their own risk.

> **Case Study**
>
> ### The Bargain Christmas – 2008
>
> In order to stimulate customer demand for Christmas 2008, the high street stores slashed prices as early as mid-November. Some stores reduced prices by as much as 75 per cent in order to persuade customers to buy. All the major stores were involved: Debenhams offered savings of 50 per cent on items for the home and partywear; House of Fraser discounted heavily; and Marks and Spencer held a special discount day where everything was reduced by 20 per cent. Another ploy was the distribution of discount vouchers to encourage customers to part with their money.
>
> *Adapted from an article in the* Daily Mail, *8th November 2008.*
>
> 1. When one store starts offering discounts, others follow. Explain why this happens.
> 2. What would happen if a store such as John Lewis did not join in the early sales? Justify your answer.
> 3. Evaluate the impact that these sales would have on the retail industry and on consumers.

Chapter 14
Presenting data effectively

As part of your controlled assessment you will be required to undertake primary and secondary research. It is very important that you understand how to present, analyse and interpret this data. Throughout this chapter we will be considering some of the different ways in which you can present your work. This will include:

- written reports
- charts
- graphs
- tables
- short summaries.

Within these sections we will also consider how to use a range of statistical techniques in order to prepare a report or short summary, which is fully supported through your research.

Written reports

The purpose of a written report is to convey the findings of research to an audience in written format. It is therefore important that a report is accurate, clear, concise and logically arranged. The term 'concise' means that the report must not contain unnecessary information. You should therefore remember that the quality of your words matter more than the amount!

In order for your report to be logical, you could try using the following headings to help structure the report.

1. The heading or title (should indicate the subject of the report).
2. The opening paragraph (explain the reasons for the completion of the report, describe what it is about).
3. The main body of the report (where you will present your findings). This section should include the analysis of your primary and secondary research.
4. Recommendations and conclusions (what you think the business should do in the light of your research and analysis).

Portfolio Tip ✓

You may decide to use a report format when completing tasks of the controlled assessment for Unit 2. You might like to use the following headings to help you structure this section.

Report

From: a student [insert your name]
To: [name of teacher]
Date: [insert date of completion]

Subject

Report on how [name of business] meets the needs of its customers, and analysis of competitor activity.

Introduction

I have undertaken research in [name of business] to establish how it is currently meeting the needs of its current target market. I will then investigate how the competitors [name them] meet the needs of the same target market. From the analysis of these results I will then consider how my selected business can better meet the needs of its target market and hopefully become more successful than its competitors.

Main body of the report

- **Paragraph 1** Describe the target market and customer needs of the target market.

- **Paragraph 2** Analyse how your selected business is currently meeting the current customer needs of the target market. This must be based on your primary and secondary research.

- **Paragraph 3** Analyse how your selected business's competitors meet the customer needs of the target market. Consider how this would impact on the target market – could it influence them to buy from the competition?

Conclusion

Pulling all your research together, describe two ideas of how your business could better meet the needs of its target market and be more successful than its competitors, making reference to the marketing mix (see Chapter 15).

Below are some examples of statistical techniques that you could use when analysing your primary and secondary research, to gain higher marks.

Percentages

Having carried out your survey, you will be required to analyse the results. If you asked 30 people if they had come to school by car today, and 5 said yes, you could present this in a number of different ways. For example, you could simply say that 5 people out of 30 had come to school by car this morning. However, it is much better if this information is presented as a percentage. To create a percentage:

- Add up the total number of respondents.

- Divide this number by the response you receive for each question, and multiply by 100.

In this instance, divide 5 by 30 and multiply it by 100:

$$\frac{5}{30} \times 100 = 16.666 \text{ per cent}$$

This should be rounded up to 16.67 per cent. You can now state that 16.67 per cent of pupils came to school by car this morning.

Activity

Present these results in percentage terms:
1. 57 out of 120 people said yes.
2. 10 out of 50 people said no.
3. 8 people out of 32 went to the cinema last week.
4. 25 out of 1,000 people flew during last month.
5. 5 out of 20 people own a cat.

Arithmetic mean

The mean is calculated by adding up all the numbers in a group, and then dividing the total by the number in the group. You could use the mean for a question that asked respondents how often they attended an event, or how often they purchased a product over a period of time.

For example: ten respondents were asked how many eggs they eat in a week. The results are shown here:

6	7	8	10	11	4	5	7	4	3

The total is 65, which is then divided by the number of respondents, ten. This gives a mean of 6.5 eggs per week.

Activity

Using the same question, calculate the mean from the following responses from 20 different people.

4	2	1	6	7	3	4	4	4	5	2	2	3	3	2	1	7	3	2	4

The median

The median is the value of the middle number, and is found by arranging the numbers in order and selecting the middle number from the list. It is the value that divides the distribution into two. This method of statistical analysis is particularly useful when there are extreme values in a series of numbers that would otherwise distort the mean.

For example:

| 6 | 7 | 8 | 10 | 11 | 4 | 5 | 7 | 4 | 3 |

First of all, arrange the numbers from the lowest to the highest:

| 3 | 4 | 4 | 5 | 6 | 7 | 7 | 8 | 10 | 11 |

The position of the median is:

$\frac{N+1}{2}$ where N = the number in the sample

Therefore $\frac{10+1}{2}$ = 5.5th number = 6.5

Activity

Using the responses from the question about how often do people eat eggs, calculate the median.

| 4 | 2 | 1 | 6 | 7 | 3 | 4 | 4 | 5 | 5 | 2 | 2 | 3 | 3 | 2 | 1 | 7 | 3 | 2 | 4 |

The mode

The mode is the most frequently occurring item in a list of numbers. For example:

| 6 | 7 | 8 | 10 | 11 | 7 | 5 | 7 | 4 | 3 |

First of all, arrange the numbers from the lowest to the highest:

| 3 | 4 | 5 | 6 | **7** | **7** | **7** | 8 | 10 | 11 |

Once they have been re-arranged, it is clear that number 7 is the most frequently occurring number. This is the mode.

Activity

Using the responses from the question about how often do people eat eggs, calculate the mode. Remember, it is the number which occurs the most frequently.

| 4 | 2 | 1 | 6 | 7 | 3 | 4 | 4 | 5 | 5 | 2 | 2 | 3 | 3 | 2 | 1 | 7 | 3 | 2 | 4 |

Graphs, tables and charts

Another way to present data is through the use of graphs. It is very easy to insert data into a spreadsheet which will then create the graph for you. However, beware! You must make sure that the choice of graph is suitable for the information you are trying to display, and that it contains a heading and also a key to each section. Often graphs appear in colour on your screen and as such the key makes sense, but as soon as they are printed in black and white, the key means absolutely nothing to the reader. Make sure that you insert the colour code. You could annotate your graph or even colour it in.

Activity

Look at the chart in Figure 14.1 and consider what is wrong with it.

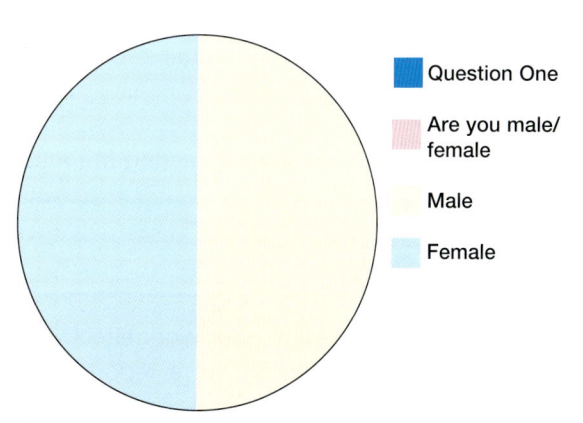

Figure 14.1 Sample chart

Short summaries

A short summary involves highlighting the important facts from a larger piece of writing. You may need to do this when analysing your secondary data. For example, you may find a relevant newspaper article that you could use within your controlled assignment. It would not be feasible for you to insert the whole article in your work, and therefore you would extract all the relevant information and write this out in a much shorter format. The ability to summarise work accurately requires high-level skills and plenty of practice.

Case Study

Great train robbery – Outrage as rail travellers face an 11% fare rise

Rail operators provoked outrage yesterday as they announced inflation-busting fare rises of up to 11 per cent in the New Year [2009].

The huge hikes, at a time of recession and economic turmoil, met with almost universal condemnation from passengers, unions, and MPs. Rail chiefs were accused of having 'a licence to print money', while critics accused the Government of using the railways to impose a 'stealth tax' on vulnerable passengers.

The increase comes into force on 2nd January 2009 in the wake of a rail repair operation expected to bring chaos to Christmas travel.

Unregulated fares, which include most cheap day returns and advanced fare tickets, will rise by an average of seven per cent, and in one case 11 per cent, the Association of Train Operating Companies announced.

Regulated fares – including season tickets, savers and standard day returns – will increase by an average of six per cent as operators are not permitted to hike them by more than one per cent above inflation.

Rail chiefs said the rises were necessary to fund major rail improvements and in line with Government policy to reduce rail subsidy by 40 per cent before 2014.

(Source: The Daily Mail, 22nd November 2008)

- Summarise this article, extracting the main points.

Summary

- Ensure that you present your work effectively. This might include laying out a report using the correct headings.

- If compiling a report, remember the following points: the title of the report should indicate what it is about, the opening paragraph should explain the reasons for its completion, the main body of the report should be where you present the findings of your investigation and your recommendations should form the conclusion.

- A short summary involves highlighting the important facts from a larger piece of writing.

Chapter 15

The marketing mix

> **Activity**
>
> Think of a product or service that you purchase or use regularly. Consider the following questions:
> - What is the product?
> - How much does it cost?
> - Where can you buy the product?
> - How is it promoted?

Through the completion of the above activity, you have described the marketing mix of your selected product/service. Having the correct marketing mix allows businesses to deliver the right product to the right people at the right price in the right place.

```
              Price
                ↓
Promotion → Marketing mix ← Product
                ↑
              Place
```

Figure 15.1 Components of the marketing mix

The marketing mix combines the following aspects:

- The product: it must appeal to the target audience.
- The price: this must be affordable and meet the requirements of the target audience.
- Place of sale: the product must be in a location which is easily accessible to the customer.
- Promotion: this must catch the attention of the correct target audience and persuade them to purchase.

By manipulating the different parts of the marketing mix, businesses are able to attract and retain their customer base.

Marks and Spencer's advertisements for food often include offers. This type of offer reduces the price but increases the level of promotion to create customer awareness. The place of sale and product remain the same. However, if customers are encouraged to purchase one product, they might buy others whilst in the store.

Product

In simplistic terms the product is the tangible, physical item that you see. However it is not quite that simple. The product can be broken down into three distinct sections:

A new washing machine has three distinct sections

- The **core product** is the benefit that the product will bring to the consumer. For example, if you purchase a washing machine, the core value is the convenience of the machine in cleaning your clothes. Another core benefit would be the time it saves for you. You are therefore able to do other things while the washing machine is washing your clothes.

- The **actual product** is the tangible physical product; in this example, the washing machine.

- The **augmented product** is the non-physical side of the product. The washing machine will have a one-year guarantee, and the company may offer after-sales service. These all form part of the added value, for which you may or may not be charged.

Activity

Working in pairs, select a product that you both know. Describe the three elements of the product:
- the core benefit
- the actual product
- the augmented product.

Price

This is the only part of the marketing mix that brings in money. The remainder of the marketing mix are costs to the business.

Price is an extremely important aspect of the marketing mix. If a business prices the product too highly, customers may not be able to afford it and therefore sales will falter. On the other hand, if the price set is too low, customers may perceive the product/service to be of low quality and therefore may avoid it. There are a number of different pricing strategies that a business can use when deciding what price to charge for their product/service.

Premium pricing

When a product is unique and unavailable through multiple outlets, the business will have a substantial competitive advantage and is able to charge a high price. The price charged will also reflect the quality and image of the product, for example first-class flights or rooms at the Ritz Hotel, London. The business would not expect to sell large volumes of the product, and so prices it highly to retain its uniqueness and special qualities.

Penetration pricing

When a market is saturated with suppliers, it can be very difficult for a new business to establish itself. One method which a business can use is to price its products below those of its competitors. Once regular and repeated custom is established, the business will need to raise its prices in order to increase profit margins.

Economy pricing

Products and services priced in this range offer 'no frills' deals at a low price. Many of the main supermarkets have their own range of 'economy' foods. These are usually aimed at people on low incomes.

Low-cost economy airfares increased in popularity with the growth of companies such as Easyjet, Ryannair and Flybe. These companies offer low-cost basic fares. The cost of the flight does not include baggage allowance and food; when these costs are included, the customer could end up paying more than with another, more expensive airline.

Price skimming

With the ever-increasing pace of technology, businesses often bring new technological inventions to the market at a high price. At the point of launch, the business will hold competitive advantage, and if the price is high, only a small percentage of the population will be able to afford the product. This enables those buyers to feel special.

Competitive advantage is not held for long as other businesses begin to supply the market, and it is at this point that the price starts to fall. It is now possible to buy a good laptop computer for just over £300. Four years ago, this might have cost in excess of £600.

Psychological pricing

This method of pricing is very common in the retail industry. Items are priced at 99p rather than £1.00, as it gives the product the image of being cheaper. A house priced at £299,900 sounds much cheaper than one that is priced at £300,000.

Product bundle pricing

The seller combines a number of products in the same package in this pricing strategy. This will help to move old stock and also stimulate sales in time of falling demand.

Promotional pricing

The retail food industry uses this method of pricing heavily. It involves using promotions such as BOGOF (buy one, get one free), 50 per cent free, buy two and get the third half-price. This method of pricing is prevalent at the time of writing, with stores trying to stimulate falling sales because of the credit crunch.

Cost plus pricing

This method considers all the costs involved with the manufacture and sale of the product. The business considers how much profit it wants to achieve, and adds this to the price of manufacturing the product:

average cost + profit margin = selling price.

In reality, very few businesses operate in such a non-competitive market or a market where customers are insensitive to price, and therefore this method of pricing strategy is rarely used for mass-produced items.

Conclusion

Even taking into account all the different pricing strategies listed above, a business has to be aware of the price that customers are actually prepared to pay for the product or service. This should be established through market research conducted by the business. The results of this research should help a business to establish the pricing strategy they could use when launching or redeveloping their product/service.

What pricing strategy would suit these products?

Activity

- Research a range of different products, at least five.
- Describe the pricing strategy you think best fits all of these products.

Place (channels of distribution)

Research has shown that although figures vary from product to product, roughly a fifth of the cost of a product is spent on delivering it to the customer. The concept of 'place' considers the various methods which businesses can use to transport and store goods, before finally making them available to the customer. The choice of distribution channel will vary depending on the product being distributed and the circumstances of the business.

All goods and services need to reach the customer in the fastest and most accessible and convenient way possible. There are two basic channels of distribution:

- direct from the manufacturer to the customer
- through the use of intermediaries.

Direct supply

This is where the manufacturer or producer decides to sell their product direct to the customer. A free-range egg producer may decide to sell eggs direct to the customer through a farm shop. Because the owner of the business is cutting out the retail shop, it is likely that they will earn more profit by directly selling to the customer. The main drawback to this method of supply is that there is no guarantee of customers visiting the farm shop, and therefore sales might be slow until a regular customer base is established. In order to do this, the producer would have to be responsible for marketing and promotions, which could eat into the profits of the venture.

With the ever-increasing use of the Internet, direct selling is becoming easier for manufacturers and producers. Manufacturers are able to sell their products direct to customers from their websites, 24 hours a day, seven days a week. For many people, the ability to shop at home is appealing and internet sales have seen a large increase over the last five years.

The use of intermediaries

Figure 15.2 shows the traditional method of distribution used by manufacturing businesses.

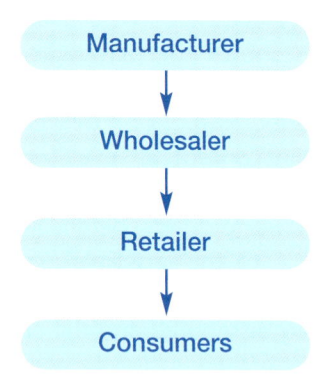

```
Manufacturer
     ↓
 Wholesaler
     ↓
  Retailer
     ↓
 Consumers
```

Figure 15.2 Traditional method of distribution

Many people still recognise this as the normal distribution chain when purchasing their goods on a daily basis. In fact, if high street shopping were to cease, many people would not know what to do with their spare time!

The role of the wholesaler is to buy items in bulk from the manufacturer. The wholesaler breaks the order into smaller consignments to be sold to the retailer. The retailer then sells the items to the consumer.

This traditional system means that manufacturers only have to deal with a few wholesalers, and so can concentrate on what they do best, manufacturing. The main drawback with the system is that there are three people in the chain who all need to make a profit. The manufacturer has to sell the product to the wholesaler for a profit. The wholesaler also requires a profit and therefore increases the unit price as the items are sold on to the retail outlets. Finally, the retail outlet adds their profit to the item before selling the items to the customer.

This can be illustrated as follows.

- The cost of manufacture of the unit is £100.
- The manufacturer adds his profit of 25 per cent, and sells it to the wholesaler for £125 (manufacturer's profit is £25).
- The wholesaler adds his 20 per cent profit and sells the item to the retailer for £150 (wholesaler's profit is £25).
- The retailer wants a profit return of 15 per cent, and therefore prices the unit at £172.50 for the customer (retailer's profit is £22.50).

Large supermarkets such as Sainsbury's and Morrisons have their own distribution centres. Due to their size, they are able to purchase in bulk from the manufacturers. These large orders go to the distribution centre where they are broken down into smaller consignments. From there they are distributed to individual stores.

The ability to purchase in bulk often means that supermarkets can secure large discounts. By removing the wholesaler from the chain of distribution, supermarkets are also removing one level of profit margin. This is one of the reasons they are able to sell their products cheaper than local shops that have to buy the same items from a wholesaler.

The marketing mix   97

> ### Activity
>
> Calculate the final selling price of the following item:
>
> - A clothing manufacturer produces a woollen scarf for £2.00.
> - The manufacturer adds a profit margin of 10 per cent when the item is sold to the wholesaler.
> - The wholesaler adds a profit margin of 15 per cent.
> - The retailer adds a profit margin of 10 per cent.
>
> Round your answer up to two decimal places.

Promotion

Promotion is one of the ways that a business can communicate with its customers. With increasing competition, it is important to keep your current and prospective customers aware of what your business is doing.

Every day we are bombarded with different kinds of advertisements trying to persuade us to spend our money. Promotional activity can be divided into two distinct types: above the line and below the line techniques.

Above the line promotion uses independent media to promote the business's goods. This can include:

- television
- radio
- cinema
- national and local press
- magazines
- outdoor advertising
- leaflets and flyers.

Below the line promotion involves all other forms of promotional activity, and will include:

A famous logo can help promote a business

- sales promotions
- competitions
- sponsorship
- public relations (press releases)
- money-off coupons
- point of sale promotion.

Before we start looking at the various different ways business can advertise and promote their products, we need to consider why businesses need to continually advertise their products and services.

1 One reason might be because the business wishes the consumer to bring forward a decision to buy. This involves offering a discount or free product. The idea is to encourage either old or new customers to buy the product at that moment in time. It is a useful way to move old stock.

2. Another reason might be to encourage loyalty to a product. This would involve offering current customers an incentive to stay with the business. This could be connected to loyalty cards or discounts for repeat and regular orders.

3. The reason for offering three goods for the price of two is to encourage the customer to stockpile goods. This is another method of moving old stock or goods that have not been selling as well as expected. The problem with this method is that the consumer then does not need to buy any further goods for a period of time. When needing to replace the product, they may return to their original choice or brand.

4. The final reason to promote is to encourage consumers to purchase and try a new product or service. These promotions would be designed to raise awareness of the new product. Hopefully consumers will be tempted to try, thereby deserting the competition.

Television

Television advertising hit our screens in 1955, transforming advertising within Britain. Television advertising is only available on commercial channels such as ITV, Channel 4 and Sky. With the ever-increasing number of commercial channels, the available time and space has increased significantly. Commercial television channels rely on the revenue raised from advertising to fund their production and purchase of programmes.

Television advertising is able to use strong images, sound, colour and special effects to gain and hold the audience's attention. Generally, the aim of the advertisement is to persuade people to purchase, rather than to provide detailed information about the product. If an advertisement is shown at prime-time, it will also attract a substantial audience.

However, television advertising is very expensive. The price will vary according to the popularity of the channel and time of showing. A business will also have to consider the production costs of the advertisement. If the advertisement features a celebrity endorsing the product, this will greatly increase the cost of production; for example, footballer David Beckham endorses Gillette razors.

If a business has decided to use television for advertising, the next decisions are which channel to use, and when to air the advertisement. These decisions will be linked to the target audience for the product. If the product is for children, it will probably be aired after school, or on Saturday and Sunday mornings when their target market would be free to watch television.

Businesses will also look at the viewing figures for different programmes and channels. Advertising between very popular programmes is

Activity

Working in small groups, think of two advertisements that are currently being shown on the television. Consider the following questions.
- On which channel do they appear?
- At what time are they aired?
- Who is the target market?
- Do you think the advertisement is appropriate, and aired at the correct time to appeal to the selected target market? Justify your decisions.

No	TV Programme – day and time	Millions
1	Coronation Street – Monday 19.32	10.60
2	The X Factor – Saturday 19.45	10.37
3	Coronation Street – Monday 20.29	10.20
4	Coronation Street – Friday 19.33	9.66
5	Coronation Street – Friday 20.31	9.54
6	Coronation Street – Wednesday 19.29	9.50
7	The X Factor Results – Saturday 22.12	8.89
8	A Touch of Frost – Sunday 20.18	8.16
9	Emmerdale – Monday 19.01	7.59
10	Emmerdale – Tuesday 19.00	7.12

Table 15.1 Viewing figures for ITV 1, week ending 26th October 2008   (Source: BARB)

No	TV Programme – day and time	Millions
1	River Cottage Autumn – Thursday 19.59	2.75
2	Gordon Ramsay: Cookalong Live – Friday 21.00	2.70
3	Jamie's Ministry of Food – Tuesday 21.01	2.51
4	The Simpsons – Thursday 18.02	2.50
5	Deal or No Deal – Monday 16.13	2.40
6	Desperate Housewives – Wednesday 22.03	2.39
7	Hollyoaks – Monday 18.29	2.30
8	Mum, Heroin and Me – Thursday 21.10	2.25
9	The Simpsons – Wednesday 18.03	2.23
10	Deal or No Deal – Thursday 16.14	2.17

Table 15.2 Viewing figures for Channel 4, week ending 26th October 2008   (Source: BARB)

much more expensive than when fewer people are expected to be viewing.

As you can see from Tables 15.1 and 15.2, the most popular programmes on ITV 1 are Coronation Street and The X Factor. Advertising between these programmes would be the most expensive airtime to buy, because they secure such large audiences. Channel 4 viewing figures show significantly smaller viewing audiences, and so it would be cheaper to advertise between The Simpsons and Hollyoaks.

Television advertising is not usually an option for medium-sized or small businesses, due to the high costs involved. It can also be quite difficult to gauge whether or not the advertisement has been successful. If there is an increase in sales, the business is unable to track the increase directly back to the advertisement.

Radio

Commercial radio is defined as a home radio service which is broadcast terrestrially or non-terrestrially, that derives revenue from the sale of advertising airtime. Commercial radio stations earn money from the advertisements that they are able to play between or during programmes. In 2003, UK revenue from commercial radio advertising reached £601 million, which represented an increase of 6.8 per cent on 2002. In terms of earning revenue, commercial radio is broken down into three sections:

- advertising on national radio stations
- advertising on local radio stations
- sponsorship of both national and local radio stations.

Commercial radio stations specialise in different kinds of music from pop to classical. They are able to target audiences effectively, and advertisements can be directly linked to the listener's profile. The ability to target audiences has increasingly made radio advertising more appealing to commercial organisations.

The way that people listen to the radio is also changing. It is now available through digital technology (DAB), the Internet and satellite television, which is playing an increasing role in the growth of this type of advertising. Ninety-three per cent of commercial radio stations are now available live on the Internet, and eighty-seven per cent of these contain local news on their websites.

Commercial radio is very important to local communities, where local stations often serve audiences with a wide range of invaluable information alongside supporting local events. In 2008, Ofcom outlined a series of revised rules which govern local radio stations. The new rules allow stations to share programming and news outside of peak hours in a bid to save the industry up to £12million per year. As a result, commercial radio's market share increased, up to 43.1 per cent during the summer of 2008. BBC radio does not carry advertisements as it is publicly funded, and it holds 54.9 per cent market share.

Radio advertising can be a relatively cheap and effective way of advertising for small to medium businesses. The downside is that people are only listening; there are no visual images to support the message. The listener may also be unable to remember telephone numbers and contact details after the advertisement has finished.

Cinema

The first advertisement to appear on cinema screens was for Dewars Whisky, used to create some memorable campaigns such as 'Careless Sneezes Spread Diseases' and 'Careless Talk Costs Lives'.

Cinema attendance saw a dramatic decline in the 1980s with the growth of home entertainment. Advertising revenue kept many screens afloat. Few customers realise that the revenue generated by cinema advertising helps to keep ticket prices low.

The industry recovered strongly through the 1990s, with young people aged 15 to 24 being the most likely to visit the cinema. The Office of National Statistics reported that in 2004 there were 171 million visits to UK cinemas, an increase of 2.4 per cent on 2003. This is the second highest number for over 30 years. In 2003 39 per cent of children aged 7 to 14 went to the cinema once a month or more. Almost all children (98 per cent) aged 4 to 9 are accompanied to the cinema by an adult. Children start to go to the cinema with friends aged 10 to 14. Over 70% of children in this age group had been to the cinema with friends.

Because films are categorised according to age-group suitability, it is very easy for businesses to target their advertising at the correct target market. Some films are aimed at younger children (for example Shrek 2) whilst others at older children/teenagers (for example Terminator Salvation which carries a 12A certificate.

This is also supported by the research that is carried out by the Cinema and Video Industry Audience Research (CAVIAR) organisation which provides the largest data bank of cinema-going profiles by film. This information allows a

The marketing mix

> **Activity**
>
> Below are some common consumer beliefs and perceptions about cinema advertising, taken from www.dcm.co.uk:
> - 'The adverts have more impact at the cinema on the big screen.' (female aged 25–34, Manchester)
> - 'Better sound and quality.' (male aged 25–34, Manchester)
> - 'It's because the adverts are quite different generally; I find them incredibly irritating on the television.' (Mother, London)
> - 'There's a touch of fantasy, the humour is great. It all adds to the experience and makes them more memorable.' (Mother, London)
> - 'They do stand out more at the cinema.' (male aged 25–34, Manchester)
> - Cinema adverts are more upmarket (than other media).
> - You see the newer adverts at the cinema.
> - Cinema ads are longer than television adverts.
> - Cinema ads have been 'specially chosen for you in the cinema' … but on television they're for everyone.
> - Cinema adverts are more entertaining
> - Cinema adverts are special, versus television adverts which are seen as 'everyday' stuff.
> - Cinema adverts are for successful products and brands.
>
> Find out if these comments and feelings reflect your age group.
>
> Design some questions on how people view cinema adverts. Ask at least ten people who regularly attend the cinema, to see if your findings support the research and comments made by Digital Cinema Media.

business to be very precise when deciding which films they should select for their advertisements.

National and local press

> **Activity**
>
> Working in pairs, see how many national and local newspapers you can name. Compare your list with the other members of the class.

Newspapers can be broken down into two types:

1. National newspapers have a readership covering the breadth and depth of the country.

2. Local newspapers are read by the people living within the circulation area. This could include daily or weekly publications.

National newspapers can be divided into two categories: tabloid and broadsheet. *The Sun* is a tabloid newspaper, and has a readership of over eight million copies per day (although it sells just over three million copies); *The Times* is a broadsheet newspaper, and has an average readership of approximately 1.6 million copies per day (selling just over 600,000 copies). A daily local newspaper in the Southampton area is the *Daily Echo*; *The Hampshire Chronicle* is a local paper that is produced weekly.

The cost of advertising is related to a newspaper's circulation figures (the number of people who actually purchase the paper). It will cost more money to advertise in *The Sun* than a local paper because of its increased audience.

On the next page are extracts from different reports on the readership and circulation figures of national newspapers. These facts should be considered when you plan your own promotional campaign.

Newspaper readership trends

In December 2007, the Lords Communication Committee reported that evidence from the National Readership Survey (NRS) showed a decline in the overall number of people who are reading daily newspapers. The figures reduced from 26.7 million in 1992 to 21.7 million in 2006. The decline in readership has been most marked among younger adults. The overall number of 15–24 year old readers fell by 37 per cent and 25–34 year old readers by 40 per cent. The number of older readers was steadier, with the number of 55–64 year old readers increasing by four per cent and the number of readers aged 65+ falling by three per cent.

In August 2008, the National Readership Survey indicated that six national newspapers have increased their readership within the last year. *The Daily Mail* increased its readership by three per cent in the last 12 months, taking its total to an estimated 5.34 million per day. *The Sun* also saw a three per cent rise to 8.03 million. *The Times* increased by two per cent to an estimated 1.73 million, while the free national Metro newspaper increased its readership to 3.12 million, a staggering increase of 35 per cent.

The Metro distributes 1.36 million copies to 16 British cities and now has a higher readership than six national dailies. This paper secures its income through the sale of advertisements, and therefore could be considered an effective way to advertise. Within the 16 British cities, it is now distributed free of charge.

Newspaper advertising is within the reach of many smaller businesses and can be an effective way of advertising. Local papers are best used to advertise businesses that operate within the circulation area, while national newspapers can be used to advertise mass-produced items, as the paper will potentially reach a very large audience. In order for a newspaper campaign to be effective, a business must first identify their target market and decide if the chosen paper will be read by the appropriate people.

Activity

Collect copies of national and local newspapers. Look through both and describe the following information.
- What businesses are advertising in the papers? Are they national or local?
- What types of products are being advertised?
- Where do they appear in the paper? At the front, left-hand side, at the back?
- What size are the adverts?
- How effective do you think the adverts are?

Summarise your findings.

Magazines

Magazines are often directly targeted at a particular market, and therefore can be an extremely effective way of reaching a specialised audience. Magazines are a more permanent form of media than newspapers, and may still be looked at several months after publication.

Specialist magazines are often based around people's hobbies and interests, for example *Your Horse*, *Country Life*, *Home and Garden*. Other general interest magazines are aimed at a particular segment of the population; for example, young women might purchase *Bella*.

Outdoor advertising

Outdoor advertising covers a range of different advertising methods which include:
- posters
- billboards

The marketing mix

Buses are an effective form of outdoor advertising

- buses and taxis
- hoardings at sports stadiums.

This form of advertising is usually permanent and located in areas which receive a lot of attention. Businesses can tailor the adverts to their target market effectively; for example, advertisements on football hoardings are linked to the likely interests of those people who attend football matches.

Posters are an extremely cheap way to advertise events such as garden fetes, a new restaurant opening up or a local charity event. They can be placed in shop windows or on local notice boards. It is illegal to put up a poster outside without authority and if done so can be removed by the local council. Posters have to be bright, easy to read and eye catching in order to be noticed by the general public. They are subject to the weather and if left outside in damp conditions might not last very long.

Billboards are placed near traffic lights, at junctions where people will have slowed down in their cars and might have time to glance at them. A standard billboard is 10 feet by 20 feet and is known as a '48 sheet'. Double billboards contain 96 sheets. Billboards are not effective for one-time sales or non-repeating sales events. They are best used as image builders. The most effective billboards contain no more than eight words and one picture, because people often travel past them at speed so the message needs to be immediate.

Buses are slow-moving vehicles, giving car drivers time to read the advertisements on the back of them. Walkers may also have time to notice the advertisements, especially if they are eye-catching.

Within large cities, taxi advertising is becoming popular. This involves the total or partial covering of the taxi in an advertisement. This can be further supported through the use of leaflets in the taxi. A taxi is on average on the road for eight hours a day. The adverts will remain clean and legible as legal requirements ensure that taxis are always kept in excellent condition. Targeting the advert at a local area is guaranteed as taxi licensing laws prohibit taxis from working outside of their registered borough.

Leaflets and flyers

Activity

Collect at least five leaflets. Aim for a mixture of leaflets that have come through your letterbox, and others that you have collected from different organisations.

Answer the following questions, making reference to your leaflets:

1 Identify each leaflet. What business does it come from? What is it advertising?
2 How many leaflets include a voucher, coupon or money-off code?
3 What size are the different leaflets?
4 Is there a common colour used?
5 Analyse the five leaflets in terms of effectiveness. Which one would most likely raise your interest sufficiently to purchase the product? Justify your choice.

Leaflet advertising involves creating an eye-catching document for the recipient, with the aim of creating awareness of the product or service. Awareness may then develop into interest and finally the purchase of the product or service. A leaflet is a self-contained sales message, and its impact is not diluted by other messages around it (which can be the case with newspaper and magazine advertising). It is a particularly effective way of promoting special offers, shop openings, or other special events.

One major advantage of using leaflets is that the campaign can be measured in terms of success. Through the use of promotional coupons, vouchers and money-off codes, the business can see how many were redeemed against the number actually distributed.

One of the problems with leaflets is making sure that they are distributed to the correct target audience.

Tourist attractions make very effective use of leaflets. They distribute them to local tourist information centres, hotels, bed and breakfasts and even competing tourist attractions. The leaflets are positioned in areas which will contain tourists, potential customers for the attraction.

Advertising distribution

Businesses have to decide to whom and by whom their leaflets will be delivered. There are a number of businesses who specialise in leaflet delivery. JM Circular (Leaflet Distribution) was established in 2003 as a family business covering Birmingham, Coventry and London. Due to increased demand for leaflet distribution packages, the business now employs 32 full-time staff, ranging from management to trained distributors.

One of the advantages of using a distribution company is that they hold a lot of data on the population and are therefore able to help a business to target their marketing campaign correctly.

Advertising distribution is one of the fastest growing methods of advertising, currently enjoying a growth rate of approximately 20 per cent per year. Research has shown that leaflet delivery has a success rate of approximately three to ten per cent, either in direct contact or sales through information on leaflets.

The fast food industry uses leaflets very successfully. Using leaflets to promote fast food, whether it be pizza, deep-fried chicken or burgers, is more likely to result in increased sales than any other type of marketing campaign.

Method of design

The method used to design the leaflet is known as 'call to action'. This encourages the customer to enquire about the product. Terms such as 'call now' and 'order now' are used within the leaflet. The success of the campaign can rely on the apathy of the consumer – such as a quick-fix solution to the problem of preparing a meal. It is also a very easy way to monitor the success of a leaflet distribution campaign; delivery to the address is final confirmation of the success.

Sales promotions

> **Activity**
>
> How many different kinds of sales promotions can you think of?

Examples of sales promotions include 'buy one, get one free', 50 per cent extra, 20 per cent reduced price, 'buy now, pay six months later', 'interest-free credit terms available'. The first three are popularly found within retail stores which sell mass-produced items that consumers purchase on a regular basis. The next two examples are often applied to larger purchases such as furniture and cars.

The aim of a sales promotion is to persuade customers to make a one-off purchase or to buy more of the selected product. It is hoped that the 'deal' will raise consumer awareness of the product and encourage people to disregard the competition. After the initial promotion, it is hoped that the consumer will turn into a repeat customer.

Competitions

A business may decide to run a competition in order to draw attention to a particular product or service. The competition could require participants making a single or multiple purchases in order to be eligible to enter the competition. Some competitions are free, as illustrated in the following two examples.

In November 2008, Zenith Windows ran an online competition, offering a prize of new double-glazing to the value of £7,000 including VAT. All the participant had to do was enter their name, address, telephone number and email address on the website. By gaining personal details of participants in the competition, Zenith had the chance to generate sales by contacting participants directly about the possibility of renewing their windows.

Outdoor company Millets joined forces with Bovril to run a photo competition in 2008. Participants were asked to send in a photograph of their favourite location to win prizes of Millets vouchers ranging from £10 to £500. To submit the photograph, the sender was asked to submit their name, address, telephone number and email address. The two companies could then target these people with news of products, special events and further offers.

Sponsorships

Increasingly in the world of marketing and promotion, sports stars and celebrities are used to promote and endorse products. For example, Jamie Oliver is believed to be paid approximately £1.2 million a year by Sainsbury's but has increased sales by approximately £1 billion. The business hopes that people will associate themselves with the selected celebrity and therefore be encouraged to purchase the product.

A number of football stadiums and television programmes are now sponsored; for example, the NFU Mutual sponsors the ITV programme Heartbeat; in October 2004 Arsenal signed a £100million deal with Emirate Airlines and their new ground has been named the Emirates Stadium.

Public relations (press releases)

Businesses use public relations (PR) to attract free, positive publicity. PR is rarely about trying to sell more goods, but instead creating a caring and professional image of the business. Local businesses are often approached when communities are trying to raise funds for local concerns and issues. This could involve donating raffle prizes for the local church fete, which in turn gives the business free publicity. It is common to see roundabouts in villages and towns planted with spring bulbs and summer bedding plants sponsored by local businesses, with a name plate to show their involvement. All of these types of events will help raise the awareness of the contributing business.

Big companies call press conferences when they are about to release a new product or service. The business will invite press, television and radio journalists to the meeting in order to release

Activity

When the UK economy headed towards recession in 2008, the retail trade offered many different promotions to boost Christmas sales. Marks and Spencer offered a one-day sale where all goods were discounted by 20 per cent. Sainsbury's issued customers who hold a Nectar Card a booklet containing eight vouchers; this provided a discount of £6 from a £60 shopping bill. The offer ran from 22nd November until 10th January 2009.

Boots the Chemist offered 3-for-2 deals on Christmas gifts and some other essential items. Morrisons started a sales promotion in mid November: if a customer spent £40 or more on four occasions, they could swap their receipts for a £20 voucher, redeemable 15th–24th December 2008.

- Explain what Sainsbury's and Morrisons were trying to achieve through these two similar sales promotions.
- Which offer do you think would have been the most successful? Justify your choice.

their plans and take questions. The business hopes that the release will become headline news.

Local businesses may try to involve local newspapers and radio stations in their activities with the hope of raising awareness of their business.

Money-off coupons

These often appear in a variety of publications or as part of a leaflet delivered to individuals. The aim is to encourage the recipient to purchase the goods. Having tried the product, it is hoped that the consumer will buy the product again.

One advantage of this type of promotion is that the campaign can be measured. The business can count how many coupons were used. Analysis can then take place to see if the methods used to distribute the coupons were effective.

Another use for money-off coupons is where customers are encouraged to collect vouchers in order to gain reduced entry into a theme park or other tourist attraction. The idea here is to encourage customers to participate in the day out but at a reduced price. These types of offers often only apply during the week outside of school holidays, when visitors to the attraction would probably already be reduced. The tourist attraction is therefore stimulating demand during a normally quieter period.

Point of sale promotion

Research has shown that a large number of consumer decisions are influenced by the promotions, posters and leaflets in a retail store. The display and positioning of products all influence the customer's decision to purchase.

Point of sale promotions include in-store posters, leaflets, tasting sessions, interactive displays and the positioning of the product. End of aisles are known to create higher sales levels, and will often include items being promoted for that week. Large companies pay a premium price to supermarkets to display their products in key positions.

Summary

- The marketing mix is made up of product, price, place and promotion.

Portfolio Tip

Within the controlled assessment, you are required to investigate prices charged by the competitors of your selected business. You also have to consider the main features of their product/service. Part of the analysis will require you to consider how the competition advertises their product.

In task four, you will be required to design your own promotional material and justify your choices.

Part of the theory covered within this chapter can be used to help you undertake your investigations, and the remainder to help create your own promotional material.

Activity

This activity will prepare you for your controlled assessment.

- Select a business.
- Describe its competitors, what products they sell, at what price and how they advertise.
- Consider the selected business's target audience, and how their methods of promotion appeal to these potential consumers.
- Suggest and justify changes that the business could make to its products, pricing structure and promotion in order to increase potential sales.

- Product – what the item is, what it can do for the consumer.
- Price – what the business can sell the product or service for.
- Place – where the consumer can purchase it.
- Promotion – how the business will inform, raise awareness of the product's existence.

Chapter 16

Costing implications

Chapter 15 explored the different types of promotional campaigns. This chapter considers the potential costs of advertising and promotional campaigns.

When designing an advertising campaign, a business must first consider the following issues, regardless of whether the potential audience is national or local. National advertising campaigns are obviously much more expensive than local adverts.

Television

The cost of advertisements is based on supply and demand. The supply of airtime is limited to approximately seven minutes per hour for advertising. This means that the greater the demand for this limited amount of time, the higher the cost.

Easter, November and the first two weeks of December are often the most expensive times to advertise. The other variable in the cost of an advertisement is the time of day, viewing figures and the number of advertisers in the same product field.

Advertising on ITV1 is sold on a regional basis. It is therefore possible for a business to target selected brands at certain parts of the country. For further information on and potential costs of TV advertisements, please see the website www.itvmedia.co.uk/default.asp.

With the continued growth of television channels, the amount of airtime has increased and therefore the price has been driven down for some smaller, less popular channels.

Radio

The cost of this type of advertising varies widely, depending on the popularity of the radio stations selected, time of day and length of advertisement. A typical slot of 25 seconds can cost around £250–£1,000 per week. An advert on Capital Radio London will cost more than a similar advertisement on a local radio station.

Radio has an official measurement system called RAJAR that provides quarterly data on a station's audience across the UK. It is therefore possible to ensure that a business places its advertisement on the correct station, catching the attention of the selected target market. In order to create maximum impact, a business is recommended to run a campaign for four weeks and then repeat it a few weeks later.

A further consideration for advertising on the radio is the design cost. The cost of script-writing, hiring actors to speak in the advertisement, music and sound effects should cost no more than approximately £200 for a small station and up to £2,000 for the most popular stations. The price starts to increase significantly if you want to include a popular song. This can cost up to £25,000 in licensing fees.

Research by Millward Brown has confirmed that radio advertising reaches target audiences at a lower cost and therefore is considered more affordable than many people realise. Justin Sampson, managing director of the Radio Advertising Board, comments on this research:

'Radio is three-fifths as effective as TV, but only one-seventh of the cost. Radio can be a much more cost-effective medium than television for advertising purposes if it is used correctly.'

Cinema

Cinema accounts for 1.8 per cent of all advertising spend in the UK, and can be up to six times more expensive than advertising on television. Cinema advertising is therefore still one of the most expensive methods of advertising, and is seen too infrequently to match the power of television. However, it does have one benefit, which is exclusivity. There are only a few advertisements shown in the typical ten-minute slot. It also has greater impact, as there is a captive audience. Cinema revenue is predicted to rise to £215 million in 2009.

Magazines

Magazines come in many different shapes and sizes. Advertisers can target their market through the use of specialist magazines such as *Country Life*. Local magazines are delivered to households, enabling small businesses to advertise locally. Research has shown that correctly targeted magazine advertising can achieve the same success rates as television advertising, at half the price. If an advertisement is placed in one of the higher readership magazines, it could increase brand awareness by 11 per cent.

There are a number of factors that determine the cost of the advertisement:

- The frequency of the publication – is the magazine published weekly, monthly or quarterly?
- The readership of the magazine: the more people who read the magazine, the greater the impact an advertisement will have, and hence a higher cost.
- The distribution area will also impact on the cost of an advertisement. If the magazine is just distributed locally, the target audience will be reduced. If the magazine is a national publication, the advertisement will reach a much wider range of people and again will cost more.
- Is the magazine purchased by the reader, or is it paid for by the advertisements within it?

As a rough guide a business should expect to pay approximately:

- quarter page – £500
- half a page – £900
- whole page – £1,200

These costs exclude the production and design costs.

Examples of magazine advertisement costs

Influence is a free magazine which is distributed throughout the UK to live music venues, record shops, rehearsal rooms and musical equipment retailers. The magazine is compiled and distributed monthly. A double-page spread costs £500 per month for advertisements and an A4 page £300 per month.

District Life Residents' Magazine is delivered by the Royal Mail to residents living in Canterbury, Herne Bay and Whitstable. It offers advertising space for as little as £99 plus VAT, and can reach 146,000 readers.

The BBC *Good Food Magazine* has a readership of 1.182 million. In a recent survey, 71 per cent of readers stated that they were influenced by seeing products in the magazine (source: *Good Food Magazine*). The charges for advertising in this magazine range from £11,000 to £17,000, depending on where the advertisement in placed within the magazine. A full-page advertisement on the outside back cover would cost approximately £16,200.

Newspapers

The cost of advertising in newspapers varies greatly, depending on the choice of the paper. Advertising in a national newspaper such as *The Sun* will cost much more than in a local newspaper. The reason for this is the readership level; Toyota Yaris found that national newspaper advertisements drove a 23 per cent increase in website visits (source: Sophus3, 2006).

The cost of advertising in *The Daily Mail* is broken down not only into size but also the day of the week. Advertising space from Monday to Wednesday is cheaper than Thursday and Friday. To advertise on the first page, front half costs £46,116 on Monday to Wednesday, but increases to £49,392 on Thursday and Friday. The most expensive slot is £80,136 for a double-page spread, front half on Thursday or Friday.

The *Evening Standard* in London has circulation figures of just over 300,000, and charges from approximately £100 for advertisements within the actual paper to £16,800 for a full page advertisement in the *ES Magazine* published on a Friday. This is a much cheaper option than a national newspaper, but the advertisement would reach a much smaller audience.

Outdoor advertising

In 2007, outdoor advertising spend reached £975.8million. The Outdoor Advertising Association has announced that the gross revenue for the third quarter of 2008 was £277,408,224. This is a 5.8 per cent decrease when compared against the same period in 2007. The use of outdoor digital screens is now the fastest growing advertising medium in the UK.

The cost of a billboard campaign varies upon the location of the boards and also the length of time the advertisement is displayed for:

- A national roadside two-week campaign will cost between £350,000 and £1,015,000, depending on the quality and number of sheets used.
- A two-week campaign using national buses costs between £409,500 and £680,000, depending on which sections of the bus are used.
- A two-week billboard campaign using the London Underground will cost between £55,660 and £134,700, again depending on the number and quality of sheets used.

Costs for advertising on taxis vary, depending on the length of the campaign and whether the taxi is fully covered. A fully covered taxi costs approximately £4,000 for twelve months and £2,500 for three months. To advertise on one side of the taxi costs £2,500 for twelve months and £1,000 for three months.

Leaflets

Leaflets are relatively cheap to produce and many quotations can be found on the Internet. Leaflet distribution has become one of the fastest growing media since 1995. www.mailboxnationwide.com states that 96 per cent of consumers acknowledge receipt of flyers, with 76 per cent of consumers acting upon the information supplied. The industry now delivers over 13 billion items door-to-door, with a value of £1.1 billion.

The main cost is the distribution of the leaflets. If this is outsourced to another company, the cost increases. However, companies that specialise in this industry can often help a business to target their leaflets accurately, increasing the potential success rate. The cost of the distribution company will vary depending on the area of delivery and whether the item is to be delivered on its own or with other promotional material.

Leaflet distributor JM Circular's website (www.jmcircular.co.uk) states that if the leaflet is delivered independently, the cost starts at £39 per 1,000 leaflets. The shared plan means that the leaflet is delivered with additional items, but the advertising does not conflict with your leaflet; the approximate cost is from £28.50 per 1,000 leaflets. For leaflets included within a newspaper, the cost starts at approximately £17.50 per 1,000. However, the paper may contain leaflets from direct or indirect competitors, and therefore might be less effective.

Leaflet distribution – fiction versus fact

The following information was taken from www.frontdoormarketing.co.uk. The data was collected by the Direct Marketing Association (DMA).

Perception: The majority of consumers do not like receiving marketing material through their letterbox.

Fact: As many as 79 per cent of recipients keep, pass on or glance at door-drop marketing material: 38 per cent keep it for at least a few days, while 13 per cent retain it for a week or more.

Perception: Consumers do not find door-drop marketing material useful.

Fact: 71 per cent of those questioned said they found free samples delivered through their letterboxes useful; 66 per cent said the same of supermarket offers, 62 per cent of money-off coupons and 47 per cent of new product leaflets.

Perception: Consumers do not find door-drop marketing as useful as they used to.

Fact: DMA research shows that consumers generally find promotional material delivered through their letterbox approximately 10 per cent more useful than they did in 1995.

Perception: Consumers who reject the medium do not find door-drop marketing material useful.

Fact: Even among those who, in research, initially claimed to reject door-drop marketing, 52–63 per cent still said they found the material was useful.

Perception: Door-drop material does not have the same impact as direct mail.

Fact: 79 per cent of people keep, pass on, read or glance at door drops – same as direct mail.

Perception: People do not keep door-drop material for a long time.

Fact: 38 per cent of door-drop material is kept for at least a few days and 13 per cent is kept for a week or more.

Perception: Door-drop marketing does not work.

Fact: 48 per cent of consumers visited a shop, sent for information, or bought a product having received promotional material through their letterbox.

Perception: Door-drop marketing does not work as well as direct mail, television or press.

Fact: 48 per cent of consumers responded to door-drop marketing material compared to 47 per cent for direct marketing, 47 per cent for television and 60 per cent for press advertising.

(Source: DMA/BMRB Omnibus, 2001)

Portfolio Tip

Within the controlled assessment, you will need to demonstrate some understanding of the costs of different types of promotions. Hopefully this chapter will provide you with a basis to make comparisons between the different costs. However, you may still need to research into the cost of advertising within your own local media. Do not forget that village or parish magazines can be a very effective and cheap way of advertising a small business that meets the needs of people living within the local community.

Activity

In order to prepare for your controlled assessment, spend some time investigating the cost of advertising in your local papers, local radio station and any other appropriate media. Keep a note of all your research as it could be useful when you attempt the controlled assignment. Keep a record of all sources in a bibliography. Chapter 18 explains how to create a bibliography.

Summary

- Different types of promotion will cost a lot more than others.
- Television is one of the most expensive methods of advertising but does have the capacity to reach a huge number of people in a very short space of time.
- Cinema is also expensive. Adverts can be exclusively shown but the audience is likely to be smaller.
- Local radio is growing in popularity and can be targeted at different market segments effectively.
- Magazines and newspapers have to be carefully selected if they are going to have the required result.
- Outdoor advertising – use of billboards, buses and taxis is growing and statistics prove it can be very effective.
- Leaflets are cheap to produce and can produce a 3-5% success rate but they have to be delivered to the correct people. This can take time and money.

Chapter 17
Reflection and review

Within the controlled assessment, you are required to analyse and reflect on how well you worked on your own and within the team. This will involve you considering the contributions you made to the team and any problems that you experienced throughout the task. You will also need to reflect on how well the team worked together in order to achieve the task.

It is important to keep your action plan up to date throughout the controlled assessment. This will help you identify where plans had to be changed and the reasons for delays or problems, etc.

In order to assess your own performance and that of others, you might like to use some of the following ideas to help structure this section of evidence.

- Were all deadlines met?
- In the group activity, did I complete my allocated jobs?
- Did other members of the group complete their set task on time?
- If deadlines were not met, what were the consequences?
- How did you/the group overcome problems?
- Did you or any other members of the group struggle with time management? Did you manage to complete the tasks within the time allowed?
- How could you improve your ability to manage your time effectively?
- How well were you able to work with other members of the group?
- Were there any communication problems? If so, how were these overcome?
- What would you do differently if you had to tackle this controlled assessment again?

Summary

- Reflection and review is very important, especially if you want to improve your overall performance. Learning is an ongoing process and everyone should reflect on what has worked well and what did not work so well, and try to improve on these angles in the future.

- Within your controlled assignment, consider whether you met all deadlines, within the group did you complete all your individual tasks, and how did you work within the group. These questions should help you start the reflection process.

Chapter 18
Sourcing work

As part of the assignment, you will be required to use a wide range of sources. This will involve the use of both primary and secondary data. Failure to acknowledge resources that you have used will be regarded as plagiarism. It is therefore very important that you record all of your sources used within a bibliography. There are a number of ways that you can source your work and these are outlined below.

Citing references in the text

If you have used a reference book as part of your research, you must state the name of the author in brackets, alongside the date of the publication. This should appear after the quote or information, for example 'Agriculture still employs half a million people in rural Britain (Shucksmith, 2000)'.

If there are two authors, the names of both should be given, for example (Jones and Smith, 2006).

If you are going to make a direct quotation from a piece of text, including page numbers is a useful reference.

Electronic references should follow the same rules as those applied to reference books and journals. They should first of all be cited by author if known, by title if no identifiable author, or by URL if neither author nor title is known.

Arranging references in a bibliography

It is usual to arrange book references alphabetically by the author's name or title of text if the author's name is not known. Within your bibliography, you should try to include the following information:

- Author's/editor's name: surname should be followed by first name. If there are three or more authors, use the first name and then 'et al'.
- Year of publication: if this is not known, use 'n.d.'.
- Title of the book/journal: capitalise the first letter of the first word and any proper nouns.
- Edition: only use this if there is more than one edition.
- Publisher: the company which published the text.
- Page numbers: these should be included if they have been stated within the main body of the text.

References for electronic resources should be integrated into the bibliography for printed sources. As far as possible, try to provide the same information as outlined above; also provide the URL and the date on which you accessed the information, as websites change constantly.

Date	Author's Name	Year of Publication	Title of book/ journal/website Edition if relevant	Publisher	Page numbers

Table 18.1 Sample bibliography

> **Activity**
>
> In preparation for your controlled assessment, design your own bibliography. In the activity on page 111 you were required to investigate the cost of different types of advertising. Use the bibliography to record all the sources you used throughout this investigation.

Summary

- Throughout the assignments you will need to make reference to wide ranging research. In order to do this you will need to compile a bibliography. You should record the following: date of research, authors name, year of publication, title of book/journal/website, who published it and page numbers used.

UNIT 3

WORKING IN BUSINESS

Introduction

> **Activity**
>
> Working in a small group, decide on a business that you are familiar with. Answer the following questions:
> - What type of business ownership is the selected business?
> - How is the business structured? Draw this if you can.
> - Identify the different departments within the business.
> - Describe the role of each department.
>
> Discuss your ideas and thoughts with other class members. See if they agree with your answers. If not, who do you think is correct?

The aim of this unit is to build upon the knowledge and understanding gained in the previous two units. The unit will investigate in more detail the internal functions of business.

This unit is externally tested. During the course of the examination, you will be required to carry out a series of 'in-tray exercises', taking responsibility for certain duties and tasks which would be required of an employee working in a particular functional area. Throughout the examination you will be required to answer questions on the paper from a number of different perspectives. The finance functional area will always be covered, with other functional areas being included as appropriate. The human resources functional area has not been included within the unit as it forms the basis of Unit 4.

It is important to note here that a number of sections within this unit have been covered previously within the textbook. Where this has taken place, the reader will be directed to the relevant section within the textbook. The examination covers a wide variety of sections, and therefore it might be best if this unit is tackled towards the end of your studies in order to ensure that you have gained the holistic knowledge required to do well in the external examination.

Working in Business is an externally tested unit

Chapter 19

Business structures – how businesses organise themselves

A builder is one type of sole trader

Sole trader

A sole trader is usually the only person working within a business and, as the owner, is responsible for all decisions and everything that happens. The owner therefore has to be skilled in many different aspects of business; for example, they would need to understand marketing and finance in order to continue to grow the business and remain successful.

As soon as the business grows, the owner would have to consider employing people. When the business reaches this stage, the owner needs to consider how to organise the business: Who would do what? What skills does each person have, and how could these be put to best use? In order to do this, the business starts to form organisational structures. These structures outline who is in control and the responsibilities of each member of staff.

Flat structure

This is a commonly used structure for businesses, and is best illustrated by using an example.

Henrietta is a qualified electrician and started working for herself in 2002. Her unique selling point is the fact she is a woman working in a male-dominated environment. Her business is very successful, and by the end of 2004 she employed three people and developed an organisational structure shown in Figure 19.1.

```
          Owner
         Henrietta
        /    |    \
Employee 1  Employee 2  Employee 3
Electrician Electrician Administration
                        and Finance
```

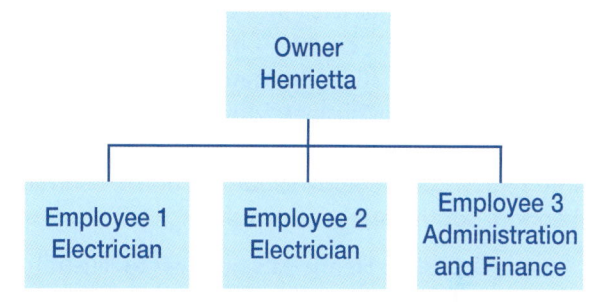

Figure 19.1 A flat organisational structure

As you see from Figure 19.1, Henrietta as owner of the business is at the top of the chart. Due to the increased workload she employed two other electricians. With the increase in customers, Henrietta became overwhelmed with paperwork. This was an area of work that she did not enjoy, and took her away from doing her actual job. She therefore decided to employ someone to take on this role for her. This was the start of specialisation, and enabled Henrietta to continue to use her skills fully and gainfully. Employee number 3 was able to cope with the administration and financial side of the business much more efficiently as they had the necessary skills, whereas Henrietta had not been trained in these areas.

The organisational chart shows that Henrietta is still in control of the business, making all the important decisions. The relatively small size of the organisational structure means that communication between employees and Henrietta will be both fast and easy. Face-to-face or telephone conversations will be easy to maintain and the management style used by Henrietta is likely to be relaxed and consultative.

Hierarchical structure

As businesses grow, they need to employ more and more people to specialise in different areas of the business. This increases the layers found within the structure. A hierarchical structure is one that contains many layers. The people at the top of the structure have the most control and power, making the decisions that are later passed down to employees further down the structure.

This type of structure enables different parts of the business to split itself into different functional areas which could include finance, administration, ICT, human resources and marketing. If the business covers the UK, they might decide to break down their departments into regions. This could include the north, central, London, south-east, south-west.

Let us consider Henrietta's business to illustrate some of the points made. By 2008 the business was so successful that Henrietta was approached by a major house-builder. It was agreed that the two businesses would merge and Henrietta would be in charge of all the electrical contracts. The new organisational structure is shown in Figure 19.2.

Figure 19.2 shows that the structure now has five layers. Major decisions will be made by the managing director in consultation with all the other directors. It will be the responsibility of Henrietta, the bricklaying director, carpentry director and marketing and administration manager to ensure that these plans are explained and carried out by the relevant site foreman, and ultimately the craftsmen at the bottom of the structure.

A hierarchical structure resembles a pyramid; there are fewer senior managers at the top of the structure than employees at the bottom of the structure. One of the benefits of this structure is that it enables employees to climb the promotion ladder. It also means that there are clear lines of communication, and employees know how they fit into the organisation. This enables a business to define job roles clearly, with everyone in the structure aware of their responsibilities.

However, due to the size of the structure, decision-making is likely to be slower as more people have become involved. The larger the structure, the more bureaucratic the organisation tends to be. This means that there are set procedures to follow which can slow decision-

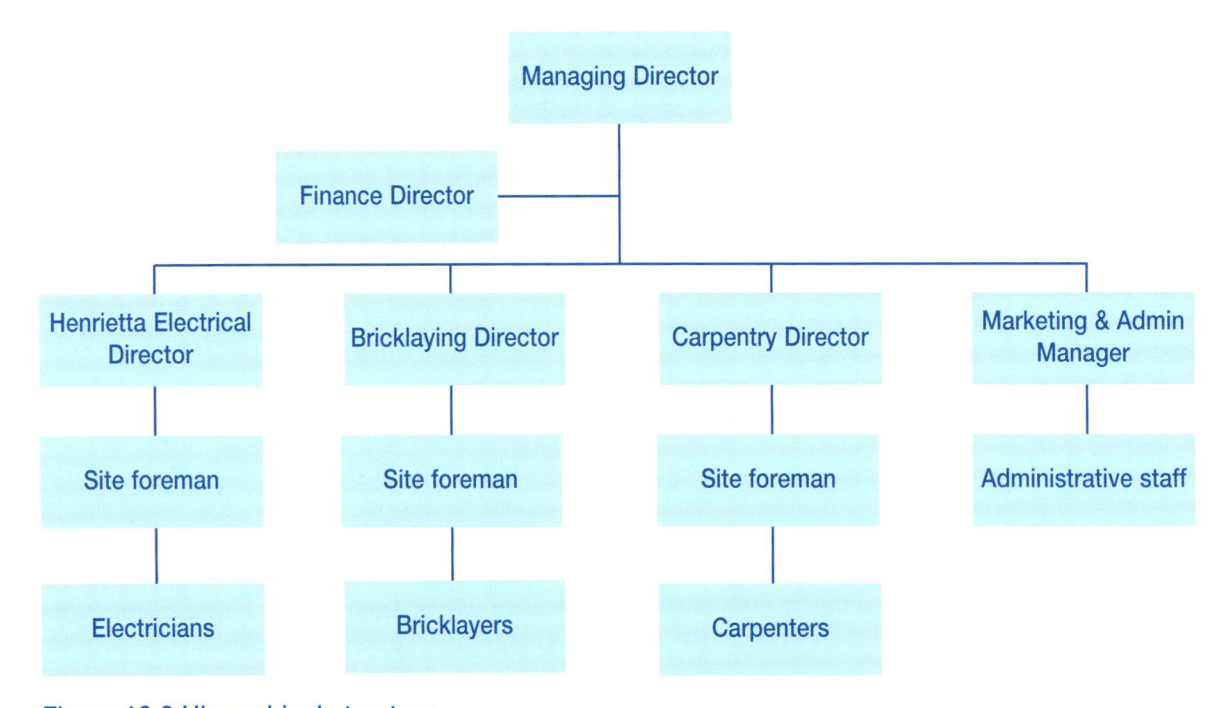

Figure 19.2 Hierarchical structure

making and communication down considerably. This could stop the business reacting to changes in the market-place quickly and maintaining the competitive edge.

This example had specific departments relevant to the construction industry. The more common breakdown of functional areas is outlined below:

- marketing
- finance
- production
- ICT
- administration
- research and development
- customer service.

This segmentation means that employees will often be working alongside other people doing similar work; for example, in the finance department you would have people working on sales and others on purchasing. There could also be a section of people working on the financial accounts of the business, preparing budgets and year-end reports for the business.

Businesses that trade and have distribution networks throughout the UK might decide to break down the organisation chart into regions. One department could focus on the south-west of England, and others on the south-east, London alone, the Midlands, north-west and north-east England, Wales, Scotland and Northern Ireland.

The business might also have regional offices to represent this split. This would enable employees living in an area to become familiar with local customers' tastes and lifestyles, enabling the business to target customer needs effectively and respond quickly to changes in the market. This could gain a competitive edge for the business.

Matrix structure

If a business wanted to undertake a special project, it might decide to put together a team of specialists. Team members would be drawn from a range of departments within the organisational structure. This is known as matrix management. An advantage of this type of team is that team members have a wide range of skills and experience; but a disadvantage is the time it takes for team members to develop an effective working relationship. There is also often a feeling of disappointment when the project is finished and team members return to their normal departments.

Team Leader – Head of the Project
- Marketing Department
- Finance Department
- Production Department
- Research and Development Department

Figure 19.3 Example of a matrix structure

Conclusion

The type of business will dictate how it is organised; for example, a hotel will have a housekeeping department, whereas a pharmaceutical company would have a large research and development department. Not all businesses divide themselves into the standard functional areas. During the examination you will have to ensure that you read the question carefully, so that you can decide the best way in which the business could be subdivided into departments.

Activity

Here is a list of five different types of business. Consider the type of departments that they would have.

1. a large garage that repairs cars
2. the local supermarket
3. a local hairdresser's salon
4. a hotel
5. the local leisure centre.

Activity

Examination practice

The following people work for a company that manufacture electrical components for the car industry. Design an organisational chart for this company:

- managing director
- finance director, cost accountant, financial accountant and two book-keepers
- marketing manager and marketing assistant
- production director, production manager, two factory supervisors, 20 employees who work on the factory floor
- administration/ICT manager, two ICT technicians, two receptionists, two clerical assistants.

Summary

- A flat structure does not have many layers of management. Employees will possibly have a wider range of jobs and work in a less structured environment. Communication will flow easily with everyone knowing each other.

- A hierarchical structure (tall) has many layers of management. Employees will understand how they fit into the organisation and what their respective jobs are. Direction is likely to be formal – employees being told what to do. Communication is likely to be slow as it has to flow through many layers.

- A matrix structure brings together specialists to work on a project. Often the team will work together for the duration of the project and then revert back to their old teams.

Chapter 20

Job roles – key activities and responsibilities

In any workplace people will have different job roles and responsibilities

Activity

If you have a part-time job or have undertaken work experience, describe your job role, what you were expected to do and any responsibilities which you had.

If you do not currently have a job and have not yet completed work experience, ask someone you know about their job. See if you can find out their job title, their normal daily activities and their responsibilities.

Share your findings with the remainder of the group. Is there a picture building up of the different kind of responsibilities and activities which people have, according to their status within a company?

Key activities and responsibilities

For a business to remain efficient, it is imperative that all employees are fully aware of their own duties and responsibilities. This is achieved in large businesses through the allocation of specific job roles. There are many benefits to this: clearly defined job roles give employees a sense of security and pride; they also enable the business to run like clockwork as everybody knows where and how they fit into the organisation. This in turn enables the business to meet customer needs due to increased efficiency and productivity, which ultimately could help the business gain competitor advantage.

A generic structure of job roles is often found within a hierarchical structure. Figure 20.1 gives examples of these roles.

Chairman
↓
Managing director/Chief executive
↓
Director
↓
Manager
↓
Supervisor
↓
Operative

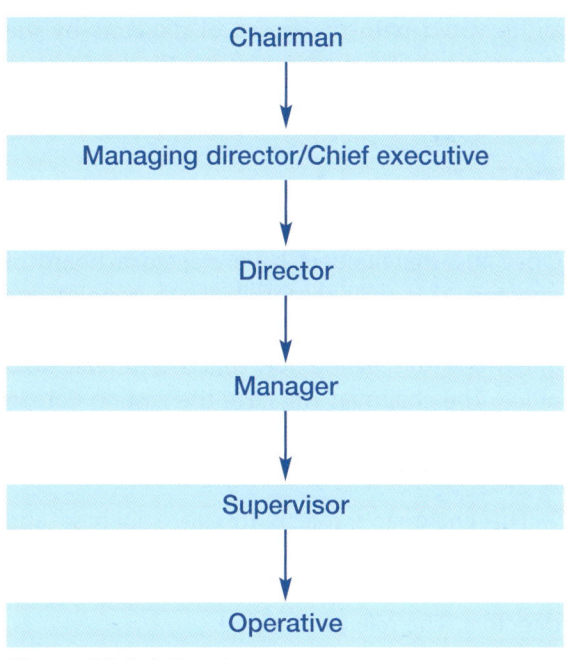

Figure 20.1 Job roles

The positions outlined in Figure 20.1 are relevant to businesses that have grown either into private limited companies or public limited companies. As you know from previous chapters, when this happens there is a divorce of ownership from control. A private limited company (Ltd) will often be much smaller than a public limited company (plc), and the owners are probably still heavily involved in the running of the business.

Major shareholders will ultimately take the top positions of chairman, managing director and directors of the business. Divorce of ownership from control in this case is much smaller, as the major shareholders form the board of directors. The board of directors are the people who make all the major decisions concerning a business.

A public limited company such as Tesco will have sold millions of shares to a wide variety of institutions and individuals; in this case, the owners of the company (the shareholders) will not have any say in the day-to-day running of the business. Shareholders vote for a board of directors at the Annual General Meeting (AGM) to run the business on their behalf. The first three positions that are outlined in Figure 20.1 – chairman, managing director and directors – will all be voted onto the board of directors by the shareholders. Their job is to run the business in the best interests of all its shareholders.

Chairman

Once the shareholders have elected a board of directors, it is their responsibility to appoint one of their own number as chairman and to determine the period for which s/he will hold office. The chairman will have the casting vote in the case of equality of votes when major decisions are being voted upon.

The chairman's role is to run, supervise and control board meetings, and s/he will work in conjunction with other members of the board of directors. The role can include:

- determining the composition and organisation of the board of directors
- confirming the responsibilities of the board in terms of management and running of the business
- planning and managing the board and board meetings
- developing and supporting all board members in order to improve the effectiveness of the board.

Managing director/ chief executive

In the private sector, the chief executive would probably be known as the managing director. The role of the managing director is to coordinate the work of the other directors and managers, and to advise them. The managing director is responsible for the day-to-day running of the business and developing business plans for the long-term future of the business. The board of directors grants the managing director the right to run the business. The role is accountable to the board of directors and ultimately the shareholders.

The role of managing director is one of leadership for the business, with the aim of motivating the workforce to achieve the overall strategic aims of the business in order to secure its long-term future. The managing director is also responsible for developing the culture of an organisation. This involves the way in which people treat one another in the company, how they communicate, and the general atmosphere of the working environment.

The managing director is required to manage everything, including staff, customers, budgets and company resources. S/he must ensure that resources are used properly to ensure that the business increases profitability.

The managing director will have regular meetings with the board of directors in order to discuss progress, future plans and any problems. The board will offer advice and guidance on how the business could improve. It is the managing director's responsibility to implement these suggestions with the idea of increasing productivity and efficiency.

The managing director is ultimately responsible for the business's affairs and therefore must ensure that it stays within the law. This will include ensuring that health and safety legislation is maintained, and equal opportunities or consumer legislation is not breached.

The board of directors

The board of directors is appointed by the shareholders at the AGM. It acts on behalf of the shareholders to run the day-to-day affairs of the business, and is directly accountable to the shareholders. At the AGM the board of directors must present a report to the shareholders which outlines the performance of the company over the last year. The report will also include strategic plans for the business and their short-term objectives.

The board of directors can be made up of executive and non-executive directors. An executive director works full-time for the business, while a non-executive director is employed part-time. Non-executive directors are invited to join the board because of their specialist skills and knowledge, and are able to offer unbiased advice as they are not concerned with the overall success of the business.

The role of the board of directors can be summarised as follows:

- Determine the business's vision and mission: decide the overall strategic plans of the business.
- Determine the values to be promoted through the business.
- Determine company policy.
- Review and evaluate present and future opportunities and threats.
- Decide upon the strategic options to be followed and decide how to implement and support them.
- Ensure that the business's organisational structure is appropriate when implementing new strategies and policies.
- Delegate authority to management; monitor and evaluate the implementation of these policies.
- Decide how new policies and strategies will be monitored, and by what criteria.
- Communicate with senior management.
- Communicate with shareholders.
- Consider the interests and opinions of shareholders.
- Achieve the support of shareholders.

Directors

Directors are in a position of trust, looking after the affairs of the business. They must always act in good faith for the best interests of the business and not for their own personal gain. Directors are generally responsible for the management of the company. They must act collectively as a board in order to take the business forward successfully.

Directors are responsible for ensuring that the company fulfils all its statutory duties. This means that the business complies with all relevant company legislation which is imposed under the Companies Act 2006. The main statutory responsibility of directors is to prepare the accounts and a report, and to present both to the shareholders at the AGM. Another area where directors have direct responsibility is the implementation of the Health and Safety at Work Act 1974. Directors become personally liable if there is a breach of this Act and an employee is injured.

Directors can have two roles within the business: they will be part of the group of people who form the board of directors, but might also have responsibility for the work of an allocated area, for example, marketing or finance.

The role of directors can be summarised as follows:

- Establish the strategic plans for their department. These will directly link to the overall strategic plans of the business.
- Establish targets to meet the strategic plans. Implement a system to monitor the achievement of targets so that results can be reported back to the board of directors.

- Work in close liaison with departmental managers, informing them of decisions made by the board of directors.
- Ensure that the business/department remains within the law.
- Receive feedback from departmental managers concerning progress and developments taking place within the department.
- Delegate duties to employees within the department.

Managers

Managers are the middle people between the senior management levels and the team that reports to him/her. The manager must ensure that communication is smooth and conveyed clearly to avoid misinterpretation.

Managers are responsible for and supervise employees who work alongside or beneath them on the organisational structure. They play an important part in the motivation and development of performance in their department.

Managers generally undertake less decision-making, as their main responsibility is to implement the decisions made by the board of directors. They will need problem-solving skills as they are often working closely with employees and consumers. Decision-making and problem-solving could include employee selection, motivating an employee who is underperforming, or implementing change within the department.

Managers need to communicate the plans and visions of the board of directors. This will involve breaking down targets for individual members of staff which are realistically achievable. Targets need to be monitored to ensure that the required progress is made. This information is then passed back to the relevant director, who will then feed back to the board of directors.

A good manager will be able to encourage their team in order to build trust and confidence within the workplace. This will help the business to achieve maximum output and hopefully retain happy, well-motivated staff.

The role of managers can be summarised as follows:

- Carry out the instructions of the director of the department.
- Allocate and organise the work of departmental staff.
- Implement relevant legislation within the department.
- Monitor the work of staff – are they meeting targets?
- Make decisions which directly relate to the department.
- Encourage and practise good working relationships.
- Receive feedback from employees, and give them feedback about the strategic plans of the business.
- Give feedback to the directors about progress and developments within the department.

Supervisors

Over recent years, the role of supervisor has steadily changed as organisations have started to realise that the best way to motivate people is to encourage and nurture them, rather than just issue instructions. This is a cultural shift, and methods of working have impacted on the way in which people now supervise their team.

A supervisor is usually in charge of a small number of employees, with the aim of ensuring that a set job is completed on time and at the required standard. They will report directly to their designated manager. Supervisors are required to monitor the progress of their team against the targets set for the department. This could involve making simple decisions in order to deal with immediate problems. Major decisions would be made in consultation with the relevant manager.

Most supervisors are promoted into the role as they were considered to be good at their job. This is obviously good for the company as they have a loyal, hardworking employee who has a sound understanding of the business. However, it could mean that the supervisor does not fully understand the responsibilities of their promoted role. Outlined below are the main generic responsibilities of a supervisor.

- Carry out the instructions of the manager.
- Work in conjunction with the manager to allocate work to other members of the team.
- Ensure that the team is adhering to legislation.
- Monitor the work of team members – are targets being met?
- Encourage and practise good working relationships within the team.
- Provide help and guidance to team members as required.
- Receive feedback from employees and pass this to the relevant manager.
- Pass information concerning the department from the manager to the team.

Operatives

These are the employees who are at the bottom of the organisational structure. They are employed to carry out tasks relevant to their position. The actual details of their work will be outlined in their job description. Most operatives are members of a team who will be working with the close support of other employees. New operatives may be closely monitored by their supervisor until they have understood their role within the business.

Outlined below are the main generic responsibilities of an operative.

- Carry out their allocated tasks as outlined in the job description.
- Follow instructions given by their supervisor/manager.
- Comply with legislation.
- Build effective and efficient working relationships with other members of the team.

Skills, qualifications and personal qualities

In order to establish the qualifications, skills and personal qualities required for each of the above job roles, a wide variety of different recruitment and selection documents were scrutinised for this section. These documents outlined the type of person each type of position required.

Chairman, chief executive/managing director and director

There is a common theme for the qualifications, skills and personal qualities that are required for all the roles that make up the board of directors.

- Degree-educated, with an MBA desirable.
- Past experience at senior level; ten years quoted on a number of advertisements.
- Experience at senior board level.
- Ability to demonstrate intellectual depth in required field; this varied according to position.
- Confident communicator, orally and face-to-face, including presentations.
- Outstanding leadership qualities.
- Proven ability to meet targets and deadlines.
- Ability to lead and motivate a large and diverse team.
- Ability to manage and drive through change.
- Proven track record of success gained within similar capacity.

Manager

- Preferably educated to degree standard.
- Relevant work experience reflecting ability.
- Ability to demonstrate good leadership skills.
- Ability to establish effective working relationships with a wide range of people.
- Ability to demonstrate analytical skills.
- Focus on detail, with the ability to work flexibly.
- Ability to coordinate several activities at once.
- Ability to cope and meet deadlines.
- Ability to motivate a team.

Supervisor

None of the recruitment and selection documents specified specific academic qualifications for the role of supervisor. This is probably because many supervisors are promoted through the ranks, based on past performance and experience within the business.

Other skills and personal qualities listed included:

- Proven history as a supervisor – sound knowledge of relevant field of work.
- Ability to plan ahead and monitor progress of team.
- Ability to lead and support team.
- Good organisational skills.
- Highly motivated with the ability to motive a team.
- Ambitious with a desire to progress to a managerial position.

Summary

- Jobs roles give employees a sense of security and pride.
- The chairman is one of the directors who has been voted to run, supervise and control board meetings.
- The Managing director/chief executive coordinates the work of the other directors and managers and is responsible for the day to day running of the business and developing business plans.
- The board of directors are responsible for organising and planning the day to day running of the business. They are directly accountable to the shareholders.
- Directors are responsible for ensuring that the business follows all relevant legislation.
- Managers are responsible for and supervise employees who work alongside or beneath them on the organisational structure.
- Supervisors are usually in charge of a small number of employees, with the aim of ensuring that jobs are completed on time and at the required standard.
- Operatives are the employees who are at the bottom of the organisational structure. They are employed to carry out tasks relevant to their position

> ### Activity
>
> **Research for external examination**
>
> Outlined above are qualifications, skills and personal qualities for job roles that have been summarised from research. It is now your turn to undertake both primary and secondary research, to see if you agree with the above information.
>
> 1 Interview a number of people in different managerial positions to discover their qualifications and what they consider to be their personal qualities and skills. Analyse your findings; do they match the results summarised above?
>
> 2 Investigate a number of recruitment and selection documents for the job roles outlined above. Establish what they outline as the qualifications, skills and personal qualities for each individual job role. You could use newspapers, magazines, trade journals and the Internet. Analyse your findings; do they match the results summarised above?

Unit 21

>Forms of communication

Good communication between workers is important to businesses

One of the key factors of a good working relationship between functional areas is the way in which they communicate with each other. The ability to communicate effectively through speaking and writing is a highly demanded skill in business organisations.

The development of technology has had a dramatic effect on communication. Often the new methods are faster, but are they always as efficient?

This chapter will look at different forms of communication:

- oral
- written
- ICT.

Oral communication

Oral communication can also be referred to as verbal communication. It simply involves people talking to one another. However, types of oral communication vary between informal and formal forms.

Informal communication occurs when we talk to our colleagues, at school or within the workplace. **Formal** communication could involve a business meeting, or a presentation where prior preparation is required to ensure that the message conveyed is accurate and unbiased.

The type of oral communication used **internally** within the business could include:

- staff/departmental meetings
- personal discussions
- presentations
- telephone conversations
- informal conversations between colleagues.

External oral communication could include:

- face-to-face meetings with clients
- telephone calls
- teleconferences or video conferences.

Face-to-face discussions

Face-to-face discussions can include anything from a one-to-one conversation with a colleague or business client, to a large meeting where lots of people offer their opinions.

One of the main advantages of face-to-face discussions is the fact that you can observe people's body language. This includes the expressions on their faces: are they happy, angry, worried? If a person you are talking to continually puts their hand in front of their mouth, this can be a sign of anxiety. The person talking is also able to use gestures in order to help illustrate the point they are making. Eye contact is very important during face-to-face conversations. If someone is unwilling to maintain eye contact, it may mean that they do not feel very comfortable with the conversation. The tone of voice used during the conversation will also convey how someone is feeling about the discussion.

Another advantage of face-to-face conversations is the ability to gain immediate feedback. Decisions can be made based on the outcome of the conversation.

One of the disadvantages of face-to-face conversations is the fact that there is no written evidence of what was said and by whom. Decisions may be later refuted.

Meetings

These can be informal or formal events which are organised in order to discuss and make decisions on the progress of the business. The annual general meeting of a limited company is a formal meeting; a team meeting may be considered informal.

Meetings have to be organised, and as a general rule 24 hours' notice should be given to employees required to attend. An agenda is prepared prior to the meeting which clearly states why, when and where the meeting will take place. The agenda should clearly explain the purpose of the meeting.

A formal meeting will be run by a chairperson, who will control the discussions and ensure that everyone remains focused on the items to be discussed. The chairperson should also ensure that everybody is given the opportunity to participate. Points raised and decisions made will be recorded and later presented as the minutes of the meeting.

- An advantage of having meetings is that it allows people to listen to other opinions, join in the subsequent discussion and be part of the final decision-making process.

- Disadvantages include difficulty in arranging meetings because of people's busy work schedules. It is also easy for discussions to lose their focus, and therefore valuable time can be wasted.

Telephone

The development of the mobile phone has dramatically changed the way in which the telephone is used. It is now possible to reach

Mobile phones are important to young people, but take care when using them . . .

people wherever they are, as long as there is a mobile phone signal. It has enabled businesses to remain in constant contact with employees who are away from the office. It has also changed the way in which young people communicate.

The Carphone Warehouse, advised by the London School of Economics, has published the results of their research. It stated that 91 per cent of children over the age of 12 years own a mobile phone, 51 per cent of ten-year-olds and 24 per cent of nine-year-olds. Young people consider it as the most important electronic device they own. Having a mobile phone gives them a sense of security, access to entertainment, social network and most importantly a sense of belonging to their peer group. People aged 11–17 years use their phones more for sending text messages than talking: on average they would daily receive or send 9.6 text messages, against making or receiving 3.5 calls. The use of a mobile phone has enabled the younger generation to remain constantly in touch with their immediate peer group.

Advantages of telephone discussions:

- Very useful when distance makes it impossible to talk to people face-to-face.
- An immediate response is achievable by using a phone. You are able to generate a discussion which can resolve a problem, help make a decision or simply pass on important information quickly.

Disadvantages of using the telephone:

- You cannot see or gauge the response of the person who is on the other end of the line.
- You must also ensure that the information you are passing on has been fully understood. It is very easy for people to misinterpret information which could cause problems in a business.
- There is no written evidence of what was said or the conclusions drawn.

Written communication

Written communication means that there is always a 'hard copy' of what was said and agreed. Written communication can take a variety of different forms and these include:

- memorandums
- letters
- notices
- newsletters.

Memorandums

Memorandums are usually known as memos. They are an internal form of communication that enable people working within the same organisation to work together. They are usually informal but grammatically correct, with paragraphs and accurate spellings.

The layout of a memo is illustrated in Figure 21.1.

MEMORANDUM

To: ....
From: ....
Ref: ....
Date: ....
Subject: ....

Figure 21.1 A memorandum

The content of the memorandum is usually short and concise. It could be used to request information, provide information or to give instructions to members of staff.

When the memorandum is finished, it is not signed.

Advantages of using memos include:

- Written evidence of what has been said/agreed.
- They can be tailored to one person or sent to a number of different people.
- Internal mail system ensures cheap and effective delivery service.
- It is easy to communicate with work colleagues without having to find them.
- They are always dated which could be useful later if they need to be referred to.

Disadvantages of using memos include:

- No confirmation that it has been received and read.
- It does not create an immediate response.
- They can be lost within the internal mail system.
- Emails have taken the place of written memos as they are fast and provide quick response and feedback (see below).

Letters

Formal business letters are used when a business wishes to communicate with its customers, suppliers and other external stakeholders. The company may wish to let customers know of special offers or discounts that they have become entitled to through their loyalty. Suppliers might receive a letter to confirm an order or to query the quality or quantity of goods received.

Letters can also be sent to employees. They could be used to convey information about a change in terms and conditions of employment, or to confirm a promotion.

Letters are used to request or provide information, give instructions, or to attract attention to new deals.

Business letters have a formal layout which must be adhered to. Language must be formal, with spellings and grammatical errors eliminated prior to posting. It does not create a good impression if the business sends out letters that are poorly laid out and contain numerous mistakes. It might put customers off dealing with the company again.

Figure 21.2 shows an example of a letter layout commonly used in business.

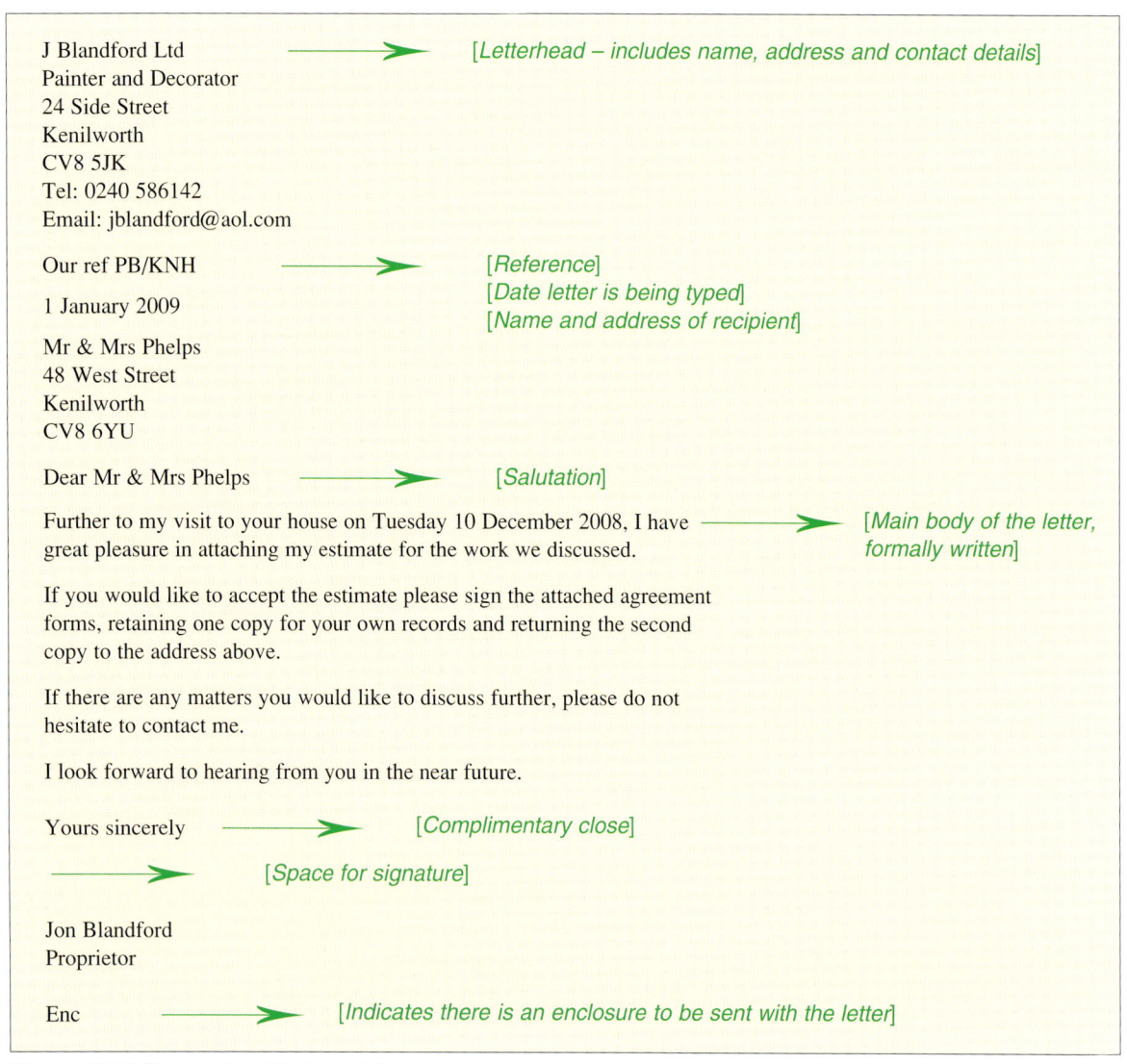

J Blandford Ltd
Painter and Decorator
24 Side Street
Kenilworth
CV8 5JK
Tel: 0240 586142
Email: jblandford@aol.com

→ [Letterhead – includes name, address and contact details]

Our ref PB/KNH   → [Reference]
1 January 2009   [Date letter is being typed]
Mr & Mrs Phelps   [Name and address of recipient]
48 West Street
Kenilworth
CV8 6YU

Dear Mr & Mrs Phelps → [Salutation]

Further to my visit to your house on Tuesday 10 December 2008, I have great pleasure in attaching my estimate for the work we discussed.   → [Main body of the letter, formally written]

If you would like to accept the estimate please sign the attached agreement forms, retaining one copy for your own records and returning the second copy to the address above.

If there are any matters you would like to discuss further, please do not hesitate to contact me.

I look forward to hearing from you in the near future.

Yours sincerely   → [Complimentary close]

→ [Space for signature]

Jon Blandford
Proprietor

Enc   → [Indicates there is an enclosure to be sent with the letter]

Figure 21.2 Example of letter style

The letter in Figure 21.2 is going to be sent to a prospective customer, and is therefore personally addressed to the people concerned. There are some occasions when businesses decide to send a letter to all their customers informing them of developments within the business. If they were to produce an individual letter to each customer, this could be time-consuming and expensive. The answer to this problem is to send a standard letter to all their customers that is simply addressed 'Dear Customer'. With the development of word processing packages, it is possible to hold customers' names and addresses on a database or special file, and the business can use a mail merge facility so that each letter is personalised.

Advantages of using letters:

- They can be kept and made reference to at a later date. This could be vitally important in the unfortunate circumstances of a dispute.

- The date can also be useful in order to establish a chain of events.

- A well-produced professional letter will help to reinforce the image of a business.

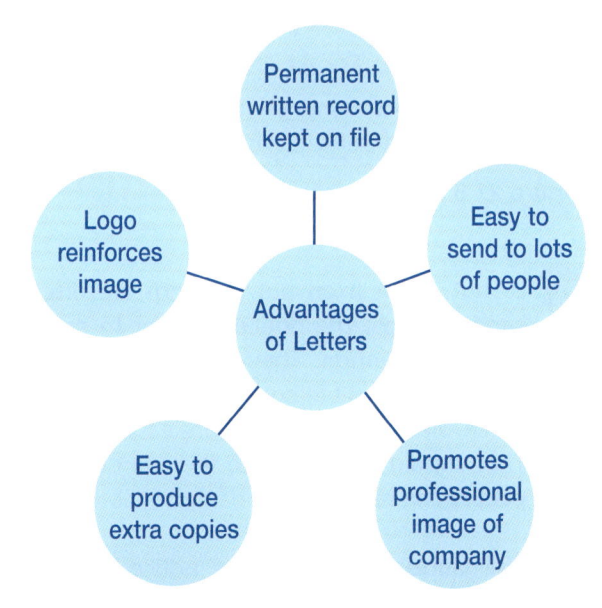

Figure 21.3 Advantages of using letters

Disadvantage of sending letters:

- A poorly laid-out and worded letter could severely damage the reputation of a business.

Figure 21.4 Disadvantages of using letters

Activity

Examination practice

Before you start to write a letter, you need to consider what you are going to say. It is important that you use concise sentences that convey the correct information.

Read the advertisement in Figure 21.5, and write a letter of application for the job, following the three questions below.

PART TIME RECEPTIONIST

Required for newly refurbished hotel due to open at the beginning of October 2009

Must be able to work evenings and weekends. No experience necessary as full training will be given. This is a great opportunity to join a new and exciting venture.

Please send your letter of application to MRS J DAWSON, PARK VIEW HOTEL, 1–16 GRAND PARADE, NEWTOWN, NO67 4HG.

Figure 21.5 Example of an advertisement

1. Identify the skills you would need to have in order to apply for this position. Refer to those skills which you think you possess in your letter of application.
2. Identify the main duties of this position. Consider what experience you can offer to support these duties.
3. Remember to state why you think you are a suitable candidate.

Notices

Notices have multiple uses within business. They can be used internally to communicate with staff. A notice could be used to announce social events, invite staff to attend a staff meeting to discuss the future plans of the business, or describe recent achievements of the business.

Internal notices informing staff of current events or successes will be placed on notice boards that all staff can access. These could be located in the staff canteen, staff room, at the entrance to the building or in each department. Formal notices that are required for legal reasons, such as health and safety notices, are displayed where all members of staff can see them. Specific health and safety notices which outline correct procedures for operating machinery will be placed by the relevant machine. Hospitals often use notice boards to display photographs of the people who work within each department. This helps members of the public to identify who is dealing with their particular case.

There is no set layout for a notice. The main purpose is to grab people's attention, encourage them to read the information and remember it. If they are required to act upon the information, it is hoped that sufficient interest is raised for them to participate in the event.

Notices are most obvious when they are colourful, make use of pictures or cartoons, use large point sizes, and are not overcrowded with information.

Advantages of notices:
- Quick way to communicate with a large number of people.
- Relatively inexpensive method of communication.
- A display notice will be a constant reminder.
- Can be eye-catching and colourful.

Disadvantages of notices:
- Cannot gauge how many people have seen and read the notice.
- Will not receive an immediate response.
- Could be easily destroyed or removed.
- Relies on people regularly looking at the notice board.

Staff Social Club

Would like to invite you to the XMAS PARTY

Where? When? How Much?

THE WALDORF HOTEL
16 December, 8pm until late

FREE TO ALL STAFF

To reserve your place contact
Sue Rogerson ext 234 before 6 December

Figure 21.6 Example of a notice

1. Layout is not fixed but headings are often centred across the notice in order to catch people's attention. They should be in large font and if possible colourful. Notices make much more impact if they are easy to read. They should be straight to the point so that people can remember the information.

2. The language used in the notice is often quite informal. Complete sentences are not required, and text is often displayed on single lines with little, if any, punctuation.

3 Different font styles and colour have been used in order to attract and hold the reader's attention. The last section of the notice informs the reader of what they have to do if they wish to attend the event.

Activity

Examination practice

Working in pairs, critically evaluate the notice in Figure 21.6. Use the questions below to help you structure your answer.

- Do you think it is eye-catching?
- Has good use been made of colour and different fonts?
- How do you think it could be improved?
- Would the inclusion of pictures/cartoons improve the overall impact of the notice? Justify your answer.
- Would this notice encourage you to attend the social event? Justify your answer.

Now design your own notice for the same event. You can change any of the information if you wish.

Newsletters

Very large businesses which have a lot of employees spread across multiple sites might decide to create a newsletter. This would contain news concerning the developments of the business, and often what individual staff have been doing; for example, if a member of staff has just run a marathon for charity, there may be an article about this. There might be photographs of the employee crossing the finishing line and information on how much money was raised. The newsletter might also contain news about people who are leaving or joining the business.

The aim of a newsletter is to keep all members of staff up-to-date with what is happening within the business. The focus is on creating a community among employees through the availability of information. It is common in large businesses for members of staff to become isolated within their own department. A newsletter helps to break down these barriers and encourages people to become more involved with the business.

Advantages of newsletters:

- Relatively easy to produce and distribute to all members of staff.
- Easy way to communicate information concerning company achievements.
- Can be motivational – employees fully informed of progress of business.
- Easy to access – can be read at any time.

Disadvantages of newsletters:

- No guarantee that all members of staff will read them.
- Have to encourage staff to contribute new articles.
- Slowly being overtaken by the use of internal intranet.

ICT communication

The way that we communicate has altered dramatically over the last ten years. Using ICT has made communication much faster and often more efficient. The younger generation now use less oral communication, choosing to use mobile phone text messages and email. Texting has even led to the development of a new abbreviated form of language being used by young people; parents often struggle to understand what their children have written in their text messages!

> **Activity**
>
> Write down how many times you have communicated with other people electronically. Then answer the following questions:
>
> - How did you send the communication?
> - What was the content?
> - Did you have to send the message?
> - Was it vitally important?
> - Was the electronic method selected the most appropriate?
> - Would a face-to-face conversation have been better? If not, why not?
> - How often do you talk to people face to face? Has this been reduced due to the availability of electronic communication?

Email

'Email' is short for electronic mail. It is a simple way of sending information and attachments via the Internet. In contrast with a letter arriving through the letter box via Royal Mail, it appears on a computer screen.

Advantages of email

The main advantage of email is the speed at which information can be sent. An email which has multiple attachments can be sent from the UK to Australia in a matter of seconds. The sender and recipient must however have access to the Internet, which would usually cost a monthly fee. There are no other fees associated with the use of email.

Email has had a huge impact on the way in which people work within a business. Only a few years ago, employees in large businesses who needed to pass on information to other colleagues would normally send a hard copy via internal mail or actually go and talk to their colleague. It is a much simpler process now. Emails can be sent internally around the business at no cost, and are able to reach a large audience through the click of a button. This ability to share information quickly does enable employees to keep up-to-date with what is going on within a business.

Disadvantages of email

It has been found that emails are a distraction to employees. Once a new email has been received, an employee is likely to stop their current activity to read the email. It can then take up to four minutes for an employee to return to their original task.

An email is likely to be responded to as quickly as a telephone call, and with an average employee receiving between 40 and 50 emails a day, this can have a dramatic effect on the overall efficiency of the business.

It is also too easy to send emails to people just for general information. It is surprising how long people spend looking at emails that are not really relevant to them. This again impacts on the overall efficiency of the business. A business should ensure that it targets its emails to specific employees in order to reduce this waste of time. To contextualise this, it is estimated that:

- 39.7 million person-to-person emails are sent per day.
- 17.1 million automated alerts are sent per day.
- 40.5 million pieces of spam (unsolicited commercial email) are sent daily.

An article in www.computerweekly.com stated that 40 per cent of workers spend at least two hours per day on email.

Another problem with email is the tone and content of messages that are being sent to customers, suppliers and colleagues. It is very easy to send an email without considering if it has been written in the correct tone and whether the content is actually accurate and suitable for its intended audience. It is also very easy to state things in emails that probably would not be said in a face-to-face conversation or on the phone. It is therefore vitally important that employees consider the content of their email, particular focusing on the person to whom the email is being sent.

Continual use of email has also changed the way in which people interact and behave towards each other in a business. It is not uncommon for employees to send an email to someone they sit next to, rather than turn around and have a conversation. This does have an impact on the culture and team spirit within a company.

In order to overcome some of these problems, an idea started in America is beginning to find favour in the UK: email-free Fridays. The company stops people sending emails on the selected day. If they need to communicate with a colleague they must either have a face-to-face conversation or pick up the telephone. For example, Liverpool City Council has banned emails on a Wednesday; computer developers Intel encourages its 150 engineers not to use email as a form of communication on a Friday; Phones4U have taken this even further and banned all internal emails.

PowerPoint presentations

PowerPoint is a programme that enables the user to produce slides to be used as a presentation. The software is now highly specialised, allowing the creator to include pictures, animations and music in order to enhance the impact of their delivery.

In order to project the presentation to a wide audience, the use of a computer software projector will be required.

If the presentation is to be shown at a trade show or exhibition, it is possible to set up the programme so that the presentation will run unattended. If the presentation is going to be used 'live', the person delivering will be able to control the flow of the slides either through the use of the computer or a remote control.

If a business needs to impart information to a large audience, a PowerPoint presentation will enhance the delivery. It can create an impact and illustrate the points being made by the presenter. It will also allow the audience to follow bullet points being made. If the audience is supplied with a handout of the presentation, this can act as a reminder, having returned to the office. It could also enable the employee to pass on information gained to other members of staff. This is known as cascading information down.

PowerPoint presentations are often ruined because the slides contain too much information or have been made so interactive that they distract from the delivery of the presentation itself. The slides should be used to support what the presenter is saying, not to interfere with the message.

Activity

Examination practice

You are currently employed by a small insurance company as a clerical assistant. Your immediate supervisor is going to be out of the office today and has set you the tasks listed below.

Choose the best method of communication for each of the tasks. Justify your answers, outlining why you think your selected method of communication is the best one.

1 Mrs Flynn telephoned yesterday to ask for a renewal quotation for her house contents insurance. It has now been calculated and is £145. Her telephone number is 01897 890754; email address JaneFlynn1@aol.com.

2 You have received a letter of complaint from Mr Hilton, concerning the length of time that it took to arrange a courtesy car after his accident two weeks ago.

3 The company is going to attend a charity ball in two weeks' time. The organisers of the charity contacted the business last week, stating that ticket sales are a little slow at the moment and asking if the business has any ideas on how it could tell more people about the event?

4 The summer staff party needs to be organised but the management team want to know what staff want to do and where they want to go. The manager has asked you to try to find this information out.

5 All customers need to be informed of a new offer that the company is about to introduce: all named drivers on a car policy will be gaining a 'no claims bonus' as long as they are not involved in an accident.

Summary

- Oral communication is also known as verbal communication. It simply involves people talking to one another. It can be formal, for example business meetings, or informal, for example a quick chat with a colleague.

- Telephones – the use of the telephone has dramatically changed over the last fifteen years. It is now possible to contact people whereever they are in the world. Telephone conversations are a quick way to talk to customers or colleagues when an immediate response is required. The disadvantage is there is no record of the conversation unless the call has been recorded.

- Written communication includes memorandums, letters, notices and newsletters.

- Memorandums are internal communication and are now less commonly used within business due to the increased use of internal email.

- Formal business letters are still used within a business. They might be sent to customers to let them know about special offers. Employees might be contacted by letter if there have been formal changes made to their contract of employment.

- Notices are a cheap and easy way to convey a message to all members of staff.

- Newsletters help keep employees informed of developments within the business. They might also include staff announcements. Their aim is to build community spirit within a business. Newsletters are often sent electronically in order to save printing costs.

- Email has dramatically changed the way that people communicate within and outside of a business. It is fast and relatively cheap. Unfortunately it also has its downside in the amount of time staff spend reading emails that are not relevant to them. Phones 4U have now banned internal emails.

- PowerPoint is a programme that enables the user to produce slides to be used as a presentation.

Chapter 22

Functional areas within businesses

Chapters 19–21 make up the 'in-tray' element of the examination. You will be required to undertake a range of practical activities using information and documents supplied within the examination paper. The activities selected will be relevant to the functional area. The finance department is always included within the paper, but the other functional areas will not always appear.

The following chapters will look at the tasks associated with each functional area, and how they all work together to complete key business activities. The functional areas you will be required to study are as follows:

- finance
- marketing and sales
- administration and ICT
- customer service
- production.

This chapter considers how the functional areas outlined above work together in order to help the business remain successful.

How functional areas work together

No department within a business can work in isolation. Although each department will have its own separate and specific role, it will always be dependent upon other departments in some form or another.

Activity

Consider the different activities that would be undertaken by functional areas within a medium to large business. You are required to match each activity to one of the following departments:

- finance
- marketing and sales
- administration and ICT
- customer service
- production.

Activities undertaken by different departments:

- Preparing accounts
- Undertaking market research
- Designing production schedules
- Paying wages and salaries
- Organising meetings
- Quality control of new products
- Dealing with customer complaints
- Organising customer surveys
- Cleaning and maintenance
- Obtaining capital
- Health and safety on the factory floor
- Visiting potential new customers
- Organising focus groups
- Distributing mail
- Organising a promotional campaign
- Sending out invoices to customers
- Supporting ICT applications
- Ordering raw materials as required
- Maintaining machinery
- General clerical support.

Finance

The finance department is responsible for money coming into and out of the business. It is therefore the hub of the business. Without finance, no marketing campaigns can take place, no wages can be paid, no raw materials can be purchased, and all other departments will grind to a halt.

The finance department allocates money to other departments to perform their specific role. It allows the business to employ staff and manufacture goods to be sold. This in turn brings money back into the business. If the flow of money is interrupted, it will have a dramatic effect on the ability of the business to continue trading.

As you can see from the article below, once a business gains substantial debts which it cannot pay, its ability to continue trading is greatly reduced. Woolworths would have been unable to undertake a marketing campaign to stimulate sales or purchase new and innovative stock in order to entice customers back through their doors.

Marketing and sales

The marketing department is responsible for researching what customers want and raising their awareness that it is available. The department works alongside sales to ensure that customers purchase the products.

The marketing and sales department has to work closely with the finance department to agree the budget for market research and subsequent marketing campaigns. They would also work closely with the production department, deciding what products customers want. This vital information will drive the production schedules. If the production department produces goods that are not required, the business will ultimately lose money.

Administration and ICT

The administration and ICT department support all the other departments within a business.

The administration side will take responsibility for the reception duties, internal and external mail. Administration supports the other departments with their clerical/admin tasks.

Woolworths

Woolworths should have been celebrating its 100th anniversary, but instead it disappeared after falling into financial trouble.

Throughout its 99-year history in the UK, Woolworths had been a well-known store for the majority of UK families. It built its reputation on Ladybird School Uniform and the legendary Pick 'n' Mix selection.

Woolworths hit major financial trouble and was offered for sale for only £1, with debts of £295million and a deficit in pension contributions of up to £100million. No buyer could be found and it finally left the high street at the beginning of 2009.

(adapted from an article in the *Northern Echo*, Deborah Johnson, 21st November 2008, www.thenorthernecho.co.uk/business)

The ICT department supports, runs and maintains the computers within the company. This could involve the development and support of an internal intranet and website which enables the business to sell goods online. If another department has problems with their computers, they would seek the assistance of the ICT department.

Customer service

The role of the customer service department is to look after the needs and wants of customers. This will involve close liaison with the marketing and sales team and production department. For example, if a customer complained to the customer service department that a product they purchased was poorly packaged and damaged when received, the customer service department would ask marketing and sales to check the packaging of similar products. If there was a fault, this would have to be discussed with the production department so that the packaging could be modified.

Production

The production department is responsible for the manufacture and quality control of products. This involves the purchase of raw materials required to make the products. The finance department would be involved in the costing of products: how much they cost to manufacture, against how much they can be sold for. Finance would also consult with production when choosing a supplier.

Production needs to keep abreast of consumer tastes and fashions, and would rely on the marketing and sales department for this information. Customer service will relay customers' concerns about products so that modifications can be made if needed. ICT support will be needed if the production line is electronically automated.

Summary

- The finance department is responsible for money coming in and out of the business. It is therefore the hub of the business. No money = no business!

- Marketing and sales are responsible for researching what customers want and raising their awareness that the product/service is available.

- The administration and ICT department supports the other departments within the business. Administration might take responsibility for reception duties, dealing with incoming and outgoing mail, typing up reports/documents for the other departments. ICT will be responsible for maintaining the computer hardware and software used throughout the business.

- The customer service department aims to meet the needs and wants of the customers.

- The production department is responsible for the manufacture and quality control of products.

Chapter 23

> Finance

This section is broken down into the following sub-sections:

- wages and salaries
- purchase and sales documents, and payment methods
- profit and loss statements
- balance sheets
- cash-flow forecast
- break even
- using ICT to prepare financial documents.

Wages and salaries

What does it all mean?

As soon as we consider becoming an employee, often the most important question is: how much are we going to be paid? Not many people go to work just for the love of their job!

Wages

Wages are paid to people who work on an hourly rate. They are often paid weekly and would receive overtime payments if they worked more than their contracted hours.

It is easier to use an example to explain how wages are calculated. Paul has just joined BP Joinery. He has been employed as a carpenter, being paid £6.80 per hour. His contracted hours are 37.5 hours per week. If he works overtime, he will be paid at time and a half, which is £10.20 per hour. In his first week, he worked 42 hours. His wages for that week would be as follows:

37.5 x £6.80 = £255

4.5 x £10.20 = £45.90

Total wages for week one = £300.90.

This is known as gross pay – the total amount of money which someone earns before deductions.

Activity

In Paul's second week, he worked his normal 37.5 hours and then an additional six hours' overtime. Calculate Paul's gross pay.

Salaries

Salaried employees are usually paid a set amount of money per year, which is divided into twelve monthly payments. Salaried employees are unlikely to be paid overtime for any work they do in addition to their normal hours. Instead they are sometimes allowed to take 'time off in lieu'. This means that they are able to take time off work when the organisation becomes less busy.

Let us consider an example. Marjorie works for a travel agent and earns a salary of £16,800 per annum (year). Her gross monthly salary would be calculated as follows:

£16,800 divided by 12 (months in year) = £1,400 per month.

> **Activity**
>
> Marjorie has just been promoted to a supervisor's position and her salary has increased to £19,200 per annum. Calculate her monthly gross pay.

Gross pay versus net pay

As you can see from the above calculations, **gross pay** is the amount of money which an employee receives before any deductions have been taken. **Net pay** is therefore the amount of money that an employee actually receives after statutory deductions have been made. Examples of deductions made by employers to calculate an employee's net pay include:

- income tax
- national insurance
- student loans
- pension contributions.

Income tax

Every day of our lives, we enjoy services that are provided by the government. You may be enjoying a free education, which will be paid for by the funds collected by the government in different ways.

One of the ways in which the government collects these funds is through income tax. This is a tax that is levied on people's earnings. How much you pay is related to how much you earn: the greater your income, the bigger contribution you make. Not all income is taxable. Everybody is entitled to at least the basic personal allowance (tax-free amount). In order to calculate an employee's correct personal allowance, they will be asked to supply HM Revenue and Customs with personal financial information. Using this information, HM Revenue and Customs will issue each employee with a tax code. This code is sent to both the employee and employer, and tells the employer the amount of personal allowance to which the employee is entitled. The basic personal allowance for the tax year 2009–10 is £6,475. This means that the first £6,475 you earn is not taxed. You will start paying income tax as soon as your income rises above your personal allowance.

There are currently two levels of taxation (2009–10). The basic rate is charged at 20 per cent on earnings from £0–£37,400. Higher rate tax is 40 per cent and is charged on earnings over £37,400.

If you are employed, your income tax will be collected through the Pay as Your Earn (PAYE) system. Your employer will deduct your tax out of your wages. You will receive your gross wages minus the tax, as net pay. If you are self-employed, you will be responsible for filling in a self assessment tax return. HM Revenue and Customs will then calculate how much tax you owe. You will be required to pay this to them by 31st January and 31st July.

If you have savings in a building society or bank and are eligible for tax, or have an income over your personal allowance, the tax will be automatically deducted from any interest you receive on your savings.

National insurance

As soon as you start work, you will also be required to pay national insurance contributions (NICs). These contributions build up your entitlement to certain social security benefits, including your state pension. The type and level of national insurance contributions you make will depend on how much you earn and whether you are employed or self-employed. You stop paying national insurance contributions when you reach state pension age, which is currently 65 for men and 60 for women, but will gradually increase to 65 for women over the period 2010 to 2020.

In order to pay national insurance, you will be issued with a national insurance number when you reach the age of 16 and leave full-time education. This is your own personal account number and you must not lose it or give it to anyone else to use. This number will ensure that all national insurance contributions and tax you pay are properly recorded on your account. It also acts as a reference number for the whole social security system.

You have to be earning at least £110 per week before you start paying national insurance contributions. National insurance contributions are charged at the following rates for the tax year 2009–10.

- If you earn above £105 a week but less than £844 per week, you will pay 11 per cent of this amount as 'Class 1' NICs.

- You also pay one per cent on earnings above £844 a week as Class 1 NICs.

Student loans

If you decide to go to university, you may find yourself taking out a student loan which is administered by the government. The idea of the loan is to help students pay their university fees and living expenses. Student loans are part of the government's financial support packages for students in higher education in the UK.

HM Revenue and Customs are responsible for collecting repayments of student loans when the borrower works within the UK tax system after leaving higher education.

An ex-student currently has to be earning in excess of £15,000 before student loan repayments become due. This is further broken down into a monthly threshold of £1,250 and a weekly threshold of £288.46. The amount to be deducted from an employee's pay is nine per cent after the threshold amount has been deducted. HM Revenue and Customs supply a CD-ROM or you can access the SL3, Student Loan Deduction table found on their website (www.hmrc.gov.uk).

However it is relatively simple to calculate: for example, as Jimmy earns £400 per week, his student loan repayment would be calculated as follows:

£400 – £288.46 (weekly threshold) = £111.54.

(This is the amount of pay that would be used to calculate nine per cent).

£111.54 x 9 divided by 100 = £10.04

£10 would be deducted from the employee's pay.

Pensions

If an employee is part of a company pension scheme, these contributions are taken out of the employee's pay before they actually receive the money. It will therefore become another deduction from their gross pay.

The payslip

All employees are legally entitled to receive a payslip. The purpose of a payslip is to inform the employee how much money they are going to/have received, which will be based on the hours worked. The complexity and layout of the payslip will depend on how the employee is paid,

Name of company	Employee No
Tax date	Employee

Pay this period £		Tax amount £
Hours	Rate £	Taxable pay this year £
Gross pay £		Nat insurance £
Net pay £		Total deductions £

National insurance No	Tax Code

Figure 23.1 Example of a payslip

whether salaried or paid by the hour. It will also contain extra boxes if deductions for student loans and pensions are being made. These deductions are unlikely to appear on your examination paper.

The payslip illustrated in Figure 23.1 is similar to one that could appear on the examination paper.

- **Name of company**: all payslips should contain the name of the business that is paying the employee.
- **Tax date**: the tax year starts on 6th April and runs until the 5th April the following year. It is therefore important that the week the payment refers to is recorded on the payslip. This means that payments can be correctly allocated to the correct tax year.
- **Employee**: the name of the employee must be stated so that ownership of the payslip is known.
- **National insurance number**: as mentioned above, this number ensures that all national insurance and tax payments are correctly allocated to the payee.
- **Tax code**: in order to calculate an employee's personal allowance correctly, HM Revenue and Customs collect information about an employee's personal financial circumstances, and with this information they provide the employee with a tax code. This ensures that each employee receives the correct personal allowance.
- **Taxable pay this period**: this is the amount of pay relevant to this payslip and will link to the tax date. This will be the gross amount which the employee has earnt.
- **Taxable pay this year**: this records the total amount of tax which an employee has paid in the relevant financial year.
- **Employee number**: some businesses give their employees a reference number. This helps recognise each individual, which is especially useful if a computerised payroll system is being used.
- **Hours**: this is the number of hours the employee has worked during this period.
- **Rate**: the hourly rate at which the employee is being paid.

- **Gross pay**: this is calculated by multiplying the number of hours worked by the rate.
- **Tax amount**: this is the amount of money due to HM Revenue and Customs. This amount will not be received by the employee, but will be paid directly to HM Revenue and Customs by the employer.
- **National insurance**: this is the contribution due, calculated on the employee's earnings.
- **Net pay**: in order to calculate net pay in this case, you need to subtract the tax amount and national insurance from gross pay. This will be the amount which the employee receives.

Example

Molly Smith is employed as a machinist at Whitehaven Curtain Manufacturer Ltd. She works a 35-hour week and is paid £6.50 per hour. Her employee number is 004567. National insurance contributions for the tax week 1st–6th December 2008 are £11.03. Taxable pay to date is £8,190, and tax payable that week amounted to £22.30. Molly's national insurance number is WM303471B. Her tax code is 65G. Her payslip is completed in Figure 23.2 on the next page.

A blank payslip can be found at the end of the textbook. This can be photocopied.

Payment methods

Having calculated how much employees are going to be paid, we now have to consider how this payment will be made.

Security is an important consideration when paying employees

Employee: Whitehaven Curtain Manufacturer Ltd	Employee No 004567
Tax date: 1–6 December 2008	Employee: Molly Smith

Pay this period £ 227.50	Tax amount £ 22.30
Hours 35 Rate £ 6.50	Taxable pay this year £ 8,190
Gross pay £ 227.50	Nat insurance £ 11.03
Net pay £ **194.17**	Total deductions £ 33.33

National insurance No WM303471B	Tax Code 65G

Figure 23.2 Molly Smith's payslip

Activity

Examination practice 1

1. Harry Mortimer works for the Whitehaven Curtain Manufacturer Ltd. Complete his payslip for the week 1st–6th December 2008. He works in the stores department, dealing with the ordering of all the raw materials. His employee and national insurance numbers are 004657 and MN203516C. His tax code is 67B. His taxable pay this period is £9,878.40. For the week 1st–6th December he worked 42 hours, and his rate of pay is £7 per hour. Tax due is £35.60. National insurance contributions amount to £17.01.

2. Paul Brown is the production manager working at Whitehaven Curtain Manufacturer Ltd. Calculate how much tax and national insurance he would need to pay from the information supplied, and complete his payslip for the week 1st–6th December 2008. His details are as follows: employee number 0048961; national insurance number MN673516D; tax code 61A. He works 40 hours per week and is paid £10.50 per hour. His taxable pay this period is £14,112. He has a weekly personal allowance of £116, and the remainder of his income is taxed at 20 per cent. He does not pay national insurance contributions on the first £105 of his wages. The remaining amount is charged at nine per cent.

(The question on the examination paper is unlikely to be this complicated and is more likely to resemble the example and question 1 above.)

Cash

Many years ago, the majority of employees who were paid weekly were paid in cash. It is now quite rare for an employee to be paid in cash. There are probably two main reasons for this:

- Security: if a company is going to pay its staff in cash, it means that they have to have a large amount of cash on the premises on pay day. This makes the business very vulnerable to thieves, and the security risk is too high.

- Developments in technology have meant that people can gain access to their money via cash machines 24 hours a day, seven days a week.

Cheques

To overcome the security issues connected to cash payments a business could write out a cheque for each employee. This becomes quite a slow process for the employee as they have to find the time to bank the cheque, wait for it to be cleared and then draw upon it. Again, due to the development of technology this method of payment is becoming quite rare.

Bank transfers

This is where the business holds the employee's bank details in order to pay them. They will then transfer the employee's wages into their bank account direct from the business bank account. The money should be available to the employee within three working days of the transaction.

BACS – banks automated clearing system

Banks automated clearing system is a company owned by the UK banks which operates a computerised payments clearing service. This is commonly used for paying employees. It was set up in order to establish a more secure and effective way to process payments. The idea was to replace the traditional methods of paying employees – cash and cheques. Over 90 per cent of employees within the UK were paid using this system during 2007.

BACS services are run alongside all the leading high street banks, and process millions of payments each week for businesses. The system has built up considerable trust and is now considered as the most risk-free method of processing payments. Money transferred through this method is available to the recipient within three working days.

Sales and purchase documentation

In order for a business to trade with other businesses and customers, it is important that it uses a range of source documents correctly. A business may deal with two very different types of customer:

- The first type of customer is business to business. This means that one business buys/sells items to another business. This will often mean that they do not receive immediate payment for the goods or services they buy (known as trade credit). If trade credit is offered, the range of source documents used increases.

- The second type of customer is when the business sells direct to the consumer. This will usually involve a cash sale, with payment made at the point of sale. This process will involve fewer source documents as there is no need to issue documents that request payment.

In order to pass the examination, you are required to understand the purpose and sequence of the source documents, and how to complete each of the documents accurately. The source documents outlined below are:

- purchase order
- delivery note
- goods received notes
- invoices
- credit notes
- statement of account
- remittance advice slips
- receipts.

Two businesses will be used to illustrate all the documents, and for all the practice examination questions contained within this chapter. The first business is a retail shop selling garden equipment, including lawn mowers, plants and accessories. Most of the plants are grown in-house. The company is known as Gardeners' Paradise and is based in Somerset. The second business is Garden Supplies, a supplier to Gardeners' Paradise.

Purchase order

When a business needs to order something from another business, it has to put the order in writing. The form that they use to do this is known as a **purchase order**. This form confirms the description and number of each item that the business requires. This will provide evidence that the business buying the goods did actually order the items. The purchase order acts as the first part of the tracking process for both the seller and buyer.

If you were to buy something by mail order or the Internet, you would be required to complete a form giving your name, address and payment details. This is equivalent to a purchase order.

Gardeners' Paradise

12–16 Long Lane
Wellington
Somerset TA43 78Y

[a] VAT Reg No 542/18956/43

Telephone: 01823 962369

Website: www.gardenersparadise.co.uk   email orders@gardenersparadise.co.uk

PURCHASE ORDER

To: Garden Supplies
Lord Street
Havant
Hampshire PO54 7YU

[b] Supplier No: 865
[c] Order No: 2007-978
[d] Date: 10 December 2008

Please supply:

Quantity	Description	Item Code	Unit price
5	Shovels Medium	Sho-786	£4.60
4	Yard brooms – red	Bro-321	£4.70

Signed [e] B Henry..

Date 12 December 2008

Figure 23.3 Example of a completed purchase order

Letters [a] to [e] are explained below:

(a) If a business has an annual turnover of over £67,000 they are required to register for VAT (2008). This means that they must charge 15 per cent VAT on all their sales. On 24th November 2008 and due to the 'credit crunch', the Government reduced VAT in order to encourage customers to start buying again. VAT has been reduced to 15 per cent until 1st January 2010 when it will rise again to its previous level of 17.5 per cent. If a business is registered for VAT, it must show this on all its sales and purchase documents.

(b) If a business deals with a supplier on a regular basis, they will usually allocate them a supplier number. This helps the business quickly find information relevant to each supplier.

(c) All purchase orders must be numbered so that they can be tracked through the business. This document will need to be linked to the delivery note when it arrives; using reference numbers makes the tracking process much easier and quicker.

(d) Purchase orders must be dated so that they can be allocated to the correct financial year. It also makes chasing items not received easier, as the date the purchase order was sent is known.

(e) Purchase orders are only valid if they are signed by an authorised member of the business.

Finance   147

> **Activity**
>
> ### Examination practice 2
>
> Blank documents for photocopying can be found at the back of the text book.
>
> Complete a purchase order form. Gardeners' Paradise wants to place the following order with Easy Lawn Ltd. The address is Unit 89, Eden End Industrial Estate, Exeter EX37 8PY. The supplier number is 742 and the purchase order number is 207-1023. Use today's date. The order is as follows:
>
> - two McCulloch Petrol Lawn Mowers 3540P at £49.99 each (item code McPL-896)
> - three Flymo Quicksilver 40S Push Petrol Mowers at £65 each (item code FIQPP-743).

Delivery notes

Having received an order, a business will need to pack up the goods ready for despatch to the customer. The next step is to create the delivery note which clearly outlines the items that have been included in the parcel about to be despatched. The delivery note is included in the parcel. Upon delivery the recipient should check the items received against the delivery note.

A delivery note is usually a multi-copy document. This means that the recipient of the goods keeps the top copy, the person/organisation who delivered the goods keeps the second copy, and finally the signed copy goes to the supplier. If a dispute were to occur concerning the condition of items upon delivery and the number and type of items delivered, the signed delivery notes can be referred to as evidence.

GARDEN SUPPLIES

VAT Reg No 897/4587/78

Lord Street, Havant, Hampshire, PO54 7YU
Telephone: 02392 453123
Website: www.gardensupplies.co.uk   email gardensupplies@aol.com

DELIVERY NOTE

To: Gardeners' Paradise
    12–16 Long Lane
    Wellington
    Somerset TA43 78Y

Date: 15 December 2008

Delivery Note No: 4578

[a]

Your order No	Customer Account No	Despatch date	Invoice No [b]	Delivery Method
2007-978	08453	15 December 2008	012658	Signed for DHL delivery

Item Code	Quantity	Description
Sho-786	5	Shovels Medium
Bro-321	4	Yard Brooms – red

Received in good condition (please comment here)...

Signed .... Date ....

Top copy Customer   Blue copy Carrier   Yellow copy Garden Supplies

Figure 23.4 Example of a delivery note

Remember that the delivery note is compiled by the supplier and signed for by the recipient of the goods. It is not always possible at the time of delivery to check the contents, and therefore the delivery note might be signed stating that the contents have not been fully investigated and checked.

An example of a delivery note is found in Figure 23.4.

The letters [a] and [b] are explained below:

(a) All of the information in this section has been taken from the purchase order. This enables both companies to check the original purchase order and helps create the paper trail of evidence. The customer account number is the reference number that has been allocated to Gardeners' Paradise from Garden Supplies.

(b) Once the goods have been delivered, Garden Supplies will send the invoice requesting payment to Gardeners' Paradise. Quoting this number on the delivery note enables Gardeners' Paradise to link all the paperwork together, enabling them to make a speedy payment.

Activity

Examination practice 3

Complete a delivery note. In examination practice 2, you completed a purchase order which was sent from Gardeners' Paradise to Easy Lawn Ltd. You now need to design a delivery note from Easy Lawn Ltd to Gardeners' Paradise and complete it with the details used in examination practice 2. You can make up a customer reference and invoice number.

Goods received notes

A goods received note is designed by the business that is receiving the goods, ie the customer. In the example we have been using, this would be Gardeners' Paradise. A goods received note is completed by the person who is unpacking the parcel and checking each item is in perfect condition. It will record exactly what has been sent. This information should tie in with the delivery note. If the business is a large company, purchases will be received by the stores department. They will complete the goods received note and then send the document to the accounts department, telling them that the goods have arrived. The goods received note can then be checked against the purchase order to ensure that all goods ordered have actually been received.

When the invoice arrives from the supplier, the accounts department will know that the goods have been received, were in good condition and so the invoice can be paid.

The goods received note is also a multi-copy document. One copy will be held by the stores or purchasing department, and the other copy will be sent on to accounts.

Figure 23.5 is an example of a goods received note.

Activity

Examination practice 4

Complete a goods received note. In examination practices 2 and 3, you completed a purchase order and then a delivery note. You now need to complete a goods received note on behalf of Gardeners' Paradise which clearly outlines the goods that have been received from Easy Lawn Ltd. The only problem is that one of the Flymo Quicksilver 40S Push Petrol Mowers has been damaged and will need to be returned.

Invoices

There are two kinds of invoices, a sales invoice and a purchase invoice.

1. A purchase invoice is received by the business from a supplier requesting payment for goods which the business has had on credit terms. Continuing with the

Finance 149

Gardeners' Paradise
GOODS RECEIVED NOTE

Supplier:
Garden Supplies
Lord Street
Havant, Hampshire PO54 7YU

GRN No: 7654
GRN Date: 17.12.08
Delivery Note No: 4578
Delivery Note date: 15.12.08

Supplier A/c No: 865

Purchase Order No: 2007-978

Carrier: DHL Checked by

Item code	Quantity ordered	Quantity delivered	Description	If damaged please record details
Sho-786	5	5	Shovels Medium	1 broom head is cracked. This item needs to be returned
Bro-321	4	4	Yard brooms – red	

White copy – stores department   Yellow copy – accounts department

Figure 23.5 A goods received note

Purchase invoice

GARDEN SUPPLIES

VAT Reg No 897/4587/78

Lord Street
Havant, Hampshire
PO54 7YU

Telephone: 02392 453123
Website: www.gardensupplies.co.uk
email: gardensupplies@aol.com

INVOICE

To: Gardeners Paradise
    12–16 Long Lane
    Wellington, Somerset TA43 78Y

Date: 17 December 2008

Your Order No	Customer account no	Dispatch No [a]	Invoice No
2007-978	08453	4578	012658

Item code	Quantity	Description	Unit price £	Net Price £
Sho-786	5	Shovels Medium	4.60	23.00
Bro-321	4	Yard brooms – red	4.70	18.80
			Total	41.80

Terms: 30 days net [b]
E & OE [c]

VAT 15%   6.27

Total due   48.07

Figure 23.6 Purchase invoice from Garden Supplies

Letters [a] to [c] are explained on the next page.

example, Garden Supplies will send Gardeners' Paradise an invoice requesting payment for all the goods that have been delivered.

2 The sales invoice is sent from a business and is a request for payment for goods supplied to a customer. Using our example, if Garden Supplies had sold 3 Flymo Quicksilver 40S Push Petrol Mowers to Landscape Designs for £95 each, they would then send an invoice requesting payment once the goods had been received.

Figures 23.6 and 23.7 are examples of purchase and sales invoices.

(a) The dispatch number is the delivery note number. The invoice contains the purchase order number and delivery note number. This allows the purchaser of the goods, Gardeners' Paradise, to link all the paperwork together. This allows the business to check that everything is in order, prior to making payment for the goods received.

(b) Gardeners' Paradise is trading with Garden Supplies. This is often referred to as business to business. In these circumstances it is usual to allow the purchaser of the goods 30 days before payment becomes due. This means that Gardeners' Paradise must pay for the goods by 17th January 2009.

(c) E & OE stands for errors and omissions excepted. This means if there is an error within the invoice, it can be altered; for example, if a business undercharges the customer due to a mathematical error, they are within their rights to send an amended invoice for the correct amount.

Sales invoice

Figure 23.7 shows a sales invoice from Gardeners' Paradise, who have sold goods on credit to Landscape Designs.

Gardeners' Paradise
12–16 Long Lane, Wellington, Somerset TA43 78Y

VAT Reg No 542/18956/43

Telephone: 01823 962369

Website: www.gardenersparadise.co.uk   Email gardenersparadise@aol.com

INVOICE

To: Landscape Designs
Wallis Road
Taunton
Somerset TA67 2WE

Date: 15 December 2008

Your Order No	Customer account no	Dispatch No [a]	Invoice No
2007-999	08467	4534	012678

Item code	Quantity	Description	Unit Price £	Net Price £
FLQPP-743	3	Flymo Quicksilver 40S Petrol Push Mowers	95.00	285.00

			Total	285.00
Terms: 30 days net [b]				
E & OE [c]			VAT 15%	42.75
			Total due	327.75

Figure 23.7 A sales invoice

> **Activity**
>
> **Examination Practice 5**
> Complete a purchase invoice from Easy Lawn Ltd to Gardeners' Paradise.

Credit note

The role of the credit note is to reduce the amount owed on an invoice. This usually happens when a customer has received a consignment of goods and then has to send some back because they were the wrong colour, damaged in transit or simply had not actually been ordered in the first place.

As you can see from Figures 23.6 and 23.7, the invoice is dispatched at the same time as the goods under separate cover. If goods then have to be sent back, the customer is actually being over-charged. The credit note will reduce the invoice by the value of the goods sent back.

Look back at Figure 23.5, the goods received note completed by Gardeners' Paradise; one broom was going to be sent back. Garden Supplies would need to send Gardeners' Paradise a credit note for the full value of the broom which had been returned. This is illustrated in Figure 23.8.

GARDEN SUPPLIES

VAT Reg No 897/4587/78

Lord Street
Havant
Hampshire
PO54 7YU

Telephone: 02392 453123

Website: www.gardensupplies.co.uk
email: gardensupplies@aol.com

CREDIT NOTE

To: Gardeners' Paradise
12–16 Long Lane
Wellington
Somerset TA43 78Y

Customer account no	Date/tax point	Invoice No	Credit note No
08453	21 December 2008	012658	25

Item code	Quantity	Description	Unit price £	Net price £
Bro-321	1	Yard Broom – Red	4.70	4.70
			Total	4.70

Terms: 30 days net
E & OE

VAT 15% £0.71
Total refund £5.41

Reason for return:..

Figure 23.8 A credit note

> **Activity**
>
> **Examination practice 6**
>
> When you completed your goods received note for goods received from Easy Lawn Ltd, one lawnmower was damaged and had to be sent back. Complete a credit note for this transaction.

Statement of account

When a business deals regularly with a customer, involving more than one transaction a month, they will send them a statement of account at the end of the month. This document is very similar to a bank statement, which summarises all the money going into and out of an account and provides the account holder with a final balance at the end of the month. In business, a statement of account summarises all the transactions which have taken place between the supplier and customer. This will include invoices sent for goods ordered, credit notes received, and payments made. The balance at the end of the month is the amount of money which the customer owes to the supplier.

The purpose of a statement of account is to save businesses time. It would not be very

---

GARDEN SUPPLIES

VAT Reg No 897/4587/78

Lord Street
Havant
Hampshire
PO54 7YU

Website: www.gardensupplies.co.uk
email: gardensupplies@aol.com

Telephone: 02392 453123

STATEMENT OF ACCOUNT

To: Gardeners' Paradise
12–16 Long Lane
Wellington
Somerset TA43 78Y

Customer A/c No: 08453
Credit Limit; £2,300 [a]
Date 31 December 2008

Date	Details	Debit (£) [b]	Credit (£) [c]	Balance (£)
Dec 1	Balance [d]			560.00
Dec 4	Cheque		560.00	000.00
Dec 13	Invoice 012678	327.75		327.75
Dec 21	Credit note – 25		5.41	322.34

Amount now due £322.44

REMITTANCE ADVICE

From: Gardeners' Paradise Customer a/c No: 08453

Date of statement: 31 Dec 2008

Amount enclosed..

Your reference date of payment..

All cheques made payable to Garden Supplies

Figure 23.9 Statement of account and remittance advice

efficient if a business paid their supplier every time they received an invoice. Instead, they can wait until the end of the month and pay off the total amount that is outstanding.

In the example, Gardeners' Paradise has been purchasing goods from Garden Supplies, and sent some back. These transactions can all be shown on a statement of account (see Figure 23.9).

Remittance advice

A remittance advice is often the bottom section of a statement of account. Its purpose is to save the customer time when sending payment. All the customer has to do is cut off the remittance advice and enclose this with their cheque. When the cheque is received by the supplier, it is easy to track down where it has come from and what it is for. If a remittance advice is not included and a customer wished to pay by cheque, they would have to write a letter explaining what the cheque was for. A remittance advice speeds up this process and enables the transaction to proceed smoothly. See Figure 23.9.

Letters [a] to [d] are explained below:

(a) When a business allows credit, it has to ensure that its customers will ultimately be able to pay for the goods they have received. One way to check the credit worthiness of a customer is to ask for credit references. These would be supplied either by the customer's bank or other regular suppliers they have dealt with over a number of years. If the reference was supplied by the bank, this would reassure the new supplier that the customer had sufficient funds to meet their debts. If the credit reference was supplied by another supplier, this would state that they had always met their repayments on time. Another way to ensure that a customer does not turn into a bad debt (someone who never pays for the goods received) is to set a credit limit. This means that the customer cannot run up a balance of greater than the set limit. In this example, the limit is £2,300.

(b) When completing a statement of account, you must remember that debit means increasing the debt – increasing the overall balance. When goods have been sold to the customer and an invoice raised, this becomes a debit entry. The customer owes the business money.

(c) Credit is the opposite of debit. All items that decrease the balance are credit items. This would include payments made and credit notes received.

(d) The opening balance is the amount of money which the customer owes the supplier at the beginning of the month. This would be for goods received in the previous month. In this example, Gardeners' Paradise owed Garden Supplies £560. This would have been for goods supplied during November. This balance is paid off on 4th December.

Activity

Examination practice 7

Complete a statement of account and remittance advice for Easy Lawns Ltd. The opening balance on the account is £237. A cheque was received for this amount; you will need to insert a suitable date. Record the invoice you sent and subsequent credit note. Clearly highlight the amount which Gardeners' Paradise owes to Easy Lawns Ltd.

Payment methods for goods

Having received a statement of account, there are a number of ways for a business to pay off the outstanding balance.

Cheque

One of the most common methods is to tear off the remittance advice slip and enclose a cheque for the required amount. This would then be posted to the supplier. Upon receipt the supplier would need to pay the cheque into the bank. Once paid into the bank, the value of the cheque cannot be drawn on until it has been cleared. This usually takes approximately three working days.

Writing out the cheques might be the job of an accounts clerk. However, they would have to ask someone in authority to sign the cheques before they were sent out. In some businesses, all cheques need two signatures, to help prevent fraud.

Figure 23.10 shows an example of a completed cheque

Figure 23.10 A completed cheque

The cheque in Figure 23.10 has been dated 7th January 2009, and made payable to Garden Supplies. It has been crossed A/C Payee Only, which means that it can only be paid into the bank account of Garden Supplies.

The amount of money is written out in words and then inserted in figures. This acts as a double check. Does the amount in words match the amount written in figures? If they do not correspond, the cheque will have to be sent back to Gardeners' Paradise. The authorised signatory is the person within the business who has the authority to sign the cheque.

Electronic transfer

With the increase use of technology, it is not uncommon for businesses to pay each other through electronic transfer, also known as credit transfers or bank transfers. They could do this using internet banking. They would instruct their bank to make the payment electronically out of their bank account, straight into that of the supplier. This is a much quicker method of payment, as it eliminates the time taken to post the letter and the supplier paying the cheque into their bank account.

Activity

Examination practice 8

Complete a remittance advice and cheque to Easy Lawns Ltd from Gardeners' Paradise for the amount of money that is owed to them. This should be the same as the balance in your statement of account. Use a suitable date.

However, there is still the time delay of three days while the money is being cleared.

Rather than using internet banking the customer could pay the supplier using BACS. This was discussed on page 145.

Cash

Cash would only be used to pay off the balance on the statement of account if it could be delivered personally. It is very unlikely that large sums of money would be withdrawn and delivered in cash. The one positive to this method is the fact that the money is instantly available to the supplier of the goods.

Due to the high security risk of holding too much cash, many businesses keep 'petty cash'. This is a small amount of money that is held within the accounts department and can be used to pay for small items. If a member of staff needed to purchase some more coffee for the staff canteen they would take the money out of the petty cash. In order to do this, they would have to ask someone in authority to sign the petty

Petty Cash Voucher			
Number	Date		
Description	Amount		
		£	P
Total			
Signature	Authorised		

Figure 23.11 Petty cash voucher

cash voucher, and then provide the receipt as evidence that they have actually purchased the coffee. Upon production of the receipt the member of staff would be reimbursed with their money. At this point, they might also be asked to sign the petty cash voucher as evidence that they have been reimbursed.

Customer to business

Sometimes a customer will purchase goods directly from a business. In order to prove that they have paid for the items, the business will issue a receipt. A receipt has two purposes:

- proof of purchase for the customer
- evidence that the sale actually took place for the supplier.

When a business is dealing directly with a customer, payment for goods could be made using cash, cheques, debit or credit cards. Through the development of technology, the most common form of payment today is probably debit or credit cards. Cheques are often not accepted at retail stores since the introduction of chip and pin.

- Debit cards allow the customer to have funds transferred straight from their account to that of the retailer. Even though the funds leave the customer's account straight away, there can be a time delay before the business actually has the funds cleared for use.
- Credit cards allow customers to pay for goods in the shop, but no money actually leaves their bank accounts. The funds leave the finance house which issues the card, for example Visa. The customer has agreed to pay the finance house at a later date. If credit card bills are not fully paid off at the end of each month, the outstanding balances are charged interest. Interest charged on credit cards is often quite high when compared against interest rates being charged on personal loans.

The importance of checking documents

There is no room for error when producing sales and purchase source documents. Even simple errors can have serious consequences for a business. It is all too easy to type in the wrong number, or even transpose numbers. If you mistakenly typed 345 metres instead of 435 metres on a purchase order, this could have severe consequences: if you were ordering raw materials and for a production line, the whole production line could run out of materials and you may miss a deadline for an order. This could affect other current and future orders, and impact on the business.

Purchase orders

As a customer, there are a number of sections that you should always check before sending out a purchase order to the supplier.

- Is the address of the supplier correct?
- Have you checked the quantity, description and item code?
- Is the unit price correct?
- Has the purchase order been signed by the authorised signatory?

Delivery note

As a supplier, there are a number of sections that should always be checked before sending the parcel and delivery note to the customer.

- Is the customer's address correct?
- Do the items packed ready for dispatch match those on the purchase order?
- Are the items listed on the delivery note actually in the parcel?

Goods received note

There are a number of sections that the customer should always check before signing and sending a goods received note to the accounts department.

- Does the goods received note match the delivery note and purchase order?
- Have all the goods ordered actually arrived?
- Are all the goods in perfect condition?

Invoice

The invoice will need to be carefully checked by both the supplier (sales invoice) and purchaser (purchase invoice). The first priority of the supplier is to ensure that the customer has been

Activity

Examination practice – possible errors in completing a purchase order

Complete Table 23.1. The first entry has been completed for you.

Error	What would happen?	Consequence
The address was not correct.	The purchase order would go to an unknown person. Eventually it might be returned to the customer.	No goods would be received which could mean the business fails to meet an order and would ultimately lose customers.
Too many items have been ordered.		
The purchase order has not been signed by the authorised signatory.		

Table 23.1

Activity

Examination practice – possible errors in completing a delivery note

Complete Table 23.2. The first entry has been completed for you.

Error	What would happen?	Consequence
Item ordered has not been packed.	The customer would receive an incomplete order.	This could delay their production process and cause the customer to let down one of their customers. The business might not deal with the supplier again.
Items are included in the parcel that do not appear on the delivery note. The customer's address is incorrect.		

Table 23.2

Finance

Activity

Examination practice – possible errors on a goods received note

Complete Table 23.3. The first entry has been completed for you.

Error	What would happen?	Consequence
One of the items in the parcel is damaged.	The supplier needs to be contacted to ascertain what they want the customer to do. The damaged item might need to be sent back to the supplier. The supplier might not want the item sent back, and will automatically give the customer a refund.	The supplier will send the customer a credit note. The customer might accept a replacement item and therefore no refund/credit note will be required.
The goods received note does not match the purchase order.		
An item that was ordered and appeared on the delivery note has not been found when the parcel was unpacked and therefore cannot be recorded on the goods received note.		

Table 23.3

---

correctly charged for all goods received. The customer's priorities will focus on how much they are being charged – is it the correct amount? Outlined below is the information that the supplier would need to ensure was correct before sending the invoice to the customer.

- Do the items outlined on the purchase order and delivery note correspond to those stated on the invoice?
- Is the unit price correct?
- Is the quantity correct?
- Has the calculation unit price x quantity been correctly calculated?
- Has the VAT been correctly calculated?
- Has the total due been correctly calculated?
- Is the invoice going to the correct address?

The customer would also check the invoice for mathematical errors but must also ensure that the invoice matches the purchase order and goods received note completed when the goods were unpacked.

Credit note

The credit note will be checked in a similar fashion by the supplier and customer. Both parties will need to ensure that no arithmetical errors have been made and that credit is being given for the correct item which is being sent back. The customer will also need to ensure that

Activity

Examination practice – possible errors on an invoice

Complete Table 23.4. The first entry has been completed for you.

Error	What would happen?	Consequence
The unit price has been incorrectly quoted.	All the additions within the invoice will be incorrect.	The customer will either be over- or under-charged. If the customer has been over-charged, they are unlikely to be very happy and will certainly make contact with the supplier. If they have been under-charged they might not contact the supplier and therefore profits could be lost.
VAT has been charged at 17.5 per cent rather than the reduced rate of 15 per cent.		
The quantity has been incorrectly quoted. Too many items have been charged for.		

Table 23.4

sufficient credit has been awarded for the returned item.

Statement of account

Before the statement of account is sent off, the supplier will need to check carefully that all entries are accurate. The supplier will need to ensure that all items sold to the customer are recorded, and that all cheques and returns have been deducted from the balance. The customer will also be checking that the opening balance is correct, that all goods are received, and that returns and payments made have been recorded accurately.

Remittance advice

This is often contained on the statement of account or in some cases, an invoice. It is important that the correct final balance has been carried down from the final balance on the statement of account to the remittance advice. It is also advisable to insert the customer's account number and date of statement on the remittance

Activity

Examination practice

Identify all the points which a supplier would need to check before a statement of account is sent to the customer. Make reference to the one you have completed. What would happen if the entries contained within the statement of account had not been added correctly? Use examples to illustrate your answer.

advice prior to dispatch, to make the tracking process easier when the customer returns the slip with their payment.

Methods of payment

If a business is using cheques as a method of payment, it is vitally important that the person writing the cheques double-checks all figures for accuracy. The amount to be paid must correspond to the balance on the invoice or final balance on the statement of account. The writer must also ensure that the figures in words and numbers agree.

If payment is being made electronically, either through bank transfer or BACS, the correct information must be used. Does the customer have the correct bank details of the supplier? If the money was inadvertently paid into the wrong account, it might be quite difficult to retrieve it. The supplier will also think that the customer has not made payment, and as such refuses to supply any further goods until any outstanding balance has been paid off. It is also important to check that the correct amount of money is being transferred.

Profit and loss account

Before exploring this section, relevant terminology for this topic is explained in Table 23.5.

So what is profit? It is the difference between the money received through the sale of goods and the amount of money left after all the expenses have been paid out.

Let us consider a very simple example. Paula is starting up in business selling second-hand cars. In her first month of trading, she has bought two cars for resale at a cost of £1,200 each, and then sells one for £1,600 and the second one for £1,800. What will be her profit?

Sales (£1,600 + £1,800)	£3,400
Less purchases (£1,200 x 2)	£2,400
Gross profit	£1,000

This shows that just through the sale of the two cars in her first month, she has made a gross profit of £1,000. However, this does not reflect the other costs she has incurred. Paula spent £200 on advertising and paid £150 for renting a forecourt. The profit and loss account is shown in Figure 23.12.

Sales revenue	The total amount of money that has been received by the business for the sale of its goods or services.
Purchases	Items that the business buys in with the idea of resale. A sweet shop's purchases would include Mars Bars, Walkers Crisps and Coca Cola. These items are bought by the shopkeeper to sell at an increased price to the customer.
Gross profit	The amount of money that has been made when the value of the purchases has been deducted from the value of the sales.
Net profit	The amount of money that has been made when you deduct the expenses of the business from the gross profit. Also, sales revenue minus expenses.
Fixed assets	Items purchased in order to help the business to run more efficiently. They have not been purchased for resale. Fixed assets include cars, computers, equipment, and machinery. These items appear in the balance sheet and not the profit and loss account.

Table 23.5 Profit and loss terminology

Activity

Examination practice

It is now the second month. Paula has sold a further three cars for a total of £8,700, for which she paid £5,000. She spent £400 on advertising, £150 on rent, and her mobile telephone expenses amounted to £40.

(a) Complete the profit and loss account for her second month of trading. Follow the layout illustrated in Figure 23.13.

(b) Complete Paula's profit and loss account for the first and second months to find her total profit. To do this you are required to add up all the sales for both months, and then all the expenses for both months. Follow the layout illustrated in Figure 23.14.

Profit and loss account for second month

	£	£
Sales		
Less purchases		
Gross profit		
Less expenses		
Advertising		
Rent		
Net profit		

Figure 23.13 Paula's profit and loss account for the second month of trading

Profit and loss account for first two months

	£	£
Sales		
Less purchases		
Gross profit		
Less expenses		
Advertising		
Rent		
Mobile telephone expenses		
Net profit		

Figure 23.14 Paula's profit and loss account for the first two months of trading

Profit and loss account for first month

Sales (£1,600 + £1,800)		£3,400
Less purchases (£1,200 x 2)		£2,400
Gross profit		£1,000
Less expenses		
Advertising	£200	
Rent	£150	£350
Net profit		£650

Figure 23.12 Paula's profit and loss account for first month of trading

Paula has made a net profit of £650 after all expenses have been deducted.

The amount of profit which a business makes will depend on a number of factors. These include:

- The number of items sold. If sales increase and all other expenses within the business remain equal, net profit will increase.
- The price at which those items are sold. If a business increases its prices and all other expenses remain the same, net profit will increase.
- How much suppliers charge for purchases. If a supplier increases its prices and the business does not pass this on to their customers, net profit will fall. If a business finds a cheaper supplier, net profit will ultimately increase.
- Level of expenses: increases in rent, or the price of petrol. If expenses increase and sales prices remain the same, net profit will fall.

In real life things are rarely so straightforward. The rapid increases in fuel prices during the summer of 2008 greatly increased the expenses of businesses, and ultimately their net profit figures fell. Fuel prices then dramatically fell throughout the autumn and winter months of 2008. This would have reduced the expenditure of businesses, allowing their profits to be restored.

The best way to consider these points is to use numerical examples. Returning to an earlier example, Yasmin is just about to open a shop selling scarves. All scarves will sell for £10 each. Yasmin is hoping that November (her first month of trading) will be a particularly cold month and sales will start strongly. She is predicting to sell 540 scarves in this month. Her expenses are

Activity

Examination practice

Complete the following tasks to show what happens to net profit. Refer back to the example above.

(a) The number of scarves purchased increases to 650. Do not forget to increase the cost of purchases (650 x £6.50). Recalculate the profit and loss account, and explain what has happened to gross and net profit.

(b) Yasmin considers increasing her prices to £12 per scarf. She sells 540 scarves during November. The purchase price remains the same. Recalculate the profit and loss account, and explain what has happened to gross and net profit.

(c) Yasmin's suppliers have increased their price per scarf. Each scarf now costs £7.50 to purchase. Yasmin sold 540 scarves during November. Sales price has remained the same (£10). Recalculate the profit and loss account, and explain what has happened to gross and net profit.

(d) Yasmin's landlord has raised her rent to £700. Sales remain at 540 scarves at £10 each. The purchase price of each scarf is still £6.50. Recalculate the profit and loss account, and explain what has happened to gross and net profit.

(e) Finally if we put all these changes together, what happens to the net profit figure? Sales increase to 650 at £12 each. The purchase price has risen to £7 per scarf and rent has increased to £700. Recalculate the profit and loss account, and explain what has happened to gross net profit after all of these changes have been included.

estimated to include her rent of £400, £200 wages for a part-time assistant on Saturday, telephone expenses of £60 and utility bills of £240. Yasmin's supplier charges her £6.50 per scarf.

	£	£
Sales (540 x 10)		5,400
Less purchases (540 x 6.50)		3,510
Gross profit		1,890
Less expenses		
Rent	400	
Wages	200	
Telephone expenses	60	
Utility bills	240	900
Net profit		990

Figure 23.15 Yasmin's forecast profit and loss account for November

Balance Sheets

Balance sheets are the second part of the final accounts that are completed after the profit and loss account has been formalised.

Before we can consider how a balance sheet is constructed we need to consider some new terminology.

Fixed assets (FA)
These are items that are purchased by the business in order to help it operate. These items will not be resold. Fixed assets include motor vehicles, equipment, machinery and computers. They usually have a life expectancy of more than one year.

Current assets (CA)
These are items that are owned by the business but have a life expectancy of less than one year. CAs are broken down into four specific sections.

Stock – these are items that have been purchased for resale within the financial year but have not yet been sold. They are in the stock cupboard and will be sold in the next financial year.

Debtors – these are customers who have received goods on credit and will pay for them in the future – usually 30 days.

Bank – this is the money the business has in its business bank account. It is a CA if there is money in the bank – not overdrawn.

Cash – this is notes and coins the business has available to spend. This money would usually be in the petty cash tin and be available to purchase small items.

Current liabilities (CL)
These are the debts of the business – the money the business owes to other people – and will consist of creditors and bank overdraft. These debts must be paid back within one year.

Creditors – if the business has purchased goods on credit these suppliers become the creditors of the business.

Bank overdraft – if the business is spending the bank's money the bank balance becomes a CL, as the business must at some stage pay this money back to the bank.

Long Term Liabilities (LTL)
This consists of money the business owes to external parties which have a repayment period of longer than one year. This will include bank loans.

Capital
This is the money the owner has invested in the business and any profits they have not drawn out of the business throughout the financial year.

Drawings
This is the money the owner(s) of a sole trader/partnership takes out of the business in order to pay for their living expenses.

So what is a balance sheet? A balance sheet is usually completed at the end of the financial year to show the current value of the business. It identifies all the items the business owns less all its liabilities – money owed to a third party. It is broken into two distinct halves.

The first half adds up all the assets and takes away all the liabilities of the business. The formula is as follows:

FA + CA – CL – LTL = top half of the balance sheet

The bottom half of the balance sheet starts with the opening capital to which the net profit of the business is added and then the drawings taken by the owner is subtracted. The closing figure is the closing capital which then becomes the opening capital of the following year. The formula would look like this:

Opening Capital + Net Profit – Drawings = Closing Capital = bottom half of the balance sheet.

Let us look at the layout of a balance sheet. We will use the example of Yasmin who has just started up her shop selling scarves. We will construct the balance sheet to represent the financial value of the business after one year of trading.

Let us refresh our memory. Yasmin started up business in November and therefore her financial year will run from 1st November to 31st October.

Yasmin's Scarf Shop
Balance Sheet as at 31st October 2010

	£	£	
Fixed Assets			
Shop Fixtures		10,000	
Current Assets			
Stock (a)	700		
Debtors (b)	50		
Bank	1,200		
Cash	50		
	2,000		
Less Current Liabilities			
Creditors	350		
Working Capital		1,650	(c)
		11,650	(d)
Less Long Term Liability			
Bank Loan		5,000	
		6,650	
Opening Capital (e)		5,000	
Plus Net Profit		21,000	
		26,000	(e)
Less Drawings		19,350	(f)
Closing Capital (g)		**6,650**	

Figure 23.16 Yasmin's balance sheet at 1st November

Finance

Explanation of terms

(a) This is the value of the scarves that Yasmin has purchased in this financial year and has yet to sell.

(b) Yasmin supplies a small boutique. This is the amount of money owed to her by the boutique for goods received on credit.

(c) £1,650 has been calculated by subtracting CL from CA. The sum is CA – CL. When you have taken CA – CL the amount left is known as the working capital of the business. This is the amount of money the business has to spend in the immediate future after all its debts have been paid.

(d) £11,650 is calculated by adding together the total of the FA to the total of the working capital.

(e) £26,000 is calculated by adding opening capital to net profit.

(f) Yasmin has taken £19,350 out of the business for her own use throughout the year.

(g) Closing capital of this year will become the opening capital of the business next year. This shows that Yasmin started the business with an investment of £5,000. She has not taken out all of her profits in drawings and therefore her capital has increased by £1,650.

Cash-flow forecast

A cash-flow forecast records all the money coming into and out of a business. Its purpose is to identify times when the business might be short of cash, or even have excess cash that could be invested. It will highlight times of high expenditure.

A cash-flow forecast will only ever be as good as the quality of the predictions made to create it. It is therefore very important that the information used within the forecast is as accurate as possible. This could involve looking at past sales figures and the cost of past expenses, or even undertaking market research to establish potential demand and costs that could be incurred.

Activity

Examination practice

Using the information complete the spaces within the balance sheet found below.

Use the layout and explanation above to help you complete this exercise.

Motor Vehicle – £6,000
Kitchen Equipment – £1,000
Debtors – £1,200
Cash – £200
Bank Loan – £6,000

Opening Capital – £12,000
Net Profit – £32,000
Drawings – £26,800

Bill's Sandwich Shop Balance Sheet as at 31st December 2008

	£	£
Fixed Assets		
Shop Fixtures		15,000
Motor Vehicle		
Kitchen Equipment		
		_____
Current Assets		
Stock	600	
Debtors		
Bank	400	
Cash	_____	
Less current Liabilities		
Creditors	1,200	
Working Capital		_____
		23,300
Less **Long Term Liability**		
Bank Loan		
		17,200
Opening Capital		
Plus Net Profit		_____
		44,000
Less Drawings		_____
Closing Capital		17,200

The cash-flow forecast will eventually be compared with what actually happened; for example, the estimated sales figures will be compared to the actual sales figures.

A cash-flow forecast helps the business in the decision-making process in the following ways:

- Ensures there is always sufficient cash available to allow the business to continue trading.
- Highlights times when there are cash surpluses that could be paid into short-term investments, in order to gain maximum return.
- Identifies times when the business will have insufficient funds to meet all its outgoings. The business will be able to arrange short-term finance such as a bank overdraft to cover these periods.
- Helps a business plan and monitors its progress. It is usually required when compiling a business plan in order to arrange a loan with a financial institution.

Example of a cash-flow forecast

Figure 23.17 gives an example of a cash-flow forecast, using the model of Yasmin's scarf shop again.

	November	December	January
Income			
Sales	5,400	7,000	3,440
Interest on investment			50
Total income [a]	5,400	7,000	3,490
Expenditure			
Purchases	3,510	4,550	2,795
Rent	400	400	500
Wages	200	300	200
Utility bills	240	240	240
Telephone expenses	60	75	55
Total expenses [b]	4,410	5,565	3,790
Opening balance [c]	240	[f] 1,230	2,665
Inflow/outflow [d]	990	1,435	[g] (300)
Closing balance [e]	1,230	2,665	2,365

Figure 23.17 Cash-flow forecast for Yasmin's shop (best case scenario)

Letters [a] to [g] are explained below. The entries are created using the following data:

- Sales in November = 540 x £10
- Sales in December = 700 x £10
- Sales in January = 430 at £8
- Interest paid on deposit account = £50 at the beginning of January
- Purchases costs for each scarf = £6.50
- Rent = £400 per month in November and December; increases to £500 in January
- Wages = £200 per month in November and January; increases to £300 in December
- Utility bills = £240 per month
- Telephone expenses = November £60, December £75 and January £55.

Calculating the balances: [a] to [g]

(a) Income: this is any money that is received into the business. It could be from sales, interest received, loans or capital being put in by the owner. All the income is added together each month and this becomes total income for the month.

(b) Total expenditure is any money that is spent within the business. It covers the purchase of items for resale, expenses of the business and the purchase of fixed assets.

(c) The opening balance is the money which the business has available to spend at the beginning of the month. This could be money in a bank account or held in cash, or both added together. In this case, Yasmin has an opening balance of £240.

(d) The inflow/outflow is calculated by subtracting the total expenses from total income. For November, total income was £5,400, total expenditure of £4,410: £5,400 – £4,410 = £990 (inflow).

(e) The closing balance is the inflow/outflow added to the opening balance. For November: £240 + £990 = £1,230.

(f) The closing balance of one month becomes the opening balance of the next. Therefore the closing balance of November becomes the opening balance of December.

(g) In January, total income was less than total expenditure. The entry is then recorded as a negative figure. One way to show this is to enclose the numbers in brackets (300) or to insert a –300. The outflow of £300 has reduced the opening balance by that amount.

What does the cash-flow show us?

The cash-flow illustrates that over the three months of forecast trading, Yasmin has an increasing closing balance. She had predicted an outflow of £300 in January, anticipating a possible decrease in sales after the Christmas rush. Due to her sound opening balance, the business is able to sustain this outflow. However, if this was to continue over the next few months, the healthy balance which she had built up would soon disappear. From her predictions, Yasmin will not need to arrange any short-term finance as long as sales continue as initially predicted.

The first set of predictions from Yasmin was based on her best case scenario. Figure 23.18 illustrates the worst case scenario. In November and December, she predicts she will only sell 90 and 220 scarves respectively, at £10 each. In January she is going to have a sale and hopes to sell 250 at £9. Yasmin has estimated that initially she will be unable to obtain discounts from her supplier so each scarf will cost £7.50. All other outgoings remain the same as before. Her opening balance remains at £240.

Activity

Examination practice

Complete Yasmin's cash-flow forecast for February, March and April using the following data:

- Sales in February = 640 × £10
- Sales in March = 580 × £10
- Sales in April = 530 × £12
- Loan received in April = £4,000
- Purchase of each scarf = £6.50 in February and March. The supplier raised the price to £7 per scarf in April.
- Rent = £500 per month
- Wages = £200 per month
- Utility bills = £240 per month
- Telephone expenses = February £50, March £65 and April £55
- New shop fittings and equipment in March = £3,500

	November	December	January
Income			
Sales	900	2,200	2,250
Total income	900	2,200	2,250
Expenditure			
Purchases	675	1,650	1,875
Rent	400	400	500
Wages	200	300	200
Utility bills	240	240	240
Telephone expenses	60	75	55
Total expenses	1,575	2,665	2,870
Opening balance	240	(435)	(900)
Inflow/outflow	(675)	(465)	(620)
Closing balance	(435)	(900)	(1,520)

Figure 23.18 Cash-flow forecast for Yasmin's shop: worst case scenario

The numbers in Figure 23.18 tell a very different story. For each of the first three months, Yasmin's expenses have been greater than her sales. As a result, she would end up with a negative £1,520 at the end of her first three months of trading. In order to continue trading, Yasmin would have to arrange some short-term finance. This could be in the form of a bank overdraft or short-term loan. On her current predictions, her balance is slowly worsening, and therefore if sales were not predicted to increase over the next nine months, this project would not be worth undertaking.

The other alternative is for Yasmin to consider how she could reduce her expenditure. Does she actually need a part-time member of staff? Is there somewhere cheaper she could rent? Could she reduce her utility bills?

Activity

Enter the numbers in Figure 23.18 into a spreadsheet. Make sure you connect all the cells with formulas. This will enable you to make changes that will be instantly calculated throughout the spreadsheet. Call this Yasmin1.

- Take out the wages for the three months. What is the new closing balance?
- Reduce the cost of purchases to £6.50. How does this impact on the figures?
- Introduce a £2,000 loan. How does this help Yasmin over the next three months? Call your final version Yasmin2.

Break even

Break even is the point where no profit or loss has been made. The business has covered its cost of production. In order to calculate break even, you will need to understand the following terminology.

- **Fixed costs**: these are costs that do not change, regardless of the levels of production. These costs are not related to production levels; for example, rent would be the same cost, regardless of the number of units produced.
- **Variable costs**: these are costs which are directly related to production, and will therefore rise or fall depending on how many units are produced. An example would be raw materials; if production increases, a greater volume of raw materials will be consumed. If production decreases, the opposite will apply.
- **Sales price**: this is the amount charged to the customer.
- **Contribution**: this is calculated by subtracting the variable cost per unit from the sales price per unit.
- **Labour**: this is always quite a difficult cost to define. If a person's wages are directly related to the production of the product, they would be variable costs. However, wages of personnel that are not related directly to production would be a fixed cost. A production line worker who was paid according to the number of units they produced would be part of the variable costs; a factory supervisor would be a fixed cost as they would receive the same wages regardless of the number of units produced.

Calculating break even

There are two ways that break even can be calculated, and you will need to know how to use both. The first method involves the use of a formula and the second interpretation of a break-even graph.

Break-even formula

The formula to calculate break even is as follows:

$$\frac{\text{Fixed costs}}{\text{Contribution}} = \text{number of units required to break even}$$

(Contribution = sales price − variable cost per unit)

An example to illustrate this formula is useful. A business which manufactures garden gnomes has calculated their fixed costs to be £30,000 per annum. Variable costs for the production of each

Number of gnomes sold	Fixed costs (FC)	Variable costs (VC) (£6 x number produced)	Total costs (TC) (FC + VC)	Sales revenue (SR) (£12 x number sold)
0	30,000	0	30,000	0
2,500	30,000	15,000	45,000	30,000
5,000	30,000	30,000	60,000	60,000
7,500	30,000	45,000	75,000	90,000

Table 23.6 Gnome manufacture figures

gnome are £6; gnomes sell for £12 each.

$$\frac{30,000}{12-6} = 5,000 \text{ gnomes}$$

This means that the business has to sell 5,000 gnomes in order to cover all their costs. As soon as they produce the 5,001th gnome, they have started to make a profit.

Drawing a break-even chart (graph)

On the break-even graph you will be plotting the fixed cost line, the total cost line and the sales revenue.

Total costs are calculated by adding together the fixed and variable costs. Sales revenue is calculated by multiplying the number of items by the sales price. The revenue is shown on the y-axis and the number of products sold on the x-axis.

In order to plot the cost and income lines on the graph, you need to calculate the information. The information on gnome manufacture is shown in Table 23.6.

Table 23.6 shows us that if the business only sells 2,500 gnomes, the total costs are £45,000 and income is only £30,000. This means that the business has made a £15,000 loss. When 5,000 gnomes are sold, the total costs are the same as the sales revenue – this is the break-even point. If 7,500 gnomes are sold, total costs are £75,000 against sales revenue of £90,000. This means that a profit of £15,000 has been made.

Figure 23.19 shows four items marked on the graph. The first is the break-even point. This is

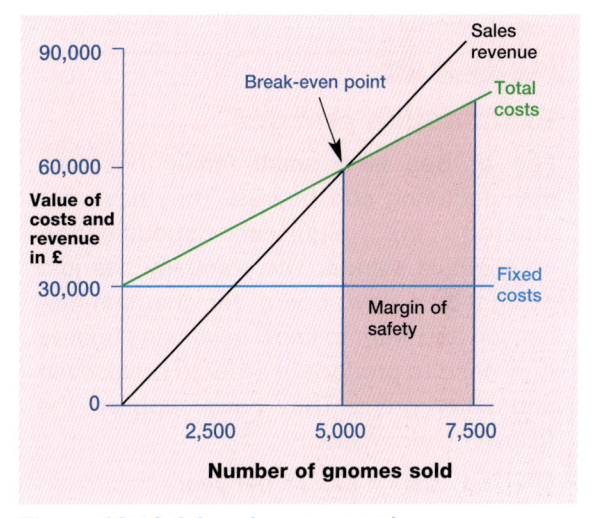

Figure 23.19 A break-even graph

where the sales revenue and total costs line meet. The space above and between the two lines represents the profit being made. The area where losses are being sustained is shown below the

Examination Tip

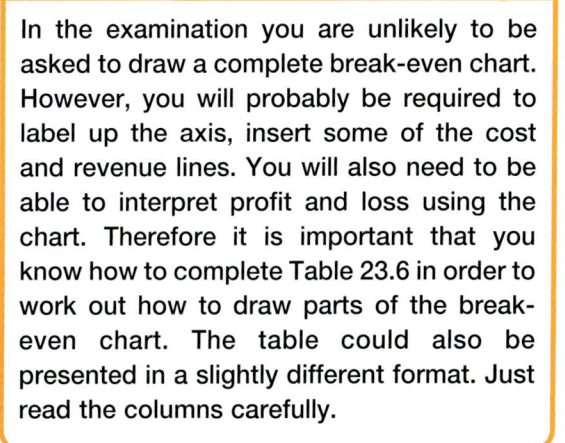

In the examination you are unlikely to be asked to draw a complete break-even chart. However, you will probably be required to label up the axis, insert some of the cost and revenue lines. You will also need to be able to interpret profit and loss using the chart. Therefore it is important that you know how to complete Table 23.6 in order to work out how to draw parts of the break-even chart. The table could also be presented in a slightly different format. Just read the columns carefully.

break-even point but still between the sales revenue and total cost line.

The margin of safety is the area between the break-even point and the number of units currently being produced. This means that if production levels fall from this point and up to the break-even point, the business will not be sustaining losses, but profit will be reducing. Current gnome production is 7,500, therefore the margin of safety will be the gap between break even of 5,000 and production levels of 7,500.

Activity

Examination practice

Fun at Sea is a small family business manufacturing surf boards. They have not entered the high-tech specification competitive market. The company has just designed a new board for the summer season and want to know how many boards they need to produce in order to break even and enter profit. They have supplied the following information:

- Fixed costs = £7,875 per year
- Variable costs per board = £145
- Sales price per board = £250
- The factory only manufactures boards that have already been ordered. Current production levels are 10 boards a week for 48 weeks of the year.

Complete the following tasks:

1 Calculate break even by using the formula.
2 Using the layout illustrated in Table 23.6, compile your own table using the figures above.
3 Create a break-even graph. Show the break-even point, margin of safety and areas of profit and loss.

Limitations of break even

Break even is a useful tool for a business to use. It indicates whether it would be financially viable to produce a product. It can be used to ascertain whether it would be cheaper to buy a product rather than manufacture it in-house. Throughout the calculation of break even, a number of assumptions are made.

- That fixed costs will remain constant, regardless of the levels of output and circumstances. However, this is not necessarily the case; eg, a landlord may increase rent payments, or utility bills may rise.
- That the sales price remains constant throughout. This is often not the case. If a business has regular customers, they may offer discounts for large orders or early payment of invoices. A business may need to reduce selling prices to move old stock.
- The only factor affecting costs and sales revenues is increase in production.
- There is the assumption that all goods are sold.
- Break-even charts generally only apply to one product.

Using ICT to produce financial documents

Computers are now part of our everyday lives and many people could not imagine working without one. Developments in technology have meant that computers also play a large part in the compilation of financial statements such as cash-flow forecasts and profit and loss accounts, and they are also able to calculate break even.

Businesses can use spreadsheets or specialised accounting software to compile their accounts or calculate break even. Specialised accounting software allows the business to input all their sales, purchases and expenses, and it will automatically calculate the profit and loss account. A spreadsheet is often used to calculate break even and produce a break-even chart.

Advantages of using ICT

There are many advantages of using ICT for financial statements, including:

- **Saving time**: once data has been input, it can be manipulated to view other outcomes. For example, if a cash-flow forecast or break-even chart has been created, new balances and break-even points can be calculated immediately by changing a few numbers.
- **Improved accuracy**: if data has been input correctly, the computer will automatically make the calculations, reducing the risk of errors.
- **Speed**: a computer is much quicker than a person at adding up and subtracting numbers.
- **Increased job satisfaction**: computers can often make an operative's job easier. For example, if an employee was asked to produce different scenarios for a cash-flow forecast, this would be extremely easy using a spreadsheet but quite tedious if they had to write out and add up the figures manually.

Disadvantages of using ICT

Disadvantages of using ICT for financial statements include:

- **Cost**: setting up the system could be a substantial part of a small business's budget.
- **Training**: may be needed to use the new systems. Some staff may feel threatened by new technology, fearing that it could mean job losses.
- **Accuracy**: data output is only ever as accurate as the information entered into the system.
- **Responsibility**: employees need to maintain the system which might mean reorganising job roles or employing new personnel.

Summary

- Wages/salary is the money an employee receives in exchange for their labour.
- Gross pay is the total amount of money an employee has earned prior to any deductions.
- Income tax is levied on earnings.
- National Insurance is deducted from earnings.
- Employees are legally entitled to receive a payslip.
- Employees can be paid in a variety of different ways – cash, cheques, bank transfers (BACS).
- Purchase orders are sent to the supplier outlining the goods to be purchased.
- Delivery notes accompany the goods. They outline what is in the parcel.
- Goods received notes are the customer's record of the goods received and the quality of those goods.
- An Invoice is sent to the customer demanding payment for goods already received.
- If goods have been returned to the supplier, the supplier will raise a credit note.
- A supplier will compile a Statement of Account for each customer they deal with on credit basis.
- Remittance advice appears at the end of the statement of account. It contains customer information and total amount owed.
- Errors in the completion of sales and purchase documents can have serious consequences.
- Net profit = total income minus total expenditure and is found in the profit and loss account.
- The balance sheet illustrates the value of the business and is calculated as total assets minus total liabilities.
- The cash flow forecast illustrates when money goes in and out of the business. It helps the business identify when they have insufficient cash.
- Break-even is the point where a business makes neither a loss nor a profit and is calculated as fixed assets divided by contribution. Contribution is calculated by deducting variable costs from the sales price.

Chapter 24

Marketing and sales

In this chapter you will be asked to demonstrate knowledge of some tasks associated with working in the marketing and sales functional area. You will need to understand how the marketing and sales functional area works together with other functional areas to ensure that key business activities are covered.

Activity

You are working for your local leisure centre which is about to launch a new high-tech gym. The marketing and sales department is responsible for creating awareness of this new facility.

In pairs, describe how the following functional areas would work with marketing and sales to ensure that the new gym is successfully launched:

- finance
- administration
- customer service.

In order to answer questions within the external examination, you will need knowledge and understanding of and skills in the following areas. (Most areas have been covered in previous chapters. Where this has occurred, you are directed to the relevant chapter.)

- The purpose of market research (Chapter 12, page 65).
- Identify different types of primary (field) market research (Chapter 12, pages 65–66).
- Identify different types of secondary (desk) research (Chapter 12, page 66).
- Suggest the most appropriate method of market research in a context and explain associated benefits to a business (Chapter 12, pages 65–69).
- Analyse and evaluate market research (Chapter 14, pages 90–91).

How can market research improve business performance?

When evaluating how the results of market research can improve future performance in a business, the first thing to discover is why a business undertakes market research; what do they want to find out?

Businesses spend time and money undertaking market research to find out different types of information, including the following:

- What do customers think about their products and services? Could they be improved/developed in order to gain market share and remain competitive? Do consumers want a new improved version of an old product, or something completely new?
- What about the durability of the product being sold? Does it actually do what it is supposed to do, and how long will it last?
- Price – what do consumers consider to be good value?
- What is the most effective way of promoting the business? Which promotional methods worked, and which were less successful?

Having collected the research, the business will then start analysing and evaluating the results.

- If consumers want the product to be adapted, developed or modernised, the business may need to consult with the research and development team to consider how these changes might be incorporated.

- If the durability of the product was shorter than expected, design teams would need to improve this in order to improve the overall quality of the product.

- If price was felt to be too high or the concept of quality was not being understood by consumers, the finance and marketing department would have to consider how these angles could be improved. Would it be possible to sell the product at a lower price, or could a promotional campaign be used to increase awareness of the quality of the product?

- If the research focused on raising awareness of the product, the marketing department will need to establish the most cost-effective way to promote the product in future. This might impact on the budget required and offered from the finance department.

The overriding aim of market research is to establish customers' opinions, needs and wants from a product. After gaining this information, the business will try to improve their performance in order to meet customers' expectations. In doing this, a business will hope to remain competitive, gain market share and ultimately increase their profits.

Promotion

You will need to study the following topic:

- Identify and explain the different ways businesses can promote goods and services – such as television, radio, newspapers, and sales promotions.

Information on this area is given in Chapter 15, The marketing mix, pages 97–109.

Advertising Standards Authority

The Advertising Standards Authority is responsible for the regulation of the content of advertisements, sales promotions and direct marketing in the UK. The authority has an extensive website www.asa.org.uk, which contains information on their role and remit. The information below has been adapted from this site.

The types of advertisement that are covered by the agency include:

- magazine and newspaper advertisements
- radio advertisements (not programmes or programme sponsorship)
- television shopping channels
- posters on legitimate poster sites (not fly posters)
- leaflets and brochures
- cinema commercials
- direct mail (advertising sent through the post and addressed to you personally)
- door-drops and circulars (advertising posted through the letter box without your name on)
- advertisements on the Internet including banner ads and pop-up ads (but no claims on companies' own websites)
- commercial email and SMS text message advertisements
- advertisements on CD ROMs, DVD, video and faxes.

Advertisements that are not covered by the ASA include:

- claims on websites (general statements made by websites should be reported to Trading Standards Department. The ASA will investigate online sales promotions such as special offers and competitions)
- television and radio programme content and sponsorship (dealt with by Ofcom)
- shop window displays
- in-store advertising
- political advertising.

(Details from www.asa.org.uk)

The main principles of the advertising standards codes are that advertisements should not mislead, cause harm or offend. The ASA judges ads against the rules laid down in the advertising codes. There are separate codes for TV, radio and non-broadcast advertising.

There are specific rules for certain products and marketing techniques. These include rules for alcoholic drinks, health and beauty, children, motoring, environmental claims, gambling, direct marketing and prize promotions. In order to ensure impartiality, the responsibility for writing the codes is taken by the advertising industry itself.

It only takes one complaint to start an investigation. Anybody can make a complaint, and most are made through the complaint form found on the ASA's website. Adjudications are published on the website on a Wednesday.

ASA adjunctions

Two complaints were made concerning an advertisement.

Advertisement

A TV advertisement for Sainsbury's showed rotating bubbles, each containing one of the following: baking potatoes, kiwi fruit, onions, plums and a packet of vegetable stir-fry. The bubbles were shown alongside other bubbles which contained the text 'Basics' and '55p'. The voice-over stated 'Right now at Sainsbury's, get on your way to five-a-day for the amazing price of 55p – healthy food, healthy deals.' On-screen text stated 'Selected stores & availability'.

Issue

Two viewers, one of whom was a registered dietician, challenged whether the advert was misleading as it suggested that potatoes counted towards the 'five-a-day' target for eating fruit and vegetables.

Response

Sainsbury's did not feel that their advertisement misled people. They believed that the voice-over clearly stated that the fruit and vegetables included in the advertisement would get you 'on your way to five-a-day'. They claimed that the advertisement was not designed to be educational but to draw consumers' attention to the reduced price of the range during the promotional period.

Assessment

The claim was upheld. The ASA noted that the advertisement showed a range of products, some of which would count towards the Government's 'five-a-day' recommendation, and some of which would not. The agency noted that Sainsbury's in-store and website information stated that potatoes did count towards the Government's 'five-a-day' campaign. The ASA decided that although the advertisement featured a wide variety of fruit and vegetables that would contribute to the Government's campaign, the voice-over coincided with the shot of the potatoes.

Action

The advertisement must not be shown in its current form.

(adapted from www.asa.org.uk, 17th December 2008)

The majority of the advertisements that we see or receive through the post conform to codes set by the industry. When the ASA upholds complaints, most advertisers agree to change or remove the advertisement, and media owners agree not to run advertisements that breach the codes. If a business fails to follow the guidance given by the agency, they will be referred to the Office of Fair Trading or Ofcom as appropriate.

A further role of the ASA is to monitor the content of advertisements independently. It also carries out research into specific sectors and public attitudes towards advertisements.

The Trades Description Act 1968 (or as amended)

You need to be able to explain the main features of the Trade Descriptions Act. This is covered in Chapter 13, page 80.

Analyse trends in promotional data

Businesses undertake a promotional campaign to increase the awareness and hopefully sales of their product or service. Having undertaken a promotional campaign, it is important to measure its potential success. There is no point in continuing to run a campaign if it is actually costing the business more than the subsequent increase in sales.

This is best illustrated with an example. A florist decided to undertake a local marketing campaign. The business ran advertisements in the local press for a month, and the total cost of the campaign was £500. The average profit on each bunch of flowers sold for £5 is £1. In order to recoup the cost of the advertising campaign, the florist would need to sell at least 500 extra bunches of flowers. If the campaign does not increase sales by at least this level, then it has not been successful and has actually cost the business money.

One way to check if a promotional campaign has been successful is to offer coupons and vouchers, as it is easy to count how many of these have been redeemed.

In general, a business will look at the sales figures for set periods prior to the campaign, during a similar time in previous years, and then compare these to sales figures immediately during and after the promotional campaign. This will provide some indication of the success of the promotion.

Case Study

Let us consider our florist again. After placing the advertisements in the newspapers throughout April, the owner decided to run a radio jingle during May.

Sales in April last year amounted to £12,000 and May £14,700. Following the newspaper advertisements, the sales for April slowly increased to £14,000, and then rapidly rose after the radio jingle was heard throughout May, peaking at £18,000.

One way to analyse these trends is to calculate the percentage change, which is the difference between the two years' sales figures, divided by the first year's sales figures.

April =
$$\frac{£14,000 - £12,000}{£12,000} \times 100 = 16.67\% \text{ increase in sales}$$

May =
$$\frac{£18,000 - £14,700}{£14,700} \times 100 = 22.45\% \text{ increase in sales}$$

This shows that the promotional campaign increased sales by 16.67% in April and then 22.5% in May. This gives an overall increase of 19.85% over the two months. Calculations are shown below.

April + May =
$$\frac{£32,000 - £26,700}{£26,700} \times 100 = 19.85\%$$

Activity

Examination practice

The florist is in the same street as a butcher. The butcher, Best Cuts, is also struggling with falling sales. More and more customers seem to be buying their meat at the local supermarket. Having heard about the success of the radio jingle, Peter (the owner) thinks he might try advertising using the same method.

Sales for February last year were £12,000 and March £11,800. The radio jingle cost £2,500 and ran through mid-January until mid-February. February's sales figures rose to £13,500 and March increased dramatically to £14,500.

- Evaluate if you think the radio jingle has been successful for Peter.
- Use a range of numerical techniques to illustrate your answer.
- Explain and show your workings.

Summary

- Undertaking market research helps businesses identify what customers think of a product/service, the durability of the product, the price customers are prepared to pay and what is the most effective way to promote the product/service.

- The Advertising Standards Authority is responsible for the regulation of the content of advertisements, sales promotion and direct marketing in the UK.

- Business must analyse whether a promotional campaign has been successful. In order to do this they need to gather data on the level of sales prior to the campaign, during the campaign and then three and six months later.

Chapter 25

Administration and ICT

For this part of the unit, you will be asked to demonstrate knowledge of some tasks associated with working in the administration and ICT functional area. You will need to understand how the administration and ICT functional area works together with other functional areas to ensure that key business activities are completed.

In Chapter 3, the administration and ICT functional area was covered. This chapter also covered key operational tasks associated with all of the functional areas. The final part of this section looked at what happened if functional areas do not operate efficiently. You should therefore have some knowledge of the areas that could be covered in the external examination.

This chapter contains other areas for which you require knowledge, understanding and skills before attempting the external examination. Some of these have been covered within previous chapters. Where this occurs, you will be directed to the relevant chapter.

Roles and responsibilities

Some of this theory has already been covered in Chapter 3. Below is a quick résumé of the knowledge that might be required for the external examination.

The main purpose of this functional area is to ensure that the business operates as efficiently as possible. This functional area supports the activities of all other departments. The key areas of responsibility are:

- **Information handling**: creation of all documents which leave or circulate around the business. Storage of documentation and subsequent retrieval as and when required. The department would also be required to record all incoming and outgoing documents.

- **Communications**: first response to telephone calls, diverting telephone calls to correct personnel, sending faxes and dealing with incoming and outgoing post.

- **Making arrangements**: this could range from booking hotels and flights to arranging parking spaces for visitors. The administration department is often responsible for arranging internal and external meetings. If the business is holding an external exhibition, it would fall upon the administration staff to ensure that all the correct arrangements had been made.

- **Stock control of stationery**: the administration staff organises stock so that for example printers do not run out of print cartridges, and there is sufficient paper to meet the needs of reprographics.

Due to the ever-increasing use of ICT to complete a range of administrative tasks, ICT technicians are now often found within the administration department. It is their role to ensure the smooth running of the computer systems.

Figure 25.1 outlines different tasks that are carried out by this functional area.

Figure 25.1 Tasks carried out by this functional area

Produce spreadsheets and update databases

There may be a question on the examination paper which requires you to explain how to use a simple spreadsheet and update a database. You will therefore need to practise both applications in order to ensure that you understand how to input and delete data in a spreadsheet or database.

Construct a letter, email, memorandum

Chapter 21 explored how to lay out and compose a memorandum and business-style letter (pages 130–131). Email composition was also covered in this chapter, on pages 134–135.

Telephone messages

Through the development of technology, the role of a traditional receptionist has changed dramatically. Often when a customer calls a business, their call is not answered by a person but by an automated machine, giving a number of options prior to reaching a member of staff. Sometimes when a customer calls a business, they will be connected immediately to the voice mail of the person they wish to speak to. Another person taking messages if the person required is not available is becoming a rare occurrence.

If you do take a call on behalf of someone else, it is important to record the message correctly. There are a number of items that you must record before passing the message on:

- date and time of the call

Activity

Examination practice

You are employed as an administrative clerk in a small family business that supplies solid fuel (coal) to domestic homes and businesses. The business experienced growth over the last six months because of the large increases in electricity and gas prices. Three members of staff (including yourself) work in the administration and ICT functional area. There are four lorry drivers including the owner.

You have a number of tasks in your in-tray for today, and the following events happen throughout the day. Decide whether you should compose an official letter, email or memorandum, or write out a telephone message.

(a) The owner of the business, Mr Barnes, wants to arrange a staff outing for the summer. It is suggested that the business organises a family barbeque at the owner's house. Wives, husbands, girlfriends, boyfriends and children are all welcome. The proposed date is 30th May. You have been asked to inform all staff, gauge their response and record how many people would like to come.

(b) At 9.15 am you receive a telephone call from Corrals, one of the business's suppliers. They would like Mr Barnes to call them back urgently on 02597 789320. Use today's date.

(c) Mr Barnes has asked you to respond to a customer who has written a letter of complaint. The letter was received two days ago, stating that Mrs Smethers had been promised her coal delivery by 11 am as she had to go to work. Unfortunately the lorry broke down and the delivery did not arrive until the next day. The driver delivered the coal as requested but left without payment. You are to apologise for the delay which was beyond the business's control, thank Mrs Smethers for her cheque which was enclosed with her complaint and communicate to her that you hope to continue supplying coal to her in the future.

- name of the caller and the name of their business if appropriate
- telephone number of the caller
- purpose of the call
- what the caller wants – do they want the recipient of the message to call back, or will they call back later?
- urgency of the call – does it need immediate attention?

You must also ensure that the message is passed on.

Welcoming visitors to a business

The welcome that a visitor receives will create an impression of a business

Activity

Working on your own, consider two occasions when you have had to enter a building as a visitor. What impression did you receive of the business, and how welcome were you made to feel?

Now compare your notes with a partner. Drawing upon your own experiences, list the factors which you think are important when welcoming visitors.

The welcome which a visitor receives when entering a business will create an everlasting impression. It is therefore vital that this impression is a positive one.

- When a visitor arrives at a business, they often need to park their car. It is therefore important that car-parking spaces are allocated to visitors. If there is nowhere to park, the visit has already become stressful.
- Having parked the car, the visitor will need clear directions on how to enter the building. Reception should be clearly signposted.
- Having found the entrance, the first person who the visitor will see is the receptionist. It is important that the visitor is acknowledged as soon as they enter the building. They should be dealt with quickly and efficiently. The visitor will need to sign a visitors' book and may be asked to wear a visitors' badge. These requirements are necessary in order to ensure the health and safety of the visitor.
- Once the visitor has been signed in, there should be somewhere aesthetically pleasing for them to sit. The person they are required to see should be notified of their arrival immediately. If the visitor is going to be kept waiting, they should be informed of the delay. Refreshments might also be offered at this stage, especially if a delay is expected to take place.

Visitor information fact sheet

Tourist attractions and hotels often have visitor information fact sheets. The purpose is to inform visitors or potential visitors of the facilities that are available. In the case of a hotel, this could include the times of breakfast, dinner and lunch, the opening times of the bar and any leisure facilities.

Individual tourist attractions use information leaflets as part of their promotional strategy. These are usually left in areas which are frequented by people visiting the locality, and also in the local tourist information centres. The fact sheets include information on the opening times of the attraction, entry prices and some information on the type of facilities available.

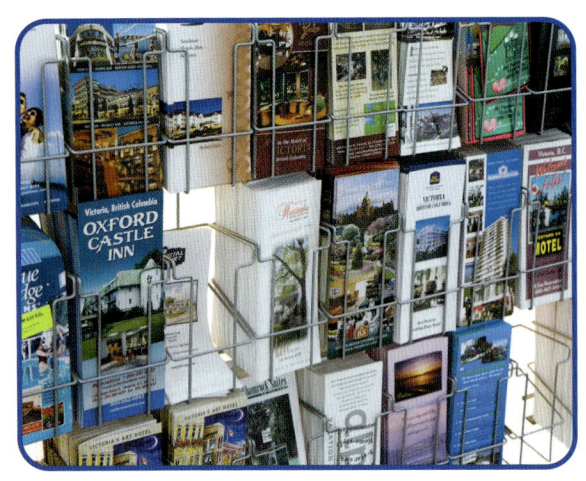

Fact sheets for tourist attractions and hotels should contain different types of information

Tourist information centres use visitor information fact sheets to provide information on what is available within their location. The link below is the fact sheet provided by the Welsh Tourist Information Board, which aims to attract visitors to the area: www.industry.visitwales.co.uk/upload/pdf/Making_most_TIC_eng010705.pdf.

A business might produce a fact sheet to outline to visitors what the business does, and to give contact details. The fact sheet might also include health and safety information, for example how to evacuate the building in case of a fire.

Activity

Examination practice

Collect a visitor information sheet from a local tourist attraction.

Evaluate how this could be improved.

- Does it contain all the information necessary to encourage you to go?
- Are the opening times, prices and directions on how to get there included?
- What else do you think should be included?
- Are the colour scheme and images effective?

Record-keeping systems

Businesses are required to maintain records for a wide range of reasons.

- Financial records must be kept for a set number of years in order to comply with financial regulations.
- Businesses need to keep track of previous and current customers in order to retain and gain their business.
- A business would need to keep records of the stock it has available in order to monitor production levels.
- A record of visitors to the business is required in order to comply with health and safety legislation. The information should consist of the date, time of arrival, the person whom the visitor was seeing, car registration number and the time the visitor left. This information could be analysed to see how many visitors the business has and the reasons for the visit.

The volume of paperwork in today's businesses is probably less than ten years ago, because of the development of technology. Even so there are very few paperless offices in existence. Hard copies of documents are often still required. It is therefore important that a business establishes an efficient and effective method of filing and retrieving documents.

Filing cabinets

Filing cabinets come in many shapes and sizes, and provide a good system for filing paperwork. Files can be organised alphabetically, geographically, numerically or in date order. In fact, systems can be totally personalised to suit individual businesses. Paper-based filing is a time-consuming task and cabinets take up space within the office. On the positive side, documents are often easily located, and security is relatively easy as all filing cabinets are fitted with locks. Most metal filing cabinets are also fireproof.

Electronic filing systems

Computerised filing is relatively easy, although retrieval of documents can be problematic if the file names cannot be remembered.

Access to documents can be extended if computers are networked within the business. This enables a business to make some information available to all or certain members of staff. Access can be limited to confidential files through the use of passwords.

If files have not been backed up, documents could be lost through computer failure. It is therefore important that documents are backed up regularly.

The impact of ICT on this functional area

ICT has probably had one of the greatest impacts on how the administration department operates in the modern business world. Computers have enabled everybody (rather than trained secretaries) to produce accurate business documents.

Word processing has enabled administrative staff to produce multiple documents easily, without typographical errors. Mail merge has enabled the production of personalised letters to a range of customers. Templates can be designed, saved and used many times, making the production of letters, reports and memorandums much quicker.

The ICT functional area has evolved with the growth of computer use. Its aim is to support the computer system within a business, to ensure that everything runs smoothly for 24 hours a day, seven days a week. The ICT department is responsible for the maintenance of existing computer equipment and the installation of new software and hardware. This functional area could also be responsible for development and maintenance of the company website. This department exists as a direct result of continued growth in the use of computers and associated software.

Summary

- See Unit 22 summary for roles and responsibilities of this department.

- Business letters, emails and memorandums must be completed in the correct format, ensuring that there are no spelling or grammatical errors.

- Telephone messages must be recorded accurately. Make sure you take the caller's number and what action the caller wants to be taken – someone to call them back, will they call again. Don't forget to record the date and time of the call.

- The welcome a visitor receives when entering a business will create an everlasting impression. It is therefore vital that this impression is a positive one.

- Visitor information sheets are mainly used by the tourist industry to inform visitors of the facilities available within an attraction. They can also be used within a business to outline the business's mission statement, health and safety policy and a map of the different departments.

- Record keeping systems can be set up in a multitude of ways. The key is that people must be able to locate documents quickly and efficiently. They must be kept securely and safely in order to meet the demands of the Data Protection Act.

- ICT has had a major impact on the work of the administration department. Computers have enabled everybody to produce accurate business documents which have an impact on the type of work some administrators now undertake.

Chapter 26

Customer service

In this chapter you will be asked to demonstrate knowledge of some tasks associated with working in the customer service functional area. You will need to understand how the customer service functional area works together with other functional areas to ensure that key business activities are completed.

In Chapter 13, the importance of maintaining excellent customer service was discussed. It is recommended that you refresh your memory of this chapter before continuing with this part of the unit.

Why businesses need to keep their customers happy

Chapter 13 looked at the consequences of not keeping customers happy. The reverse happens when customers feel that the business meets and even exceeds customer expectations.

In order to achieve maximum customer satisfaction, businesses have to understand the differing needs of their customers. Having established what customers expect from the business, they would hope to retain their current customers and gain new ones.

Let us consider a leisure centre as an example. The centre discovered that families were staying away because there were no family changing facilities. It therefore decided to re-arrange the facilities they currently had in order to segregate an area especially for family changing. The temperature in this area was raised so that young children did not become cold, and playpens were purchased so that young toddlers could be contained while their father or mother dried themselves. Families gradually began to return to the centre as their needs had been met. They also told their friends and families, and new customers started arriving as well. The centre also increased its reputation and became well-known for being family-focused.

While undertaking this development, the leisure centre had to be careful that it did not deter any of its other customers, for example serious competitive swimmers. Facilities for these had to be maintained as well. It is pointless for a business to meet the needs of one group of people and then upset another group.

Different types of customer services

Businesses offer a range of services, information and advice in order to meet the needs and expectations of their customers.

Activity

Working in pairs, write down the services that your local leisure service offers its customers.
- Identify how the centre conveys information to its customers – on notice boards or leaflets for example?
- How does this information help to meet customer expectations?

In the external examination you will be required to comment on how customer service could be improved in a given context. In order to do this well, it is often best to start evaluating the customer's experience from the moment they approach the business, and what they would expect to happen from this point. Try to put yourself in the position of the customer. For example imagine that you are a young parent with a small child who has just arrived at the local supermarket to do the weekly shopping. Outlined below are your needs when you arrive:

Parent and child parking is one example of a customer service

- Car-parking space with plenty of room for opening the back doors to lift the child into and out of the safety seat.
- Shopping trolley with a child seat and safety harness.
- Wide, clearly signposted aisles.
- Toilet facilities which include baby changing facilities in both male and female toilets.
- Staff available to give advice on the location of items.
- Help with packing the shopping.
- Ease of payment.
- Customer service desk if goods need to be returned or complaints made.

An electrical store selling washing machines or televisions would have to develop some of the services listed above in order to meet the needs of their customers. Sales assistants would need expert knowledge of the goods being sold so that customers could be given advice prior to purchase. Large goods may need to be delivered, and this option would need to be discussed with the customer. A unique selling point of a business might be free local delivery. Guarantees would also form part of the sale, and this information would need to be conveyed to the customer.

All businesses need to have a system in place to deal with complaints. It is important to remember the saying, 'the customer is always right'. Complaints made by all customers must be taken seriously and a resolution found that suits both the customer and business. As mentioned earlier, a complaint dealt with efficiently will often mean that the customer will return to the business.

Different types of businesses will need to supply their customers with different types of information. Businesses offering a service need to supply their customers with a price list, opening times and the services on offer. A business selling products will focus on what the product is capable of doing, its advantages and disadvantages over alternative products.

Improving customer service

Using the information provided in a scenario, you may be required to suggest improvements to customer service within your external examination. The current situation will influence your evaluation. Below are some points you should consider when making recommendations on how to improve the customer service offered by a business:

- What product/service is the business offering?
- Who are the target customers?
- What are the needs of the customers?
- How many of these are being met?
- If some needs are not being met, how could the business change in order to meet them?

Consequences of ineffective customer service

This area was covered in Chapter 13, pages 83–84.

Responding to a customer enquiry/complaint

Writing messages, letters and emails has been covered in Chapter 13. Within this chapter, you were also asked to reply to a letter of complaint. When dealing with a complaint through a written medium, it is important to remember the points below:

- Thank the writer for their complaint.
- Always acknowledge the complaint being made.
- Do not accuse the writer of exaggeration or inaccuracies.
- Always offer a solution or compromise.
- Invite the writer to make further contact if they wish to discuss the matter further.

Explaining emergency procedures

Businesses have a wide variety of different emergency procedures depending on the nature of their business; for example, a business manufacturing fireworks would have a very strict code on what to do in case of fire, and how to evacuate the building.

All businesses need to have systems in place in order to deal with emergency situations such as fire alarms, gas leaks and bomb scares. This will involve the evacuation of the building. As part of health and safety training, all businesses need to inform their employees how to evacuate the building, should an emergency occur. Employees need to recognise the signal that alters them to these situations (usually the continuous ringing of the fire bell). Employees must be aware of the route to their evacuation point. This is usually a car park or other safe area in the near vicinity of the building.

Businesses must run regular evacuation practices to ensure that all employees are familiar with the procedures in place. Businesses must also ensure that visitors are aware of the evacuation procedures. Fire doors must be clearly labelled and easy to see, and evacuation instructions should be visible on notice boards.

On the back of hotel bedrooms there are always evacuation procedures so that guests are fully aware of what they need to do in case of an emergency.

Under RIDDOR (Reporting of Injuries, Diseases and Dangerous Occurrences Regulations 1995), employers are required to report work-related accidents, diseases and dangerous occurrences. An employer needs to report:

- death
- major injuries
- accidents resulting in over three days' absence due to injury
- diseases
- dangerous occurrences
- gas incidents.

Under the Health and Safety (First Aid) Regulation 1981, all employers must have a fully stocked first aid kit. They are also required to record all injuries or accidents in an accident book.

Customer service data analysis

Within the in-tray exercise in the external examination, you may be asked to analyse some customer service data, which may have been collected through the use of questionnaires. You will need to draw some conclusions from this data. For example, customers may be stating that they are unhappy with a particular aspect of the business. You will then need to consider how this could be rectified in order to keep customers happy.

Activity

Describe the fire procedures that are currently in place within your own school or college. Where do you have to congregate? How do you know which doors to exit by and where to report? How is this information conveyed to you?

Summary

- If customers' needs are not met they are unlikely to return to the business.
- Customer service can take many different formats depending on the type of business involved.
- To improve customer service businesses will need to find out their customers' opinions on the service already available.
- A complaint dealt with fairly and efficiently by a business will often cement the relationship between the customer and the business.
- Businesses must ensure that training to deal with emergency procedures is part of health and safety training.

Activity

Examination practice

Sally runs a small café in the town centre that has a regular clientele. Originally the café focused their early morning trade on serving a traditional English breakfast. However, competition has increased. Within a half a mile radius, Starbucks have moved in and McDonald's also offer breakfast options. Sally diversified into specialised coffee and muffins to attract customers away from Starbucks. The café still offers the traditional English breakfast for regular customers.

Diversification has proved highly successful, with the number of customers passing through increasing dramatically. However, this increase has meant that standards of cleanliness have begun to decline, as staff cannot keep tables clean as well as keeping up with serving customers. The only waitress is now mainly occupied behind the counter, serving coffees.

A week ago, Sally received a letter from one of her regular customers, Mr Ted Brownlow, who has eaten breakfast at the cafe for the last five years. Ted was very unhappy: he had to wait 15 minutes, tables were dirty and the friendly banter of the good old days has disappeared. This prompted Sally to ask some customers to complete a customer survey. She was really taken aback by the customers' replies:

- 98 per cent considered the food to be good value for money
- 86 per cent rated the food as excellent quality
- 50 per cent thought the service was much too slow
- 47 per cent stated that tables were not cleared quickly enough, making it difficult to find somewhere to sit
- 73 per cent stated that the customer service they received was inadequate and could be improved.

1. Describe the problems facing the café.
2. Using the customer service data above, analyse the main problems facing the café.
3. Evaluate how you think customer service could be improved within the café to meet customer needs identified in (2) above.
4. Evaluate the consequences to the café if it fails to meet the needs of its customers.
5. Assume the role of Sally and compose a letter to Mr Ted Brownlow, explaining what you intend to do to improve customer service and make things more like the 'old days'. In order to complete the letter you will need to design a logo for the café. Make up addresses for the café and Mr Brownlow which are relevant to the area in which you live.

Chapter 27
›Production

In this chapter you will be asked to demonstrate knowledge of some tasks associated with working in the production functional area. You will need to understand how the production functional area works together with other functional areas to ensure that key business activities are completed.

The practical 'in-tray' element will require you to have knowledge, understanding and skills in order to do the following:

- Suggest the most appropriate method of production in a given context.
- Make an informed choice on the design of a new product to meet the needs of a target market based on research provided. You will be supplied with all the relevant data and three possible different methods of production. You will need to select and justify your choice of production method.

The role of the production department is to ensure that products are produced in the right quantities, at the right time and for the lowest cost. One of the major decisions that has to be made is how the product should be produced.

The external examination will require you to have knowledge of the three different methods of production.

- job
- batch
- flow
- cell.

Job production

This method of production is for specific 'one-off' individual items. Products are made from start to finish to the customer's own specification and design. There is no repetition of orders, and production has to be planned around each individual order as it arrives.

Each order has to be costed individually. It can be difficult to have standard costs as each product is unique.

Job production requires a wide range of equipment. Machines are often grouped together according to function. Individual items move around the machinery in a variety of different ways, thereby creating a unique item.

This is often the most labour-intensive form of production, as each item is individual and requires a high degree of technical skill. Items produced exclusively for a client will often be very expensive because they are unique.

Management of this method of production is complex due to the uniqueness of each product. Resources have to be planned carefully to ensure that orders are met on time, and that machine and labour time is used effectively in order to minimise unit costs. Motivation within the workforce is often high as each order is different, and pride can be taken in producing high-quality individual items which meet the customer's specific requirements. Examples of this kind of production could include a commissioned picture, birthday cake or wedding dress.

Characteristics of job production

- Focus on the customer rather than what the market demands.
- Expensive, unique product.
- Flexible, motivated and highly skilled workforce.
- Machinery and equipment to meet the demands of a variety of different tasks.
- Careful management to ensure that resources are available to meet demand.

Batch production

This method of production bears similarities to both flow and job production.

Repetition is involved, as identical products are made in set numbers. Unit costs are therefore lower than in job production, as a number of identical products are being produced at one time.

Each batch of products moves through the production process simultaneously. When a sufficient number of a particular batch has been produced, production is then switched to another product. This may involve making changes to the production line to allow for subtle changes between the different batches. The time in which the machines are not producing because they are being altered or cleaned between batches is known as 'downtime', and has to be factored into production scheduling.

Batch production allows a business to meet demand for products when they are required, and to keep ahead of changes in customers' tastes and fashions. A good example is the production of wallpaper. Different designs can be made according to customers' current demands. Bakeries also use batch production, switching between different types of breads and cakes.

One of the problems with batch production is that it can lead to holding high levels of stock. A variety of different stock is required for each batch of products produced. This will take up space within the factory, and also ties up money in stock that is waiting to be used. There is also the possibility that stock could deteriorate or become damaged, increasing the expenses of the business.

Characteristics of batch production

- Lower unit costs than job production, with lower priced products.
- Higher proportion of semi-skilled or unskilled labour.
- Higher capital costs, with more machinery involved in the production process.
- Economies of scale: due to the increase in production numbers the business may decide to purchase raw materials in bulk securing discounts. This means that the cost of raw materials per unit reduces.
- Specialised machinery and equipment required because of highly automated production and assembly lines.
- Production process layout designed to minimise movement of parts and sub-assemblies.
- Easier to apply budgeting techniques as products being produced are standard.

Flow production

This is used for mass-produced items that are standardised in shape, size and characteristics, for example televisions. Items pass along a conveyor belt where each item is subjected to a series of repetitive processes. Car manufacturers also make use of this kind of production method.

As large numbers of identical items are being produced continuously, the overall unit cost of each item is reduced. Businesses are able to purchase raw materials in bulk and therefore benefit from economies of scale.

The development of specialised production lines has led to an increased use of automated machinery, which greatly increases the initial capital cost of production (capital costs refer to the large sums of money required to buy the machinery required to produce the product). Machinery is able to work for longer periods of time without needing a rest, and consistency can be guaranteed. Problems do arise if machinery breaks down. This can cause long periods of downtime on the factory floor, when no items are being produced and employees have no work to do.

Using machines means that fewer employees are required. Flow production also enables the business to make maximum use of the division of labour. Each person on the assembly line only has a number of small tasks to perform, before the product moves on to the next stage of production. The requirement for skilled labour is therefore greatly reduced. The workforce can become demotivated as jobs are extremely repetitive.

In order to become very effective, careful organisation and planning are needed to ensure that production flows continuously from one process to the next without any 'bottle-necks' occurring.

Due to the complex nature of the production line, a business must be sure that the items they are producing are in sufficient demand. This demand must also be stable, enabling the market to remain profitable. Products such as Mars Bars are mass-produced, with the manufacturer aware of current and past sales trends.

Characteristics of flow production

- High capital investment costs.
- Low skilled or unskilled labour required.
- Repetitive work, which could cause demotivation within the workforce.
- Lower priced product due to benefits of mass production and economies of scale.
- Specialist machinery and equipment which is inflexible.
- Production layout designed to minimise disruption in the flow of production.
- Highly automated production and assembly lines.
- Easy to apply budgeting techniques as products being produced are all the same.

Cell production

One of the problems with flow production is the possibility of the workforce becoming demotivated because of the repetitive nature of their work. One way to overcome this is to organise the production line in a group of self-contained units, known as cells. Each cell is responsible for a significant part of the finished article. Rather than each employee only carrying out one small task, each is multi-skilled in a number of roles. This helps avoid boredom and enables the workforce to become multi-skilled.

Cell production is all about 'team working'. Team spirit is developed and each worker becomes committed to the work of the team, thereby improving working relationships and the quality of the finished article. The cell is often responsible for the organisation of staff rotas, holiday and sickness cover, and could become involved in the recruitment and selection of new team members. Cells deal with other cells as if they were customers, which ensures that the finished product sent down the production line is of high quality: cell one would not want cell two to send back their completed unit because the quality was insufficient.

Potential problems with cell production

In order for cell production to work efficiently, management has to consider and overcome a number of possible problems.

- The workforce has to be prepared to work in teams and support one another.
- The business may have to change the way it currently orders stock in order to meet the needs of cell production. More stock may need to be held.
- Cell production may mean that machinery is not used as efficiently and intensively as before.
- Allocation of work to each cell has to be managed carefully to ensure that each team has sufficient work.
- Too much work might overwhelm teams and reduce the quality of items being produced.

- Recruitment and selection processes must support the concept of team work.

Characteristics and benefits of cell production

- Team working can improve working relationships, with communication enabling employees to work more efficiently.
- The workforce becomes multi-skilled which could make them more adaptable to production changes in the future.
- A motivated workforce takes a pride in their work.
- Quality of individual item improved – each cell takes 'ownership' of each unit produced.

How to choose the method of production

When analysing the type of production process a business should use, the following points should be considered.

- The nature of the market – is this large or small? Will the market-place sustain thousands of items being produced on a daily or weekly basis? Does the customer want exactly the same product many times? If so, flow production could be a suitable method. If the market wants a unique one-off product, job production would be more suitable.
- Can the business afford the high capital costs involved with developing a fully automated production line? If so, the business could start to move towards batch or flow production if there is sufficient demand for their products.
- Is the business able to produce and sell sufficient items in order to bulk-buy raw materials? This will help cut unit costs as the production line becomes automated. This could support either batch or flow production methods.

Evaluating different types of production

In reality, the differences between the different types of production methods are slowly becoming blurred. With the increase in the use of computerisation within a business, items produced on an automated assembly line can be individualised according to a customers' wishes; for example, on the Ford production line in Swaythling, each Transit van has been sold prior to manufacture. Due to the just-in-time stock control system, specialist features can be included on the van as it travels around the production line; for example, special seats can be fitted, and the vehicle can be left- or right-hand drive.

In the past, the manufacture of individual items has been very important to the survival of the small business. They could be under threat because of the capability of complex, computerised robots that are now used in manufacturing. There will always be some demand for small-scale highly-skilled businesses to manufacture truly unique products.

Evaluating the impact of technology on production methods

Technology has greatly changed the way that manufacturing is carried out. It has greatly reduced the workforce. The complexity and diversity of robots within the production process has changed the skills required by employees. The need for highly-skilled craftsmen has probably been reduced, but employees need to understand how to control and work the computer system that controls the robots.

The ever-increasing flexibility of machines has also meant that businesses are able to individualise items being manufactured on a production line.

The downside to automated production is the huge investment that is needed in order to establish an efficient production line. This could deter small businesses from being able to compete against established businesses.

Activity

Examination question

Sonny wanted two new dog kennels and runs. He had looked on the Internet to find possible suppliers. He wanted to know that the kennel had been manufactured by the supplier. As this was going to be quite an expensive venture, he decided to order the single dog kennel and run first. If this one was of sufficient quality, he would then order the double dog kennel and run.

After looking at different websites, he contacted the first company, Dogs R Us. They offered three different ranges of kennels, and each range was made either in single or double sizes. When he telephoned the company, they said that as all kennels were made on the site, the customer just had to order the kennel and it would be delivered within six weeks.

Sonny was happy with the initial arrangements. Unfortunately, things did not turn out as expected. The kennel took 16 weeks to arrive, and was then only delivered after Sonny threatened the company with Trading Standards. The kennel was of good quality and Sonny was happy with the end product.

This experience had discouraged Sonny from ordering the double dog kennel from the same company. A friend recommended a local company, Sheds For All Occasions, who normally only manufacture sheds. Sonny explained what he wanted, and took some drawings and measurements with him. The owner of the business was interested in the project and said he could build what Sonny wanted, which would be delivered and erected within three weeks. The owner rang on a few occasions to check measurements and requests. The kennel arrived on time and Sonny was pleased with the result. It had been a real pleasure to deal with this second business, as they had kept their word and supplied a high-quality product.

1 What type of production method did Dogs R Us use?
2 What are the advantages and disadvantages of this type of production method?
3 What type of production methods did Sheds For All Occasions use?
4 What are the advantages and disadvantages of this type of production method?
5 How do you think Sheds for all Occasions met the customer's expectations?
6 If Sheds For All Occasions wanted to expand into building dog kennels, what type of production methods would you recommend they use? Justify your answer.

Summary

- Job production is the production of specific 'one-off' individual items
- Batch production involves the production of a number of items on a repetitive basis.
- Flow production is used for mass-produced items that are standardised in shape, size and characteristics.
- Cell production is not a type of production but how employees are grouped together on the production line. Each cell deals with a particular part of the production process with individuals undertaking a variety of different roles.

BUSINESS AND YOU

UNIT 4

Introduction

The most important asset for any business is its employees. Without enthusiastic, motivated employees, businesses may never be able to realise their true potential. When recruiting new staff, businesses must take care to ensure that the right people are appointed through a carefully considered recruitment and selection process.

In order to complete the controlled assessment for this unit, you need to gain an insight into the recruitment and selection processes from a number of perspectives. As part of your controlled assessment, you will be required to select and then apply for an advertised post. These posts will be located in the Controlled Assessment booklet supplied by OCR. You will be required to undertake the following tasks:

- Complete application documents in response to an advertised job role.
- Investigate and consider a number of key issues related to the recruitment and selection process.
- Produce an induction programme for a new employee.
- Investigate the skills required for a more supervisory position.

Activity

One of the roles of the human resources functional area is to support all members of staff while they are at work. This can take many formats, as we shall see throughout this chapter. A similar role is carried out in the majority of schools through a tutorial or pastoral care system.

Within your school, someone will be responsible for the pastoral care of pupils. Spend a few minutes considering the services which this part of the school offers to pupils.

- Identify all the different help and support that this department offers pupils.
- Explain how you think this role helps pupils settle into school when they first arrive.
- Analyse why this role is important within a school. What benefits does it bring to the smooth running of the school and to individual pupils?

Chapter 28
The human resources functional area

The human resources functional area has an important role within any large business. It is responsible for the recruitment and selection of employees, and is also heavily involved in ensuring the welfare and safety of all employees. The department has to ensure that all equal opportunity legislation is maintained and that no employee is victimised or suffers harassment while at work.

This chapter explores the main activities of the human resources functional area.

Employing and maintaining staff

> **Activity**
>
> Ask ten different people to define the role of the human resources functional area. Make a note of your different answers. Compare these to the rest of the class's responses.

Is this the right image for an interview?

Most people who answered your question probably stated that the main responsibility of the human resources functional area is the recruitment of staff. We must not forget that the most important asset of any business is its staff. It is therefore very important that the process used to employ these employees is fit for purpose.

The process of recruiting a successful employee is expensive and takes time. If the wrong person is employed, the consequences are often costly and the whole process has to start again. An unhappy, demotivated member of staff will not work to their full capacity, and can often disrupt a whole team.

The recruitment process

The recruitment process starts with the identification of a job vacancy. This could be created by a member of staff leaving, a member of staff gaining an internal promotion or the business expanding. Having established that a job vacancy does exist, the next step is to decide what the new employee will be required to do.

These decisions will help formulate the job advertisement and job description. These two documents outline the duties, skills and qualifications which the applicant will need in order to fulfil the vacancy.

The next step is to decide how applicants will apply for the position. Will they need to write a letter of application, complete an application form, or simply telephone for an interview?

If the applicants are required to apply in writing, the next step is to consider how many people will reach the interview stage. This process is known as shortlisting, and involves matching the applicant's skill, qualities and qualifications against those outlined in the job description and person specification. Applicants whose qualifications and experience meet the requirements will be called for interview.

After the interview stage there will, hopefully, be a successful candidate who will be offered the post.

This process is further illustrated in Figure 28.1.

The recruitment process is examined in more detail in Chapter 29.

Staff retention

Having employed a new member of staff, it is very important that they remain within the business for as long as possible. This will ensure that the business runs efficiently with little disruption to staffing.

In order to retain staff, the business must ensure that their working environment is suitable and their needs and wants are met, where possible, for example supplying a member of staff who works at a computer with a special chair if they suffer from back problems. Caring for staff also means ensuring that they are safe within the workplace and that the work they undertake is valued by their immediate managers and owners of the business. A quick 'thank you' and words of encouragement go a long way to making staff feel valued when they have made an extra effort.

If an employee becomes unhappy within the workplace, it is the responsibility of the human resources functional area to ensure that the matter is dealt with swiftly and fairly. The functional area will be responsible for designing grievance procedures and ensuring that they are accessible to all staff. If an employee wishes to take up a grievance with their employee, the process must be fair and the outcome will hopefully meet the needs of both parties.

Labour turnover

One way to measure how effectively a business is retaining its staff is to calculate the labour turnover. This measures the number of employees who leave in a year against the total number of permanent employees. If the percentage is high,

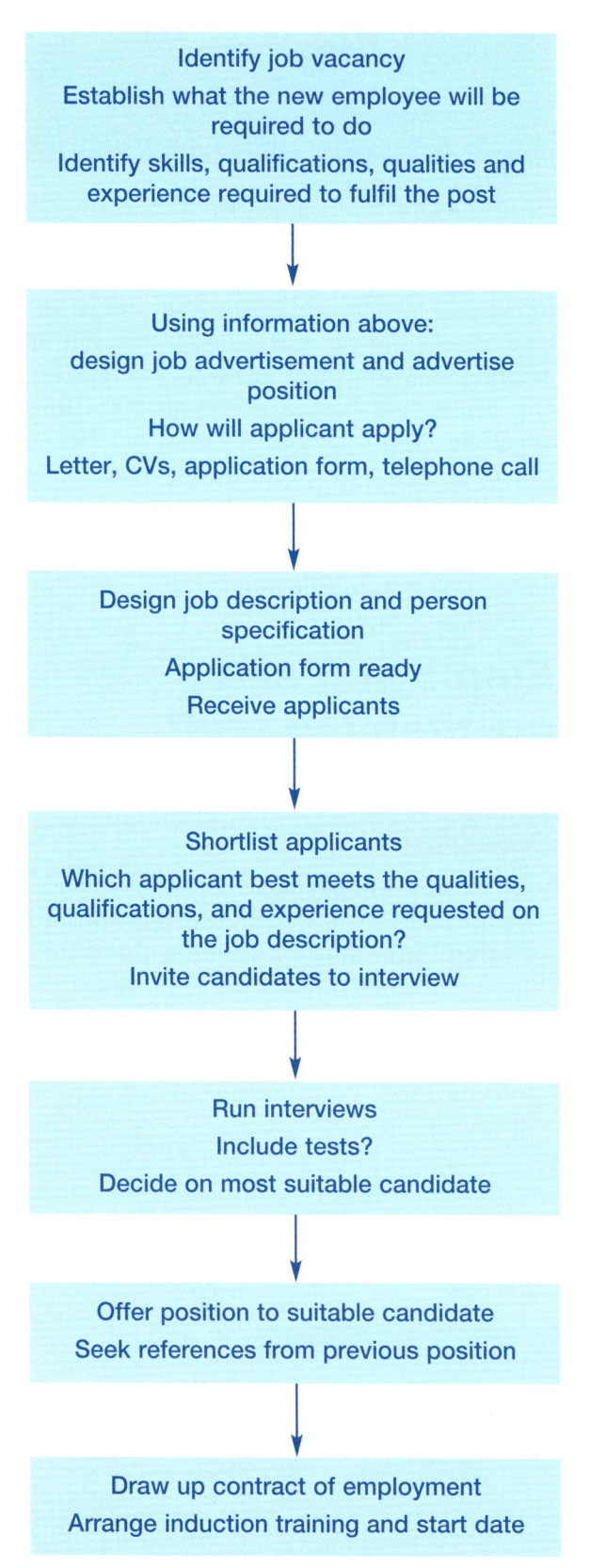

Identify job vacancy
Establish what the new employee will be required to do
Identify skills, qualifications, qualities and experience required to fulfil the post

↓

Using information above:
design job advertisement and advertise position
How will applicant apply?
Letter, CVs, application form, telephone call

↓

Design job description and person specification
Application form ready
Receive applicants

↓

Shortlist applicants
Which applicant best meets the qualities, qualifications, and experience requested on the job description?
Invite candidates to interview

↓

Run interviews
Include tests?
Decide on most suitable candidate

↓

Offer position to suitable candidate
Seek references from previous position

↓

Draw up contract of employment
Arrange induction training and start date

Figure 28.1 The recruitment process

this would indicate that the business is not very good at retaining its employees. If the ratio is low, there could be two possible reasons. One is that the business has created a good working environment and current employees have no desire to leave. The other is that unemployment is high and as such employees are unable to find an alternative position.

Training for new employees

Identify training needs

When a new member of staff is recruited, they should have the necessary qualifications and experience to tackle their new job role. However, the new employee's skills and experience might not match exactly the tasks they will have to perform in the position; for example, although the employee is computer-literate, they might not know how to work a specific computer program that now forms part of their new position. To develop this example, a hotel might have specialist software for reservations. The newly recruited employee has used a reservations system in their last job but it was not the same as this one. They will therefore need to be trained on the new program.

In addition to this, it is important that a business keeps its staff up-to-date in order to remain competitive in the workplace. Technology, working practices and even legislation frequently change. If a business is to ensure that the staff are able to cope with demands made upon them, it will need to ensure that training is offered as and when required. A well-trained member of staff will not only be more efficient but will also suffer less stress while carrying out their duties.

Appraisal

Individual training needs can be identified during the employee's yearly appraisal. An appraisal involves the employee's line manager discussing with the employee on a one-to-one basis their progress throughout the year. They will review targets that were set for the previous year and evaluate whether or not they have been achieved. New targets will be agreed for the following year. These targets help employees stay motivated, and can be linked to the development of skills which could ultimately help them achieve promotion in the future. The aim of an appraisal is to encourage employees to review their own progress, and consider where and what they would like to be doing in the future.

Training methods

Having identified the training needs of the staff, the human resources functional area must then organise this training in the most cost-effective way. Training can either be run within the business by the business, which is known as 'on-the-job training'. Alternatively employees can be sent away for training, which is referred to as 'off-the-job training'. Sending employees away on training courses is often an expensive option, so businesses have to ensure that any money spent in this way will be a real benefit to the business.

There are a number of different ways that staff can be trained, which are summarised in Table 28.1 on the next page.

Procedures, laws and legislation

Employers have a duty of care towards all their employees. Part of this process is supported through the legal system, which ensures that employees are fairly treated while in the workplace. Employment law is covered in detail in Chapter 30, pages 208–216.

Ensuring that legislation is followed correctly is the role of the human resources functional area. This department is responsible for interpreting the law and compiling documentation which outlines to employees their rights and responsibilities within the workplace. Should an employee feel they have been unfairly treated and decide to take

Type of training	Description
On the job: job shadowing	This involves working alongside another employee who shows the new recruit what to do. This is a relatively cheap way of training the new employee, but they can learn good and bad habits at the same time. The effectiveness of the training is dependent on the ability of the employee who has been tasked to take on this role. Have they actually been trained? Are they aware of what is expected of them? An example of job shadowing is an experienced employee showing a new employee how to operate a till.
Computer-based training	Employees can be asked to work through a computerised program to train them in a certain aspect of their job. This type of training is quite common with health and safety training. The advantage is that the program can be used by a large number of new recruits, and is relatively cheap to run and easy to organise. The disadvantage is that the employee has to be prepared to engage with the program.
In-house training	A member of staff within an organisation could be allocated the task of training other employees. This could be linked to the release of new legislation. For example, the Sex Discrimination Act has recently been updated, requiring businesses to pass this information on to all their employees. An in-house training session would ensure that everybody was aware of the new rules for compliance.
Off the job: external courses	This involves members of staff attending courses which are run by external agencies away from the business. The costs of this type of training are relatively high. The employee will have to be paid, and is not actively doing any work while they are attending the course. Travel expenses will also have to be paid and the cost of the actual training could be quite high. On the positive side, employees often enjoy leaving their place of work; being sent away on a course can make them feel special and appreciated. This can help to maintain motivation and enthusiasm. Employees are often more receptive to the information they are being given at these types of events. Another advantage is that the employee who attended the course can pass this information to their colleagues upon their return.

Table 28.1 Different training methods

their case to an industrial tribunal, a member of staff from the human resources functional area would represent the business. This person would have been involved in the whole procedure and would defend the position of the company.

Providing a safe working environment

The main legislation that covers safety in the workplace is the Health and Safety at Work Act 1974. This Act clearly sets out the responsibilities of both employers and employees in ensuring a safe working environment. Although it is the responsibility of the employer to ensure that all employees work in a safe environment, it is also the responsibility of the employee to ensure that they work and behave safely within that environment. The Health and Safety at Work Act is covered in more detail in Chapter 30, pages 214–216.

Internal security systems are an important part of ensuring safety within the workplace. Employees need to know that unwelcome visitors cannot enter their place of work.

> **Activity**
>
> Consider how your school/college ensures your personal safety.
> - Describe the health and safety policy of your school/college.
> - How is security maintained within your school/college?
> - Describe how the health and safety policy could be improved.
> - Analyse and evaluate the effectiveness of the security systems in place within your school. How could these be improved? Justify your answer.

It is often the role of the human resources functional area to ensure that security within the workplace is maintained. This might involve the employment of security staff, installation of CCTV and organisation of night patrols to ensure the security of the building. Security systems can also include the issuing of photographic identification which must be shown and worn when in the building. It can also involve the use of swipe cards which allow access into certain sections of the building. All of these areas will be under the control of the human resources functional area.

Summary

- Employees are one of a business's most important assets. It is important that the correct people are employed and that they are looked after to ensure they remain with the business.
- The recruitment process starts with the identification of a job vacancy. The next stage is to work out what tasks the new employee will be expected to undertake.
- From this two documents are created. The job description describes the duties the position entails and the person specification outlines the type of person required.
- Before the post is advertised the business has to decide how applicants will apply. Will they send in their CV or complete an application form?
- The interview panel decide who to interview.

> **Activity**
>
> **Controlled assessment task**
>
> As part of a task in the controlled assessment, you are required to:
>> Identify and describe the main activities of the human resources functional area.
>
> In order to gain maximum marks for this section, you need to provide a thorough description. This will involve using more than one resource to develop the content of your evidence.
>
> Interview at least two people who are in paid employment, to establish the role which they feel the human resources functional area plays in their working lives. You could focus your questions around the following themes:
> - What part did the department play in your initial application, interview and subsequent appointment?
> - What policies has the department issued to you, such as staff handbook, health and safety policy?
> - How is training arranged within your place of work?
> - What is the health and safety policy? How is it monitored?
> - What security measures are in place within your place of work?
>
> Remember, the focus of this task must link back to the responsibility that the human resources functional area has for these separate areas. These interviews will form part of your evidence for the section on effective research – Chapter 33.

Interviews are conduced and hopefully the correct person for the job will be appointed.

- Labour turnover is the number of people who leave against the total number of permanent employees.
- Training needs are identified at a staff appraisal. This is where the employee and line manager discuss the employee's progress throughout the year.

Chapter 29

The recruitment process

In order to complete this section of the controlled assessment, you need to understand that when applying for a job vacancy, applicants are required to complete a range of different recruitment and selection documents. How successfully these are completed will affect whether or not an applicant is called for an interview. An application full of spelling mistakes and crossings out is unlikely to impress a potential new employer.

In order to undertake task 1 of the controlled assessment, you will need to investigate a range of different recruitment and selection documents. This initial research should help you to complete recruitment and selection documents for the second bullet point within task 2.

Before you can start any investigations, you will need to understand the key terms in this area, and recruitment and selection documentation.

In Chapter 28, a brief overview of the recruitment and selection process was given. The focus of the controlled assessment is the recruitment and selection process from the potential employee's perspective. Before this process can begin, the employer has to create the awareness of the position through the use of internal or external advertising. Having raised awareness of the vacancy, the employer is then responsible for supplying potential applicants with greater details concerning the vacant position. It is at this point the controlled assessment begins.

Within the Controlled Assessment booklet supplied by OCR, you will find five different job vacancies. Each one has:

- an advertisement
- a job description
- a person specification.

The advertisements will give you a brief outline of the position available. This could include working hours, qualifications and experience required for each post. There will also be details on how to apply for the position. The job description will outline the key tasks for each position; the person specification describes the qualifications and skills that the position requires.

The purpose of these three documents is to help the potential applicant decide if they have the right skills, qualifications and personal attributes to be able to undertake the role described. The applicant who best matches the requirements has a greater chance of being called for interview. There is not much point in applying for a position if you do not have any of the skills, qualities or experience requested.

There are a number of ways in which a business can request applicants apply for their vacancy. These include:

- application forms
- CVs
- letters of application.

Application forms

These are documents that have been designed by a business in order to request the same information from each applicant. Application forms are usually three to four pages long and can often be quite daunting to complete. To accompany the application form, some businesses include a form that requests information concerning the applicant's ethnic background and disabilities. This is to help the business monitor the variety of people who apply for vacancies, and helps to ensure that the business does not breach equal opportunities legislation.

Application forms will usually contain the following headings.

The recruitment process

> ## Activity
>
> ### Portfolio practice (1)
>
> When you have completed your GCSEs, you may wish to continue your education at school or within a separate sixth-form college. Investigate your local colleges to see if they have an application form that has to be completed before being offered a place at the college. Then complete the following tasks:
>
> - Obtain a hardcopy of the college's application form.
> - Photocopy the application form.
> - Complete the application form.
> - Show your completed application form to your teacher.
> - Following your teacher's advice, complete the second copy of the application form.

- personal details
- education and professional qualifications
- previous and present responsibilities and duties
- previous employment
- relevant skills, abilities, knowledge and experience
- other relevant information
- references
- declaration (signature) that all information given is accurate etc.

One of the advantages of using an application form is that all applicants supply the business with the same information, and so can be easily compared. The form can also be used again for future vacancies.

Application forms can be difficult to design. They need to be easy to complete and have clear instructions. Another disadvantage is that the same application form may be used for managerial as well as operative positions. This might mean that the form becomes over-complicated for lower skilled applicants or over simplified for highly skilled positions. This can dissuade some applicants from applying for the position. There is also the cost of sending out application forms to all interested parties. This problem has been somewhat overcome with the growth of online application forms, which are now widely used.

Curriculum Vitae

The Latin term 'curriculum vitae' is abbreviated to CV, and means 'course of life' or a history of career so far.

Not all businesses use application forms; instead, they request potential applicants to submit their CVs supported by a letter of application. It is therefore very important that your CV catches the potential employer's attention, as it might be your only chance to promote yourself for the position. If the person responsible for perusing all the CVs is not impressed by its layout and content, you are unlikely to have the opportunity to meet them face-to-face.

There are many different ways in which a CV can be laid out, but it is usual to include the following information:

- Name: often centred at the top as a heading
- Contact details: address, email address, telephone numbers
- Date of birth: you do not have to include this since the Age Discrimination Act came into force in October 2006
- Education and qualifications starting with the most recent
- Work experience

Activity

Portfolio practice (2)

As part of task 1 in the controlled assessment, you are required to undertake research into a number of different recruitment documents created by a range of different businesses. You may find the websites in Table 29.1 of interest.

Website address	Content
www.hants.gov.uk/jobs.htm	Advertises all vacancies available within Hampshire County Council. Direct access to job descriptions, person specifications and online application forms.
http://www.tfl.gov.uk/tfl/search/?keywords=jobs	The London Underground also advertises vacancies on the Internet. Information concerning the position is available and applications are again made online.
http://www.ons.gov.uk/job	Detailed website that clearly outlines requirements for each position and terms of employment. Applications can be made online, or hard-copy documents can be requested.
http://www.asda.jobs/	This is an interesting link which enables the reader to find out about Asda and its working conditions. You are able to search for different jobs, and the site clearly explains how you should apply. It is probably the most eye-catching of the four sites.

Table 29.1 Application forms on different websites

- Personal profile: this could include voluntary work, hobbies and interests. Comments made here should link to the skills being requested within the job description and person specification.

Advantages of CVs

- There is no need to produce an application form.
- You can evaluate the candidate's communication skills by the presentation of their CV.

Disadvantages of CVs

- It is much more difficult to compare the qualifications, skills and qualities of the different candidates.
- Gaps in education or employment can be masked more easily than in an application form.

Activity

Portfolio practice (2)

The following two websites have some excellent information on how to write a good CV. They are well worth looking through; use the information to create your own up-to-date CV:

- http://careersadvice.direct.gov.uk/helpwithyourcareer/writecv/
- http://content.monster.co.uk/

Letters of application

Some businesses ask potential applicants to include a letter of application in support of their application form or CV. The business is then able to evaluate the writing skills of all applicants. The advertisement might also request the letter to be handwritten rather than word processed.

Any letter you send must be correctly laid out. Letter-writing has been covered within Chapters 21 (Forms of communication) and 25 (Administration and ICT). When writing a personal business letter, it is quite acceptable for the address to be blocked on the right-hand side of the page rather than on the left. The remaining layout is the same as the business letter.

When compiling a letter of application, the writer must remember to consider the skills and qualities being sought within the recruitment documentation. The letter will enable the writer to demonstrate that they have these skills. Examples can be given of when these skills have been utilised; for example, if the job requires good team work, the writer could discuss their time playing for a local football, netball or cricket team, or training for a local athletics club; commitment and good time-keeping could be related to the paper-round carried out for two years.

Some useful phrases that could be used within a letter of application are outlined below:

- I am writing in response to your advertisement in [*insert where you saw the advertisement*] on [*insert date*].
- Having read through the person specification and job description, I feel that I am able to demonstrate the following skills and personal attributes. [*Relate the skills required to your own personal experiences. Do not forget voluntary work, hobbies, interests or roles of authority taken on at school.*]
- I look forward to hearing from you in the near future.
- If there is any further information you require, please do not hesitate to contact me.

In order to write an excellent letter you must take your time. Draft it out, ask someone else to check it through, and then draft the final version. Make sure that you have checked your spelling and grammar.

Activity

Portfolio practice (3)

You have seen the following advertisement in your local newspaper. You are required to draft a letter of application, enclosing your CV created in the activity above. Having completed your initial draft, ask either one of your peers or teacher to check it for you before completing the final document.

TRAINEE ACCOUNTS ASSISTANT

An ideal opportunity exists for someone who wants to enter the exciting world of accountancy. Training will be offered to the right candidate who will be supported through the Association of Accountancy Technician's Qualifications.

A suitable candidate will have achieved at least five GCSEs grade C or above, to include Maths and English. Computer literacy will also be an advantage. The ability to work within a small friendly team is paramount.

If interested please submit a letter of application and CV outlining your qualifications, skills and qualities and two referees to:

Ms G Goodrich
Arthur Roach Accountants
Slough Road
Gloucester
GL76 2UY

Closing date for applications: two weeks from date of advertisement.

Figure 29.1 A sample advertisement

Writing a good application letter takes time

Completing documents accurately

In order to understand the importance of presentation and accuracy, spend a few minutes considering the reasons for completing an application form or writing a letter of application and CV. The reason is that you think you might like the job. The sole purpose of these documents is to impress the reader so that you will be given the opportunity to attend an interview. The reader does not know you, and the only impression which they can receive about you is based on the statements you have made, the layout of your documents and any spelling and grammatical errors you have made.

The other important fact to remember is that your application may be one of many. If this is the case, the reader will decide very quickly whether to read it further or discard it. Obviously, you want them to read it all and then call you to interview. In order for this to happen, you need to ensure a number of things.

- Have you followed a standardised layout?
- Have you followed instructions (application form)? For example, if you were asked to write in black ink, have you done so?
- Is the information easy to follow and understand?
- Have you linked your responses to the requirements of the position: job role, qualifications, skills and attributes?
- Do not include irrelevant information.
- Are there any spelling, grammatical or typographical errors?
- Have you read the document through to make sure that it makes sense?
- Have you included all the relevant information requested?
- Is the tone of the language appropriate? Formal language must be used.
- Ask someone to check the final documents prior to submission.
- Make appropriate amendments.
- Set aside sufficient time to complete the job well; first impressions really do count.

The last point you need to remember when completing an application form, CV or letter of

Activity

The following sections are extracts from different CVs and letters of application. Read them through carefully and then decide how they could be improved. Rewrite each one correctly.

(a) 'Dear Sir/Madam …

Yours sincerely'

(b) 'Dear Mrs Smith

I saw your job advertisement and would now like to apply for the position.'

'I have lots of experience working in a team cause I play football every Sunday for my local club.'

(c) This extract is taken from a CV:

'Qualifications
gcse english -C
gcse maths – C
ocr nationals in ict – merit'

(d) 'I think i would be suitable for the job as i have done this kind of work before. I used to work in the local pub collecting glasses so I know how to talk to people. I am reliable and don't often turn up late for school although I do sometimes oversleep and miss the bus. This does not happen that often though and would not stop me coming to work on time.'

(e) 'In my last job I used to do loads of different stuff. I sometimes used to answer the phones and take messages. I would also book customers into the hotel if the receptionist was not about.'

application is that no statements which you make should contravene equal opportunity legislation. It would not be a good idea to state that you do not like working with older people or people who have disabilities. The legal dimension is covered in greater depth in Chapter 30 of this unit.

Activity

Portfolio practice (4)

If you have completed portfolio practice activities 1, 2 and 3, you should now have a completed application form, CV and letter of application.

Exchange your final documents with a partner. Look through all the documents, considering if they would get you an interview. You could use the following criteria to help you make your judgements. Do not forget to comment on the good points, as well as areas that could be improved.

- Is the layout of each document correct?
- Are the documents easy to read with sentences making sense?
- Are there any spelling or grammatical errors?
- Does the information match the requirements of the job/position?
- Would you interview the potential applicant? If not, why not?

This information should help you create your own documents in task 2 of the controlled assessment.

Summary

- An application form allows the potential employer to collect the same information from all applicants. It makes the selection of candidates for interview easier as all have been required to answer the same questions.

- Curriculum Vitae (CV) means 'course of life' or a history of career so far.

- A letter of application allows the applicant to tell the potential employer about themselves and why they think they are suitable for the position. It also enables the employer to see if the applicant can lay out a business letter correctly and use the English language effectively – no spelling or grammatical errors.

- If you are applying for a job it is imperative you present your work neatly and accurately in order to create the correct impression.

Chapter 30
The selection process

Advertising a vacancy is only half of the story; the hard part is selecting the correct person for the position. The recruitment and selection process takes a lot of time and often costs a business a lot of money. Advertisements have to be placed and members of staff have to take time away from their normal duties in order to conduct interviews. If the wrong person is recruited, they will not be able to cope efficiently in the role and be unproductive. Extra training may be required to enable the employee to undertake their normal duties. All of this costs a business time and money which ultimately reduces its ability to earn profits.

Shortlisting

If a job advertisement attracts 30 applicants, it would be far too expensive to interview them all. A business will shift through all the applicants to select the most suitable. This process is known as shortlisting. The system must be robust to ensure that potentially suitable candidates are not excluded and unsuitable ones included.

It is very important that these decisions are based on common criteria and not personal preference; for example, it would breach equal opportunities legislation if all female applicants were excluded because the person responsible for shortlisting felt that the position would be better filled by a man. Due to the Employment Equality (Age) Regulation 2006, it is now also illegal to exclude candidates because they are felt to be too old or too young.

One way to ensure that there is no discrimination is to photocopy all the applicants' documents and blank out their names and personal details. This will ensure that each candidate is judged on their merits and not the preconceptions of the selecting committee.

Often a business will start looking at the documentation to see if it has been completed correctly. If instructions have not been followed, the applicant might be rejected immediately. The next criteria might be based on spelling and use of grammar. If the documents are full of errors, this might also mean an instant rejection.

The applicants' documentation should match the skills and qualities requested within the advertisement, job description and person specification; for example, if the position advertised was for a shop assistant, an essential skill would be customer service experience. All those candidates who had no customer service experience might be rejected at this point.

An interview is a chance for the interviewer and the job applicant to ask questions

The interview process

Having undertaken the selection process, the business now needs to invite these hopeful applicants to an interview. An interview must be a two-way process. The initial aim is for the prospective employer to see the applicant and consider if they would be suitable for the position and fit in with the current members of staff. It is also an opportunity for the applicant to discuss the position further and actually decide if they would like to work for the business. The applicant might be offered the position but decide that the business is not for them and so decline the offer.

Activity

Figures 30.1 and 30.2 show a job description and person specification for the trainee accounts assistant. Using these two documents, consider the criteria you would use to shortlist potential applicants for the position. What skills and qualities would your new employee need?

Arthur Roach Accountants Job description

Post: Trainee accounts assistant

Accountable to: Accountant

Location: Gloucester office

Job summary: To assist with the preparation of clients' financial accounts. To include book-keeping and compilation of accounts ready for submission to HM Customs & Revenue.

Hours of work: 9.00am – 5.30pm (total one hour break per day)

Salary range: £12,000 – £14,000 depending on age and experience

Principal responsibilities:

(1) Undertake general book-keeping duties to include the input of sales and purchase ledgers for clients.

(2) To provide cover for reception staff as and when required.

(3) To undertake other clerical duties.

Figure 30.1 A job description

Arthur Roach Accountants Person specification

Post: Trainee accounts assistant

Education/qualifications:
Essential: GCSE English
GCSE Mathematics
IT qualification
Ability to communicate effectively both verbally and in writing

Desirable: Ability to use SAGE Accounts although training can be provided

Experience:
Essential: The ability to work within a small team effectively
Desirable: Previous experience of working with customers

Skills/ability/knowledge:
Essential: Willingness to gain AAT qualifications
Desirable: Keyboard skills
Accuracy and neatness
Time management

Other requirements:
Must have a pleasant personality, good sense of humour and be prepared to work flexible hours as and when required. Willingness and flexibility to assist with a variety of different jobs.

Figure 30.2 A person specification

Different interview methods

There are a number of different ways in which to conduct interviews.

Group interviews

A popular method used by large superstores is to invite a number of applicants for a group interview. The applicants are given a variety of different tasks to undertake. The interview panel will make observations on how they meet set criteria; for example, how well do they work within a team environment? Applicants that pass the group interview will be called for an individual interview. Part of the interview process might be to ask an applicant to undertake a day's work to see if they fit into and like the working environment.

Informal interviews

Interviews for lower skilled positions generally involve the applicant being invited to the business at a certain time, and being seen by a member of the human resources department and a member of staff from the department they are about to join. The interview will often be quite informal and consist of a series of questions that will focus on the following areas:

- qualifications, previous experience (related to job description and person specification)
- current or last job, work experience, school achievements
- questions related to application form or CV (connected to hobbies, interests or personal statement)
- what the applicant feels they can bring to the position/business
- why they want the job
- future aspirations (where do they want to be in five years' time?).

The purpose of the interview is to establish the character and personality of the applicant and whether or not they have the skills and qualifications required. By keeping the atmosphere comfortable and non-threatening, the interviewers should be able to establish a good rapport with the interviewee. Creating an atmosphere of mutual respect makes it easier to establish a good dialogue, aiding the decision-making of whom to employ.

As an interviewee, it is important that you ask as many questions as possible to ensure that you are happy with the information being supplied about the position. A potential employee needs to ensure that they really would like to work for the organisation. If this was you, do not forget you would be there for over 35 hours a week, for approximately 48 weeks a year!

Interview tests

Some organisations set their employees tests to check that they possess the skills and abilities stated within their recruitment documents. An applicant for a retail sales assistant's post may be asked to participate in a role-play situation. This will enable them to demonstrate their ability to talk to customers on a one-to-one basis. If the situation involves conflict, it will give the potential employer an idea of how calm an individual can remain in a stressful situation.

The test could involve answering a telephone, or undertaking a written or numerical exercise in timed conditions. Managerial positions might require the applicant to give a presentation on a selected subject. This enables the candidate to demonstrate their ability to present information to a group of people, in a stressful situation.

Effective interviews: employer's perspective

Having gone through all the trouble and expense of arranging the interview, it is imperative that the process runs smoothly. A chaotic interview will not give a very good impression to the potential applicant; in fact it might put them off! The first thing to consider is, what is the overall aim of the interview?

A smoothly-run interview will impress an interviewee; a chaotic one might give a different impression

- Produce a suitable candidate for the job.
- Provide the candidate with information.
- Treat all candidates fairly and equally.

Bearing these three points in mind while conducting the interview will help the employer run a fair and successful interview. But what makes an effective interview?

Plan the questions

- Use information from the candidate's application form, CV or letter of application when preparing questions to ask. Make them relevant to experience outlined in these documents.
- Look for gaps in education or employment, and ensure that you ask questions about these.
- Ensure that none of the questions you ask are discriminatory (see pages 211–213).
- If more than one person is running the interview, ensure that each one knows who is asking which questions. It is usually best to split questions into categories, with each member of the interview team responsible for a set section.
- Plan responses to questions that the candidate might ask during the interview. Consider the information that the candidate may want to know about the organisation.
- Ensure that questions are open-ended and do not just require a 'yes' or 'no' answer.

Making arrangements for the interview

- Make sure that the interview room has been booked and is prepared with drinks or stationery available as required.
- Decide on the best layout of the room. Is it best to sit behind a desk which can create a communication barrier, or to sit in comfortable chairs in a circle? Could a round table be used? Think about the impression and environment you are creating for the applicant.
- Establish if the candidate has any special needs prior to the interview so that these can be met.
- Make sure there are no interruptions. Ensure that mobile phones are turned off and that telephone calls to the interview room are diverted.
- Brief members of staff who will meet the candidate when they will be arriving and the role they are expected to play within the interview. The reception staff need to be aware of the names of potential candidates and the time they are due to arrive. They also need to be aware of the procedures for waiting applicants. Should they be offered refreshments?
- Allow sufficient time for each interview, with some spare time between candidates. This will ensure that candidates are not rushed and if one interview does overrun, other candidates are not kept waiting for long periods of time.
- Come to each interview with an open mind; you must not be biased towards a particular candidate.

Keeping records of the process

During the interview process, it is usual for the interviewer to make notes of candidate's responses. This helps the interviewer(s) make their final decision. It can be quite difficult to remember the exact responses of the first applicant if you then saw five other candidates.

- Back up interviews with detailed notes. These should be written up as soon as possible after the interview.

- Only record what was actually said and decisions that were made.

- Candidates that were not appointed and make a complaint to an employment tribunal have the right to ask for copies of any notes that were made during the interview process. A business may need to defend their decision in a discrimination case relating to the process.

Interview format

The format of the interview often follows the outline below. Some potential introductory phrases have been included.

- Welcome the candidates, putting them at ease:
  'Did you have a good journey here today?'

- Introduce yourself and the other people present:
  'Hello, my name is Ravi, I am the human resource manager, and this is Julie, the production manager. We will be conducting the interview today.'

- Explain the structure of the interview:
  'I will be asking you general questions concerning your past work experience, and then Julie will ask questions concerning your current position. The final set of questions will be shared between us and will focus on your hobbies and interests. You will then have time to ask questions. At the end of this stage, you will be asked to undertake a computer literacy test, after which you will be free to go. We will contact you within one week of the interview.'

- Outline the company background and the role, and where the job fits into the organisational structure.

- The candidate should be encouraged to answer questions fully concerning their skills and experience relating to the position. This might require some probing on the part of the interview team.

- Allow the candidate time to think: do not rush them.

- Keep control of the interview. If the candidate starts to digress, bring the conversation back to the relevant points.

- Do not forget to ask the candidate if they have any questions at the end of the interview.

- If you have not already done so, inform the applicant of the next stage in the recruitment process: for example, second interviews, tests and estimated timescales.

- Thank the candidate for their time and interest in the post.

Activity

Using the advertisement, job description and person specification for the position of trainee accounts assistant, prepare a set of questions for one candidate who is aged 16, has had a weekend paper-round and is just about to leave school with ten GCSEs, grade A–C. Their hobbies and interests include participating in sports, reading and cycling.

Effective interviews: employee's perspective

The most effective interview you can have is one where you are offered the position! This section will examine what an applicant needs to do to ensure that this is the end result when they attend an interview.

Preparing properly for an interview can have excellent results

Before the interview

- Undertake research into the background, history and future plans of the business. You may be asked what you know about the business.
- Make sure before the day of the interview that you know where you are going.
- If the business is not too far away, it is often a good idea to undertake a 'dummy' run to ensure that you know exactly how long the journey takes.
- Check that you have suitable, clean clothes for the interview. Suits may need to be dry cleaned.
- Consider some questions that you could ask at the end of the interview process. Plan at least six, although some may be answered during the course of the interview.
- Ensure that you fully understand the format of the interview. If you are required to complete an activity prior to the interview, make sure that you leave sufficient time to do this to your highest standard.

During the interview

- Shake hands with the interviewers confidently.
- Listen carefully to questions; ask questions if you do not understand.
- Speak clearly and slowly.
- Do not fidget.
- Look interested – lean forward.
- Do not lounge back on your chair with a bored expression.
- Ask questions when invited to do so.
- Seek clarification of any aspect of the position you are unsure of.

Activity

Portfolio practice

Within task 3 of the controlled assessment, you are required to identify potential questions you could be asked at interview. This activity will enable you to start considering this area of knowledge.

You have been invited to interview for the position of trainee accounts assistant.

- Describe ten questions and possible answers that you might be asked at interview. Your responses should relate to your personal circumstances.
- Identify six questions that you could ask at the interview.

Legislation covering the selection process

Please see pages 211–213 for coverage of this section.

Informing applicants of the interview outcome

After attending an interview, an applicant must be informed of whether or not they have been appointed. There are a number of different ways that this could be conducted.

The successful applicant

It is usual for the successful applicant to be contacted first, to see if they are prepared to accept the position under the terms and conditions being offered. Often the applicant is telephoned soon after the interview and verbally offered the position. This could be subject to the receipt of references from previous employers. If the applicant accepts the position, they will be offered the job formally in writing, probably within a couple of days.

The unsuccessful applicant

Once the successful candidate has accepted the position, the unsuccessful candidates are then either telephoned or contacted in writing, informing them that they have not been successful on this occasion.

If the Internet has been used to advertise and receive applicants for the position, candidates might hear of their success or failure via email. This will have been clearly explained to applicants at their interview.

An applicant who has been unsuccessful at the interview stage has the right to verbal or written feedback on the reasons they were not selected. This is to help applicants develop their interview techniques in order to help them secure employment in the future. It is at this stage that applicants may wish to appeal against a business's decision and take the matter to an employment tribunal. As mentioned above, the notes made during the interview are then made available to the failed applicant.

Employment legislation

Employment legislation has steadily grown since World War II, and exists to stop employees being exploited by employers. The Employment Act 2002 and legislation protecting workers from discrimination on the grounds of age, gender, sexuality, disability and race are all important. However, the most comprehensive piece of legislation that maps out employees' rights is the Employment Rights Act 1996.

The Royal Courts of Justice, home to the Court of Appeal

Activity

Ask someone you know if they would let you have a look at their contract of employment. Describe the terms and conditions that are set out in the document.

The Employment Rights Act 1996

The Act was first introduced by the Conservative Government in 1996, but has been amended by the Labour Government since 1997. The Employment Rights Act outlines employees' rights at work, detailing what they can expect from their employer and defining the way in which they should be treated. The Act is split into a number of different sections, which are briefly outlined below.

Statement of initial employment particulars

The statement outlines the terms and conditions of the employee's employment, and should be supplied within two months of employment. The statement is often referred to as the contract of employment and should contain the following details:

- The name of the employer and employee.
- The date on which employment began.
- For temporary contracts, the expected termination date.
- The place of work and address of employer.
- The job title and brief description of the position.
- The rate of pay, frequency of payment, any bonuses, and methods of payments; this section guarantees the employee payment even if the employer is unable to provide work during the employee's normal working hours.
- The hours of work.
- Holiday entitlement.
- Maternity and paternity leave; maternity leave is covered in detail within the Act to ensure that pregnant women and their partners are not discriminated against unfairly.
- Terms relating to sickness including notification of sickness, pay and statutory sick pay.
- Pension arrangement; if there is a company pension scheme, the contributions that will be collected by the employee and contributed by the employer.
- Length of notice which the employee is entitled to receive or required to give to terminate employment.
- Disciplinary and grievance procedures; the document should clearly outline disciplinary and appeals procedures, and whom to speak to.
- Any other specific collective agreements affecting terms and conditions of work; perhaps a special arrangement that has been established between the employer and trade unions.

Right to itemised pay statement

All employees have the right to receive an itemised payslip which contains the following information:

- The gross amount of wages or salary.
- The amount of fixed or variable deductions from pay (this would include taxation, pension contributions, student loan etc.).
- The net amount of wages.
- The method of payment.

Enforcement

If the contract of employment does not clearly explain the grievance procedures, the employee must be allowed access to a document where this is outlined. This document must explain the procedures that should be followed if the employee wishes to take a grievance to an industrial tribunal.

Protection of wages: guaranteed payment

This section states that an employee must not lose wages because the employer is unable to supply him/her with work; for example, if a production worker is unable to continue working for four hours due to a machine breakdown, the employer is not allowed to reduce his/her wages because they were effectively sitting idle for four hours. This is only applicable if the employee has been employed continuously for a period of not less than one month.

In the retail environment, an employee working on the cash tills will be liable for any shortage of cash that is discovered at the end of the day. If the employee has been found to have been acting illegally, they are legally bound to pay the whole amount back. However, if the error was genuine, the employee would be liable to repay the equivalent to ten per cent of their gross pay for that day. For example, if Baljeet found his till was £20 short and his gross earnings were £38.50 for the day, he would only be liable to pay back ten per cent which would be £3.85. The same rule applies to stock deficiencies.

Sunday working for shop and betting workers

If an employee was not originally contracted to work on a Sunday, they cannot be forced to do so.

Protection from suffering detrimentally while in employment

All employers have a duty of care to look after the health and safety of all their employees. Employers must ensure that they do not ask employees to undertake tasks that would be considered dangerous to their health. Employers also have a duty of care to ensure that the demands being made upon the workforce are reasonable and not likely to cause undue stress.

Time off for public duties

An employer must permit employees time off in order to undertake any public duties. This could include the role of justice of the peace, member of the police authority or a member of the board of prison visitors.

This section also covers the right to look for work and arrange training if an employee has been made redundant. The employee has the right to be paid during this time off.

Women also have the right to attend antenatal care during working hours without losing pay. Employee representatives (trade union reps) are allowed time off work with payment in order to carry out their trade union duties.

Suspension from work

If an employee has been continuously employed for more than one month, they are entitled to be paid for up to 26 weeks if they are suspended for work on medical grounds.

A female employee who becomes pregnant and who may not be able to continue with her current role due to the pregnancy, may be suspended from work on medical grounds with pay. If appropriate, she must be offered alternative work that would not endanger the pregnancy.

Maternity rights

All women are entitled to time off before and after the birth of their child with payment. Statutory maternity leave is made up of 26 weeks 'ordinary maternity leave' and 26 weeks 'additional maternity leave' regardless of how long the employee has been employed, how many hours the employee works or how much the employee earns. An employee will be entitled to statutory maternity pay for 39 weeks if she has been employed by the same employer at least 26 weeks into the 15th week the baby is due. She must be earning an average of £95 per week.

Termination of employment

The Act sets out the notice periods required before an employee's contract can be terminated.

- Less than two years' continuous service: one week's notice.
- More than two years' but less than twelve years' continuous service: one week's notice for each year of service.
- Twelve years' (or more) of continuous service: not less than twelve weeks' notice.

If an employee is being dismissed, they have the right to a written statement giving particulars of the reasons for their dismissal. This should be automatically provided by the employer.

Impact on the recruitment and selection process

Prior to advertising the post, the employer must ensure that the exact details of the position have been clarified. The details that are used within the job description and person specification will feed into the successful applicant's contract of employment.

The terms and conditions of employment should also be fully explained to all potential applicants, so that there are no surprises for the employee after having been offered the position and received the contract of employment.

The Sex Discrimination Act 1975

This Act makes it illegal to discriminate against anybody on the grounds of their gender or marital status. It works equally for men and women. This applies when recruiting and deciding the terms and conditions that will be offered to an employee, as well as when decisions are made about who will be promoted, transferred, receive training or have their contract terminated.

There are two types of discrimination: direct and indirect.

- Direct discrimination is where an employee has been treated less favourably because of their sex; for example, a woman is not shortlisted for a post because the team currently consists only of men. Sexual harassment is also considered a form of direct discrimination. Harassment is when an employer or another employee makes unwanted sexual advances to another member of staff.

- Indirect discrimination is when a condition is applied equally to men and women, but its actual nature makes it detrimental to the majority of one sex, for example requesting that all potential applicants must have the ability to lift and carry 25kg. This criterion would be much more difficult for women to achieve than men.

Harassment

The Sex Discrimination Act has been amended to ensure that it complies with the Equal Treatment Directive, a piece of European Union legislation. All changes came into effect on 6th April 2008. The changes impact on two key areas: discrimination on grounds of pregnancy or maternity leave, and harassment.

The definition of harassment has been extended from sex-based harassment to include conduct related to a person's sex; for example, if

Discrimination on the grounds of gender, race or disability is illegal

a male employee makes rude, sexually-based comments about women to both male and female colleagues, this will now be considered harassment because the comments relate to sex, regardless of who heard the comments. Previously, the male employee could state in his defence that the comments were made to both male and female colleagues and were therefore not sexual harassment.

The change in definition also means that if a person witnesses sexual harassment against a colleague of the same sex by a person of the opposite sex, s/he could also claim sexual harassment if s/he can prove it has made his/her environment intimidating.

The liability of employers has also been extended. If the employer is aware that a member of their staff has been harassed on at least two occasions previously and it happens a third time, the employer could be liable for taking no action to protect the employee.

Making a claim for sexual discrimination becomes much easier for women under the new amendments. Women will now only have to show that they have received less favourable treatment because they are pregnant, or have exercised their rights in relation to maternity leave.

Impact on recruitment and selection

During the compilation of all recruitment and selection documents, the employer must ensure that there are no comments that would cause offence or discriminate against either sex. During the interview process, the selection panel must ensure that all applicants are asked the same range of questions, and no questions would discriminate against either sex. The interview panel must also ensure that they do not have any preconceived ideas concerning the type of person they want to fulfil the position, and therefore judge each candidate against the skills and qualifications required and not personal preferences.

All these rules would apply equally to implementing the Race Relations 1976 and Disability Discrimination Act 1995.

The Race Relations Act 1976

The Race Relations Act 1976, as amended by the Race Relations (Amendment) Act 2000, makes it unlawful to discriminate against anyone on grounds of race, colour, nationality (including citizenship) or ethnic or national origin. Racial discrimination is not the same as racial prejudice. The definition of racial harassment is defined by the Commission for Racial Equality:

> 'An unwelcome or hostile act or series of acts carried out on racial grounds'.

Under the Act, it does not matter if the discrimination is deliberate or not. The key question is whether or not the employee was treated unfavourably because of their race. The Act protects all racial groups, regardless of their race, colour, nationality, and religious beliefs, national or ethnic origins. The amended Act of 2000 imposes general duties on many public authorities to promote racial equality.

The Act covers every part of employment and includes:

- recruitment
- terms and conditions
- pay and benefits
- status
- training
- promotion
- transfer opportunities
- redundancy and dismissal.

The law allows a job to be restricted to people of a particular racial or ethnic group where there is a 'genuine occupational requirement', for example a request for an Indian employee to work in an Indian restaurant.

There are four kinds of discrimination:

- **Direct discrimination**: where a particular job is only open to people within a specific racial group, for example 'white person required to join current sales team'.
- **Indirect discrimination**: where working practices or criteria would disadvantage certain members of a racial group, for example the introduction of a dress code that might disadvantage certain racial groups.
- **Harassment**: permitting behaviour that offends a particular race or group of people, and creates a difficult working environment.
- **Victimisation**: treating someone less favourably because they have made a complaint concerning racial attitudes and behaviour within their workplace.

It is the responsibility of the employer to stop any discrimination that takes places within the workplace. Failure to do so could result in legal action being taken against them.

The 2000 Amendment to the Act encourages businesses to take 'positive action'. This involves an employer providing support and encouragement to a particular racial group. This is only acceptable where a specific racial group is under-represented in a particular workplace. As part of the support package, the employer is allowed to offer the group special training and encourage members of the racial group to apply for particular positions.

Where the above criteria have been applied, it is permissible to state on an advertisement that applications from a certain racial group will be particularly welcome. This does not allow the employer to discriminate favourably towards this group; the recruitment decision must still be based on the merits of each individual candidate.

The Disability Discrimination Act 1995 (DDA)

The Disability Discrimination Act 1995 (section 4) made it unlawful for an employer with more than 15 employees to discriminate against a disabled person. On 1st October 2004, the Disability Discrimination Act was updated to include employers with fewer than 15 employees. The Disability Discrimination Act 2005 (DDA 2005) builds upon and extends the previous provision.

The development concerns the definition of disability. Under the 1995 legislation, disability was defined as a person having physical or mental impairment which had a substantial and long-term adverse effect on their ability to carry out normal day-to-day activities. The 2004 Act changes some of these definitions:

- It removes the requirement in the Act that a mental illness must be 'clinically well-recognised' before it can count as an impairment for the purpose of the DDA. People suffering from a mental illness will still have to prove that their impairment has a long-term and substantial adverse effect on their ability to carry out normal day-to-day activities.

- People with HIV, cancer and multiple sclerosis (MS) will now be deemed to be covered by the DDA effectively from the point of diagnosis, rather than from the point when the condition has some adverse effect on their ability to carry out normal day-to-day activities.

Employers must not discriminate against disabled employees or job applicants because of their disability. The 2004 Act also makes it unlawful for an employer to discriminate against a job applicant or employee who has one of the above conditions. The employer may have to make reasonable adjustments to the workplace if they already have a disabled employee, or a disabled person applies for the job.

It is quite common for businesses to request information about disability on their application forms. The form will ask if the applicant is registered disabled, and for details concerning their disability. Some businesses state that they will offer an interview to all disabled people who are suitable for the position and able to fulfil the tasks required for the job. Reasonable adjustments to the way in which an employer recruits staff could include:

- making application forms available in large print or Braille

- allowing applications to be made in formats other than writing (such as audio tape)

- providing a sign-language interpreter for interviews

- holding interviews in an accessible location.

The Equality and Human Rights Commission

Prior to 1st October 2007, the Sex Discrimination Act was overseen by the Equal Opportunity Commission; the Race Relations Act was overseen by the Commission for Racial Equality; and the Disability Discrimination Act was overseen by the Disability Rights Commission. In October 2007 these organisations were merged to form the Equality and Human Rights Commission.

The role of the commission is to work towards the elimination of discrimination, reduce inequality, protect human rights and build good relations, ensuring that everyone has a fair chance to participate in society. The new commission brings together the work of the three former equality commissions and also takes on responsibility for the other aspects of equality: age, sexual orientation and religion or belief, as well as human rights.

The Equality and Human Rights Commission is a non-departmental public body established under the Equality Act 2006. This means that it is accountable for its public funds, but independent of government. For further information concerning the work of the commission, see the website: www.equalityhumanrights.com.

One of the focuses of the commission is to encourage employers to involve employees in the development of equal opportunities policies. This helps to ensure that all members of staff are aware of their responsibilities and are prepared to follow the rules and regulations.

The commission has recommended how employers can avoid breaching equal opportunities legislation during the recruitment and selection process. These are summarised below.

- Each individual should be assessed according to his/her personal capability to do the job.
- Any qualifications or requirements for the position that effectively inhibit applications from certain groups of people should only be retained if they are justifiable in terms of the position being advertised. This could include sex, marital status, disability or race.
- Age limits should only remain if they can be justified.
- The arrangements for determining who will be awarded the position must not discriminate on race, sex or disability or age.
- Advertisements must not indicate or imply that the position is suitable for a man, woman, married or unmarried person, a particular race or the able-bodied.
- If vacancies are to be filled by promotion or transfer, they should be offered to all eligible employees.
- Recruitment based on word-of-mouth must be avoided as it may prove biased to one particular section of society.
- Tests must relate specifically to the position and be accessible to all applicants.
- Tests should be reviewed regularly to ensure that they remain relevant and free from bias.
- When interviewing, it is unlawful to discriminate on grounds of sex or marriage, race, age or disability by refusing to offer employment based on sex or marital status, race, age or disability.
- Applications for men and women should be processed in exactly the same way.
- All personnel involved in recruitment and selection should receive training in equal opportunities.
- Questions must relate to the position being advertised. If the position involves travel or unsociable hours this must be discussed objectively, with no questions being asked about childcare or domestic obligations.
- Questions relevant to marriage plans or family intentions must not be asked.

Health and Safety at Work Act 1974

The basis of UK health and safety law is the Health and Safety at Work Act 1974. The Act sets out the general duties which employers have towards employees and members of the public, and employees have to themselves and each other.

According to the Health and Safety Executive, 200 people a year lose their lives at work; 150,000 people suffer non-fatal injuries; and a

Commission helps secure landmark accessibility ruling for disabled people

In the first ruling of its kind, a judge has ordered the Royal Bank of Scotland to install a lift so that a wheelchair user can have the same access as any other customer.

Furthermore, in recognising the embarrassing treatment which a young man experienced at the hands of the bank, he was awarded £6,500, the highest ever compensation payout in this kind of case.

In taking the case against the bank with the support of the Equality and Human Rights Commission, David Allen, a 17-year-old wheelchair user from Sheffield, has secured a historic legal victory.

It is unlawful for businesses and public bodies to treat disabled people less favourably. But since the Disability Discrimination Act came into force in 1995, a judge has never before ordered an injunction to force an organisation to make physical changes to its property so that disabled people can gain access.

David Allen's legal battle began when, contrary to signage outside his local branch of the bank and information posted on its website, he found that he could not gain access. In a catalogue of incidents, David had to discuss his current account details in the street, breaching his right to confidentiality. The bank then suggested that he should use the nearest accessible RBS branch, even though it was a 10-mile journey and amounted to a two-and-a-half hour round trip by bus.

In handing down his judgment, Judge Dowse said:

> 'In the light of the findings I have made, it is plain that David has suffered from discrimination and that he has suffered from considerable embarrassment caused by the Bank'.

On hearing the Court's decision, David Allen said:

> 'I am glad that justice has been done. I only wanted them to comply with the law and provide disabled access so I could get into my bank like my friends.'

(Source: adapted from www.equalityhumanrights.com, 16th January 2009)

---

further two million people suffer from ill-health caused or made worse through work. So what is health and safety about? The Health and Safety Executive's definition is:

> 'Preventing people from being harmed by work or becoming ill by taking the right precautions and providing a satisfactory working environment.'

For further information on the work of the Health and Safety Executive, visit their website: http://www.hse.gov.uk/pubns/indg259.pdf.

The Act requires all employers as far as is practicable to ensure the health and safety of their employees. 'Reasonably practicable' means that the degree of risk in a particular job or workplace needs to be balanced against the time, trouble, cost and physical difficulty of taking measures to avoid or reduce the risk.

The Act requires employers to do the following:

- Provide safe access to premises.
- Maintain safe machinery, equipment and systems of work.
- Provide safe and healthy premises, for example adequate toilets, heating, lighting and ventilation.

- Provide safety training for employees.
- If there are more than five employees, produce a safety policy statement, of which all employees must be aware.
- Provide a safe environment for visitors to the premises.
- Keep an accident book in which details of any incidents are recorded.

While employers have a duty of care for employees' health and safety, employees also have clear responsibilities under the Act. These are listed below:

- Take reasonable care at all times for the health and safety of themselves and others in the workplace.
- Use safety devices when required.
- Cooperate with employers on all safety matters, including training.

The Management of Health and Safety at Work Regulation 1992 stated more specifically what employers are required to do to manage health and safety under the Health and Safety at Work Act 1974. The Act includes the following sections.

- Management of Health and Safety at Work Regulation 1992 requires employers to carry out risk assessments; make arrangements to limit risks; appoint competent people; arrange information and training for all staff.
- Workplace (Health and Safety and Welfare) Regulations 1992 cover a wide range of basic health, safety and welfare issues such as ventilation, heating, lighting, workstations, seating and welfare facilities.
- Health and Safety (Display Screen Equipment) Regulations 1992 set out requirements for work with Visual Display Units (VDUs).
- Personal Protective Equipment at Work Regulations 1992 require employers to provide appropriate protective clothing and equipment for their employees.
- Provision and Use of Work Equipment Regulations 1998 require employers to guarantee that equipment provided for use at work, including machinery, is safe.
- Manual Handling Operations 1992 cover the moving of objects by hand or bodily force.
- Health and Safety Information for Employees Regulations 1989 require employers to display a poster telling employees what they need to know about health and safety.
- Employers' Liability (Compulsory Insurance) Regulations 1969 require employers to take out insurance against accidents and ill-health to their employees.

The main focus of this Act was the need to carry out risk assessment. Risk assessment involves the identification and elimination of hazards. The Health and Safety Executive defines hazards and risks as follows:

'Hazard means anything that can cause harm (eg chemicals, working from a ladder). Risk is the chance, high or low, that someone will be harmed by the hazard.'

Risk management is an ongoing process and needs to be fully supported by management. The process involves the following steps:

- Methodically identifying the hazards/risks surrounding your business activities
- Assessing the likelihood of an event occurring; how great is the risk?
- Understanding how to respond to these possible events.
- Putting systems in place to deal with the consequences.
- Monitoring the effectiveness of the risk management approaches and controls.

Impact on recruitment and selection

Part of the recruitment and selection process is to invite people into the organisation in order to show them around and conduct a one-to-one interview. While visitors are on site, it is important that their safety is considered.

Each applicant should sign a visitors' book. This ensures that if an incident were to take place, the emergency services would be aware that there are extra people within the building. Prior to the interview process, it is usually advisable to inform applicants of the fire procedures; for example, is the fire bell going to be tested this morning or afternoon? At all times, applicants must be accompanied by a member of staff so that if an evacuation becomes necessary, they can be shown to the nearest fire exits and the congregation area after leaving the building.

Activity

Portfolio Tips

In task 3 of the controlled assessment, you are required to discuss how the above legislation impacts on the selection process for your chosen job role. In order to prepare for this activity, read through the legislation, making notes on how each piece of legislation will impact on the selection process for the position you have applied for.

Break down the selection process for your selected job role into the following categories:

- advertisement
- job description
- person specification
- application form (if used)
- shortlisting
- letters inviting candidates to interview
- interview.

Under each of these sections, consider how each Act would impact on each of them. For example, the advertisement must not use language or images that could cause offence to either sex. If it did, it would breach the Sex Discrimination Act. The wording must not include a sentence such as 'able-bodied people required' as it would breach the Disability Discrimination Act.

Summary

- Once all the applications for a position have been received the business will need to shortlist those it wants to interview.

- Interviews are a two way process to decide who would be most suitable for the position.

- In order to run a successful interview time must be spent on planning. Questions must be carefully considered and relevant to the applicant and post being interviewed for. A room must be booked and all members of the interview panel informed of the date, time and the role they will play throughout the interview.

- A record must be kept of the applicant's responses in order to help the employer make the final decision. They may be used if an applicant feels they have been discriminated against.

- Interviewees should plan carefully. Undertake research into the business, make sure you have carefully considered what you will wear and know how to get to the venue. Prepare answers to questions you might get asked and make sure you have planned some questions that you could ask at the end.

Chapter 31

> Induction

What am I expected to do? Where do I start?

Induction is a training process which provides a new employee with details about where they are working, what their job entails and who they will be working with. The complex part is designing a package that will provide all the information the new employee needs, without overwhelming them.

The purpose of induction

Every employer has a duty of care to their workforce. This includes making sure that they can do their job safely and competently. The best way to do this is by having an induction programme. A good induction programme will help the new employee to do the following:

- Become familiar with their position and therefore maximise productivity and profitability.
- Feel motivated as soon as they join the company.
- Be aware of health and safety issues relating to their position. This will help reduce accidents but also ensures that the employer is fulfilling their legal obligations.
- Understand the culture of the business, including how it works, and core values and beliefs.

Although an induction process takes time and money, it helps to ensure that employees get a good grounding in the work, preventing them from making lots of mistakes in the long term. This investment could also make the difference between staff remaining with the business or looking for an alternative position. The highest level of staff turnover is usually among new employees.

New employees who have not experienced an induction programme are neither likely to understand the organisation nor their role within it. This may lead to:

- poor integration into the team
- low morale, particularly for the new employee
- reduced productivity
- failure to work to their highest potential.

The key to a good induction programme is organisation and preparation, both before and after the employee begins work.

Before the employee begins work

- Tell other members of staff that a new employee is starting and what their role will be within the team/business.
- Prepare the new employee's work area, organising any equipment that they will need to do their job.
- Prepare an information pack about the job.
- Prepare an induction checklist so that the new employee is aware of what will be covered during their induction programme.
- Ensure that all members of the induction team are fully aware of the part they will play within the induction programme.

- Ensure that any training required (such as ICT) is organised prior to the employee arriving.

After the employee begins work

- Ensure that the new employee feels welcome when they arrive.
- Allocate one person to look after the new person throughout their first day.
- Ensure that they are aware of the location of facilities: toilets, kitchen, canteen, tea- or coffee-making facilities.
- Ensure that they are familiar with the equipment they need to use.
- Aim for the employee to complete some work on their first day. This will help them relate to the position they will be undertaking, and can help them settle into their new position and begin to feel part of the team.
- Ask the employee to complete the induction checklist. This can be signed off when it is completed.
- Ask for feedback throughout the process in order to help improve the programme for future new entrants to the business.

What to include in an induction programme

Starting a new job can be extremely stressful. It is therefore important to remember that the new employee is only able to take on board a limited amount of information at a given time. It is unlikely that a new employee will remember all the rules and regulations if they sit in a room and have to listen to someone talking to them for their entire first day. It is much better to plan the process so that the rate of delivery allows the employee to understand and take in all the information. This might mean that the induction process is broken down into a number of different sessions, each being delivered by a different member of staff. The general information that should be included is outlined below.

Business background/history

A good place to start is to provide some information on the background and history of the business. It might be a good opportunity to introduce them to the senior management team. Future plans for the business could also be explained during this session. The thought of joining a fast-moving, highly focused company could prove motivating for the new employee.

Administration

- Contract of employment: it is often a good idea to go through this with the employee as part of the induction process. This could cover issues such as disciplinary and grievance procedures, what to do if unable to attend work due to sickness or accident, hours of work, etc.
- Copies of company policies and procedures for accidents: this could include the staff handbook.
- Uniform requirements.
- Details of the company pension scheme (if applicable).

Health and safety

An employer is legally bound to provide employees with necessary health and safety information to carry out their job safely. Employees must be provided with a copy of the business's health and safety policy. Employees are required to sign this document to state that they have read and understood its contents and implications.

Employees must be informed of the fire safety procedures and what to do if the alarm sounds. This should be delivered on the first day, so that every employee is aware of what to do in an emergency situation. If the employee is entering a very hazardous environment, such as a production line, they must be shown all the potential hazards and the precautions that must be taken.

Employees should also be told where they are allowed to smoke outside the building, and be shown drugs or alcohol policies if these exist.

If the position involves the use of machinery, the employee must be trained how to use the machinery safely. The trainer must ensure that the employee fully understands any associated risks and has been supplied with correctly fitting safety clothing and equipment.

It is becoming common for employees within an office or retail environment to be shown a health and safety video or DVD to illustrate the business's policies. An alternative method is to use an interactive computer programme.

Tour of the building

Where am I? I don't know how to get back to my desk

Workers will need to know the layout of the building and where all the facilities are located. This might involve introductions to different members of staff, and explanations of where to go for lunch or make tea and coffee if there is no designated canteen. A tour of the building will help the new employee orientate themselves.

Introduction to colleagues

All new employees should be introduced to the team they will be working with. Ideally this should be one at a time, rather than en masse. This should enable the employee to have a quick chat with each team member, enhancing their feelings of well-being. Employees should also be introduced to their:

- line manager
- fellow employees responsible for human resources and training
- health and safety officer
- trade union/employee representatives.

Introduction to the job

Employees will need to be given an explanation of what their new position entails. This could also include how their role fits in with the aims and objectives of the organisation. This gives the new employee a sense of belonging to the team and the importance of their own individual role, and could enhance motivation.

Office systems

Employees will need to be fully conversant with any office equipment they are required to use. This will help them achieve maximum productivity quickly and with reduced stress.

Rights and responsibilities as an employee

This section has been covered under the Health and Safety at Work Act 1974 in Chapter 30, page 216. During the induction process, the employer should take time to explain their expectations of each employee. This will ensure that the new employee is fully aware of their responsibilities and what they can expect from their employer. This could include the business's polices on time-keeping and expected behaviour while at work.

Details of on-the-job training

If the position involves the new employee gaining new skills, it is important to explain how these will be delivered. This might consist of shadowing someone doing the job for a few days before being left on their own. It might involve more complex on-the-job training that lasts a number of weeks or months. It is important that the new employee understands how this will be delivered, the progress they are expected to make and how this will be measured.

Reviewing the induction programme

Having established an induction programme, it is important to review it regularly, particularly if a variety of different personnel are being employed. It is vital that the needs of each and every new employee are met, rather than imposing an old induction programme on the theory that 'this is what we have always done'. For example, school-leavers might need more time for orientation to their new role as this might be the first time they have entered the workplace; it might also be useful to allocate more time to health and safety regulations and expectations, as young people are often unaware of risks in the workplace.

Activity

Portfolio tip

Task 4 of the controlled assessment requires you to design an induction programme suitable for your selected job role.

- Think of the information you would need in order to fulfil this role.
- Using the above section, make notes on what you think should be involved in the induction programme for this position.
- Draft out your ideas.

Summary

- A good induction programme will help a new employee settle into the business. They will be given information concerning the business, their own role within the business and have met their fellow colleagues.

Chapter 32
Promotion

The recruitment and selection process is an extremely expensive process. It costs money and time to complete successfully. Employees are now recognised as a business's most valuable asset. Bearing this in mind, it is worth trying to ensure that a good candidate remains within the business. There are three advantages to using this strategy:

1. The employee is already familiar with the business and how it works.

2. They have established a good employment record.

3. It is cheaper to recruit and select internally than externally.

If an employee wishes to gain internal promotion, it is important to recognise their own skills and realise which new skills they need to develop. If the employee began work as an operative, they will have learned their supervisor's responsibilities and duties by working alongside them and being managed by them. Learning on the job may enable them to take on the new responsibility without requiring too much further training.

Activity

Portfolio building

Let us consider again the position of trainee accounts assistant for Arthur Roach Accountants. The list below summarises the duties, qualifications and skills required for the position.

- Assist with the preparation of clients' financial accounts.
- Include book-keeping and compilation of accounts ready for submission to HM Customs & Revenue.
- Undertake general book-keeping duties to include the input of sales and purchase ledgers for clients.
- Provide cover for reception staff as and when required.
- Undertake other clerical duties as required.
- GCSE English.
- GCSE Mathematics.
- IT qualification.
- Ability to communicate effectively both verbally and in writing.
- Ability to use SAGE Accounts although training can be provided.
- Ability to work within a small team effectively.
- Previous experience of working with customers.
- Willingness to gain AAT qualifications.
- Keyboard skills.
- Accuracy and neatness.
- Time management.

Promotion

- Pleasant personality, good sense of humour.
- Prepared to work flexible hours as and when required.
- Willingness and flexibility to assist with a variety of different jobs.

At interview, you were able to demonstrate all these qualities and have been fulfilling the role admirably since joining the business. You have now been working in this position for four years. You have moved from being the trainee account assistant to qualifying as AAT Technician. Due to continued growth of the business, a new position of office supervisor is being created. The role of the office supervisor is to oversee and organise the work of the four trainee accountants, the receptionist and one other clerical position.

Another aspect of the role is arranging work schedules to ensure that deadlines are met and all members of the team work effectively to achieve maximum productivity. You are hoping to apply for this position.

In task 5 of the controlled assessment, you are required to use your selected job role in order to consider the skills and competencies required for promotion and how your day-to-day activities might change in a supervisory job role. In order to help you prepare for this task, work through the tasks below.

- Which extra activities would you have to undertake on a daily basis as the office supervisor?
- Which skills and competencies would you need to develop in order to undertake this role?
- What training might you require in order to fulfil this new role?

One way to gain this information is to investigate office supervisor roles on the Internet. Reading a range of different job descriptions and person specifications will help you to identify the skills that you will need for this position.

Types of training programmes

Training can be broken into two different sections: on-the-job training and off-the-job training. See also Chapter 28, pages 193–194 for more information.

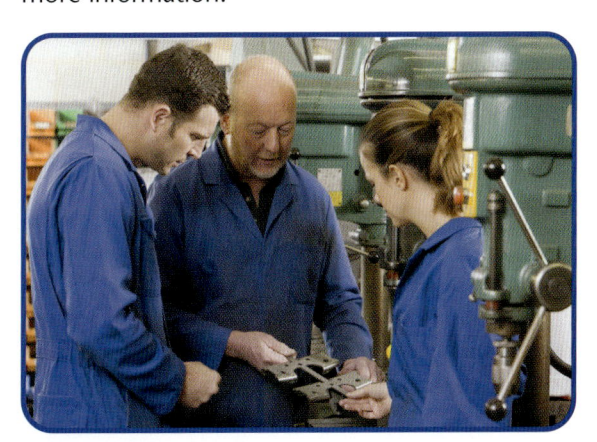

On-the-job training

On-the-job training

This is training provided while the employee is fulfilling their regular duties. It takes places within the workplace during a normal working day. It can take a variety of different forms:

- **Demonstration**: the employee is shown and guided through a task or process by a fellow colleague or supervisor. This enables the employee to perform the task to the required standard.
- **Job shadowing**: the employee watches an expert perform the task. The employee observes the stages carefully so that they can perform the task to the same standard on their own.
- **Observation**: the employee is observed fulfilling their duties. At the end of the observation, the employee is provided with feedback on their performance.

- **Coaching**: the employee learns new skills and has the opportunity to practise the skills with the coach before using them in the workplace. Effective coaching involves the reviewing of the employee's performance to ensure that s/he is able to use the new skills effectively.

- **Mentoring**: a new employee is partnered with an experienced employee so that they can discuss performance. The experienced employee is known as the mentor and the employee they are guiding is known as the mentoree. The mentoree should be able to discuss their progress and problems with their mentor.

One of the major benefits of on-the-job training is the fact that training takes places within the workplace. Employees are undergoing their training while carrying out their day-to-day duties. This means that the training is less disruptive to productivity. The cost of this type of training is often much cheaper than off-the-job training.

There are some disadvantages to this method of training:

- Employees might not take it very seriously as they are still carrying out their normal duties.

- If a fellow colleague is delivering the training, they might also be teaching bad habits to the employee. The person delivering the training may not have received any formal training on how to become a trainer, and therefore their methods could be less effective.

- Training is easily interrupted when being undertaken within the workplace. There may be other distractions which make the learning environment quite difficult.

Off-the-job training

This is training that is provided away from the employee's usual place of work. Employees will not be undertaking their usual duties and therefore can give the training their full attention. Off-the-job training may take place on the same site or off site. The training might still be run by

Off-the-job training

employees of the business, or an external training agency hired by the business.

An advantage of this type of training is that the employee may feel more receptive to the training as they have been removed from their normal working environment. It may give them a chance to discuss ideas with employees from the business or employees from another organisation. This can reinforce the training they are receiving. If they are working with other employees from the same company, it also allows them to bond and become more cohesive as a team.

A disadvantage to off-the-job training is the actual cost. It can be very expensive to hire external trainers. There is also the cost of lost productivity. While the employee is being trained, they are not at their desk doing their job. The actual benefits of the training must be weighed against the negatives, to establish whether the investment will provide a positive return.

Different training timescales

Another consideration when planning a training programme is how long the training should last. One consideration will be the type of training that is to be delivered. A one-off training session requires the trainee to absorb all the information on the day of the training. This might be quite difficult, and some aspects of the course may be forgotten when they return to their place of work.

Training spread over a longer period of time allows the trainee to go back to work and put their new-found knowledge and skills to good use. If they are going to return to training later, it also enables them to ask questions about difficult areas. The disadvantage of ongoing training is the need for an employee to be away from their job role for longer periods of time. Again, the likely gain has to be weighed against the overall costs of the course and loss of productivity.

Costs incurred by training

The idea of costs has already been discussed, so in summary the costs of on-the-job training include the following:

- The employee will be less productive throughout the training period.
- If the trainer is a fellow colleague, they will not be doing their job while training the new employee; further loss of productivity.
- The training may disrupt other members of staff and reduce overall productivity within the department.

The costs of off-the-job training include the following:

- The potential costs of the course; external training courses are often expensive.
- Possible travel expenses of employees.
- Loss of productivity while the employee is on the training course.
- Other members of staff becoming resentful that they have not been sent on a course, and therefore becoming less efficient.
- Will the employee learn enough to increase their efficiency and ultimately cover the cost of the investment in the training?

If training is ongoing, the costs will increase as the employee is away from their workstation for longer periods of time.

Activity

Portfolio building

Within task 5 of the controlled assessment, you are required to produce a suitable training programme to equip you with the skills and competencies needed for a more supervisory job role.

In the last portfolio building exercise you identified the skills and competencies you would need to undertake the role of office supervisor. Referring to this list, use the Internet to investigate a number of courses that could offer you training in these skills and competencies. Using this research, devise your own training programme to meet your identified needs.

You may find the following websites of interest:

Learn Direct: http://www.learndirect.co.uk/browse/

Welcome Host delivers customer service training: http://www.welcometoexcellence.co.uk/

A private company offering a range of different courses: http://www.businesstrainingworks.com/Steps/Step%20Two.html

Summary

- Promoting an existing employee can prove motivational as the employee feels valued by the business. It means the employee is familiar with the business and has a good employment record. Internal recruitment is often cheaper than external recruitment
- On the job training is training that is undertaken while the employee carries out their regular duties.
- Off the job training is conducted away from the employee's regular work station.
- Training can be expensive with many costs to be considered.

Chapter 33
> Effective research

This section was covered fully within Unit 2, Chapter 12, Understanding the market.

Appendix 1

➔ Blank documents

Purchase order

Gardeners' Paradise

12–16 Long Lane
Wellington
Somerset TA43 78Y

[a] VAT Reg No 542/18956/43

Telephone: 01823 962369

Website: www.gardenersparadise.co.uk   email orders@gardenersparadise.co.uk

PURCHASE ORDER

To: [b] Supplier No:
                                                     [c] Order No:
                                                     [d] Date:

Please supply:

Quantity	Description	Item Code	Unit price

Signed [e]   ....

Date

Delivery note

EASY LAWN LTD

VAT Reg No

Unit 89, Eden End Industrial Estate, Exeter EX37 8PY
Telephone:
Website: email

DELIVERY NOTE

To: Date:

                                                                                             Delivery Note No:

[a]

Your order No	Customer Account No	Despatch date	Invoice No [b]	Delivery Method

Item Code	Quantity	Description

Received in good condition (please comment here)..

Signed .... Date ....

Top copy Customer   Blue copy Carrier   Yellow copy Easy Lawn Ltd

Goods Received Note

Gardeners' Paradise
GOODS RECEIVED NOTE

Supplier:

GRN No:
GRN Date:
Delivery Note No:
Delivery Note date:

Supplier A/c No: **Purchase Order No:**

Carrier: DHL Checked by

Item code	Quantity ordered	Quantity delivered	Description	If damaged please record details

White copy – stores department   Yellow copy – accounts department

Purchase Invoice

EASY LAWN LTD

VAT Reg No

Unit 89, Eden End Industrial Estate
Exeter
EX37 8PY

Telephone:
Website:
email:

INVOICE

To: Date:

Your Order No	Customer account no	Dispatch No	Invoice No

Item code	Quantity	Description	Unit price £	Net Price £
			Total	
Terms: 30 days net				
E & OE			VAT 15%	
			Total due	

Credit note

EASY LAWN LTD

VAT Reg No

Unit 89
Eden End Industrial Estate
Exeter
EX37 8PY

Website:

Telephone:

email:

CREDIT NOTE

To:

Customer account no	Date/tax point	Invoice No	Credit note No

Item code	Quantity	Description	Unit price £	Net price £
			Total	

Terms: 30 days net
E & OE

VAT 15%
Total refund

Reason for return:..

Statement of Account

EASY LAWN LTD

VAT Reg No

Unit 89
Eden End Industrial Estate
Exeter
EX37 8PY

Website:

Telephone: email:

STATEMENT OF ACCOUNT

To:

Customer A/c No:
Credit Limit;
Date

Date	Details	Debit (£)	Credit (£)	Balance (£)

Amount now due

REMITTANCE ADVICE

From: Customer a/c No:

Date of statement:

Amount enclosed..

Your reference date of payment..

All cheques made payable to Easy Lawn Ltd

Index

accountants 3
accounts 18
   balance sheet 18, 161–3
   charities 7–8
   profit and loss account 18, 159–61
   Registrar of Companies 5
action planning 61–3
   examples of headings 63–4
   reflection and review 112
administration and ICT 19, 175
   impact of ICT 179
   interdependence of functional areas 137–9
   record-keeping systems 178–9
   roles and responsibilities 175
   telephone messages 176–7
   welcoming visitors 177–8
advertising 97
   Advertising Standards Authority 171–3
   assessment of effectiveness 173
   cinema 100–1, 107–8
   leaflets and flyers 103–4, 109–10
   magazines 102, 108
   national and local press 101–2, 108–9
   outdoor 102–3, 109
   radio 100, 107
   television 98–9, 107
   under-represented racial groups 212–13
after-sales service 79–80
aims of businesses 22–3
animal welfare 42–3, 85
Annual General Meeting (AGM) 5, 122, 123
appraisals 35–6, 193
arithmetic mean 90
articles of association 5
auctioneers 3

BACS (banks automated clearing system) 145, 154, 159
balance sheet 18, 161–3
banks 14, 15
   Bank of England: Monetary Policy Committee (MPC) 55, 56, 57

bank transfers 145, 154, 159
batch production 185
bibliography 113
billboards 103, 109
board of directors 123–4, 125
bonus payments 24
branded goods 78
break even 166–8
buses 103, 109
business organisation *see* organisation
business rates 13–14
business start-up
   activity, types of 10–11
   capital 2, 3, 4–5, 18
   reasons 10
business-to-business e-commerce 38–9
business-to-individual e-commerce 39

capital 162
   partnerships 3
   private limited companies 4–5
   public limited companies 5–6
   sole traders 2
   start-up 2, 3, 4–5, 18
capital goods 11
cash payment 144, 154–5
cash tills and shortages 209–10
cash-flow forecasts 163–6
cell production 186–7
Certificate of Incorporation 5
chairman 122, 125
changes
   in business environment 42
   consequences of not making 44–5
   in customer demands 42–3
   employees dealing with 33
   to existing business practices 43–4
charities 7–8
charts, graphs and tables 91
   break-even chart/graph 167–8
cheques 144–5, 153–4, 159
chief executive 122, 125

Index

cinemas
   advertising in 100–1, 107–8
   direct and indirect competition 86
citing references in text 113
closed questions 69
coaching 224
communication, forms of 127
   ICT 133–5
   oral 127–9
   written 129–33
companies
   advantages and disadvantages of limited 6
   private limited (Ltds) 4–5, 121–2
   public limited (plcs) 5–6, 122
competition 84
   consequences of ignoring 88
   direct or indirect 86–7
   market data 85–6
   market share 84–5, 88
   monitoring competitors' actions 86–7
   surveys 86
   ways to stay competitive 87
construction 10, 11
consumer goods 11
consumer price index (CPI) 52, 57
contract of employment 34
   induction process 219
   statement of terms and conditions 208–9
cost plus pricing 95
costs
   promotional campaigns 107–10
   training 225
creativity and innovation 32–3, 87
credit cards 155
credit crunch 14, 43, 95
credit notes 151, 157–8
credit sales 17
creditors 17, 162
current assets 161
current liabilities 162
curriculum vitae (CV) 197–8
customer(s)
   after-sales service 79–80
   changing demands of 42–3
   complaints 181–2
   databases 38
   legislation protecting 80
      Sale of Goods Act 1979 (as amended) 81–2

      Trade Descriptions Act 1968 80–1
   market segmentation 72–5
   needs 75–7, 88, 180, 181
   poor service, impact of 83–4
   power 76–80
   pre-sales service 79
   price and quality 78
   satisfaction 22, 82–3, 180
   service department 180–3
      interdependence of functional areas 137–9
   stakeholders 26–7
   surveys 82, 86
   value for money 79

databases 37, 38, 176
debit cards 155
debtors 161
delivery notes 147–8, 155
demographics 85
desk/secondary research 66
   presentation of data 89–92
desktop publishing 37
directors 123–4, 125
dis-economies of scale 6
Disability Discrimination Act 1995 213, 215
discrimination
   direct and indirect 211, 212
   disabilities 213, 215
   Equality and Human Rights Commission 213–14
   race 212–13
   sex 211–12
distribution methods
   leaflets 104, 109
   products 87, 95–6
dividends 5, 23
division of labour 4
drawings 162

e-commerce 37, 38–9, 40
economic factors
   exchange rates 15, 53–4
   inflation 52–3, 56, 57
   interest rates 54–7, 155
economy, national 14–15, 42, 85–6
   risk-taking in a downturn 45
economy pricing 94
efficiency 19
email 37, 38, 40, 134–5

Index

emergency procedures 182
employees
   appraisals 35–6, 193
   bonus payments 24
   dismissal, reasons for 210
   enterprise 32–3
   expectations 34
   flexible working practices 32
   good working relationship between employer and 35–6
   job roles 121–6
   job rotation 33
   legal framework *see* employment legislation
   maternity rights 210
   minimum wage 13, 28
   notice periods 210
   PAYE and National Insurance 13, 141–2
   payslips 142–3, 209
   pension contributions 142, 209
   promotion ladder 118, 222
   recruitment *see* recruitment process
   reward schemes 35
   stakeholders 27, 29, 30
   student loans, repayments of 142
   Sunday working 210
   suspension from work 210
   terms and conditions 208–9
   time off 210
   training *see* training
   wages and salaries 140–5, 209–10
employers
   duty of care 210, 218
   expect from employees 34
   good working relationship between employees and 35–6
   legal framework *see* employment legislation
   stakeholders 27, 29, 30
employment legislation 35, 182, 208
   Disability Discrimination Act 1995 213, 215
   Employment Rights Act 1996 208–11
   Equality and Human Rights Commission 213–14
   Health and Safety at Work Act 1974 194–5, 214–17
   Race Relations Act 1976 212–13
   Sex Discrimination Act 1975 211–12
enterprise 32–3
environment 22
   sustainability 48–9, 50

equal opportunities 34, 201
   disabilities 213, 215
   Equality and Human Rights Commission 213–14
   gender and marital status 211–12
   race, colour, nationality and ethnic/national origin 212–13
estate agents 3
estate managers 3
ethics
   business aim: ethically responsible 22
   consequences of unethical trading 48
   higher-welfare chicken 42–3, 85
   meaning of 47
   operating in ethical manner 47–8
exchange rates 15, 53–4
external environment, changes in
   customer demands 42–3
   economy 14–15, 42
   impact on business activities 11–12
   new competitor 12–13
   regulations 13–14
extractive industries 10, 11

farming 42–3, 44
field/primary research 65–6
   presentation of data 89–92
finance 17–18
   balance sheets 18, 161–3
   break even 166–8
   cash-flow forecast 163–6
   credit notes 151, 157–8
   delivery notes 147–8, 155
   goods received notes 148, 149, 155
   ICT, use of 168–9
   importance of checking documents 155–9
   interdependence of functional areas 19, 137–9
   invoices 149–50, 155–7
   payment methods
      goods 153–5, 159
      wages and salaries 143–5
   profit and loss account 18, 159–61
   purchase orders 145–6, 155
   remittance advices 153, 158–9
   sales and purchase documentation 145–59
   statements of account 152–3, 158
   wages and salaries 140–5, 209–10
financiers 28
fixed assets 159, 161

Index

flexible working practices 32
flow production 185–6
flyers and leaflets 103–4, 109–10
focus groups 65
franchises 7
functional areas 17, 118, 119
   administration/ICT *see* administration and ICT
   finance *see* finance
   human resources *see* human resources
   inefficient operation of 19–20
   interdependence of 137–9
   marketing *see* marketing and sales
   operations *see* production department

goods received notes 148, 149, 155
government 28, 30
   statistics 66
graphs, tables and charts 91
   break-even chart/graph 167–8
gross profit 159
growth
   aim of businesses 22, 23
   example of business 15
   profit versus 23

harassment 211, 212
health and safety 18, 28, 30, 123, 182
   employee and employer expectations 34, 195, 210, 215–16, 219–20
   Health and Safety at Work Act 1974 194–5, 214–17
   induction of new employees 218, 219–20, 221
helplines 80
holidays in UK 57
housing market 56
human resources 18, 191
   databases 38
   labour turnover 192–3, 219
   procedures and legislation 193–5
   recruitment *see* recruitment process
   safe working environment 194–5
   staff retention 192–3
   training *see* training
   see also employment legislation; health and safety
hybrid cars 85

ICT 133–5
   administration/ICT functional area 19, 179
   electronic filing systems 178–9
   roles and responsibilities 175
   voice mail 176
   different types of 37
   financial documents, production of 168–9
   purpose of ICT in business activities 38
   upgrades: potential benefits/drawbacks 39–40
   use of ICT in economic activities 38–9
income tax 13, 141
incorporation 5
individual-to-individual e-commerce 39
induction 218–21
industrial tribunals 194, 209
inflation 52–3
   interest rates and 56, 57
innovation 32–3, 87
insurance brokers 3
insurance, employers' liability 216
intention to buy scales 69
interest rates 54–7
   credit cards 155
Internet 32, 37, 40
   banking 154
   'checkout' pages 87
   customer information 79
   direct selling 96
   helplines 80
   market research 66
   newspaper advertising 108
   radio advertising 100
   sourcing work 113
interviews 202–7
invoices 149–50, 155–7

job production 184
job roles 121–5
   skills, qualifications and personal qualities 125–6
job rotation 33
job shadowing 194, 221, 223

labour *see* employees
labour, division of 4
labour turnover 192–3, 219
land agents 3
leaflets and flyers 103–4, 109–10
legislation 35, 123, 182, 193–4
   Disability Discrimination Act 1995 213, 215
   Employment Rights Act 1996 208–11

Index

Equality and Human Rights Commission 213–14
Health and Safety at Work Act 1974 194–5, 214–17
Race Relations Act 1976 212–13
Sale of Goods Act 1979 (as amended) 81–2
Sex Discrimination Act 1975 211–12
Trade Descriptions Act 1968 80–1
letters 130–1
licences, drinks 13
Likert scales 69
limited liability
   companies 4–6, 121–2
   partners 3
local community 28, 29
   commercial radio 100
   public relations 105
long term liabilities 162
long-term versus short-term 23
loss leaders 87
loyalty cards 83, 98

magazines 102, 108
managers 124, 126
managing director 122, 125
manufacturing 10, 11
   distribution 96
market research 65
   improving business performance 170–1
   presentation of data 89–92
   pricing strategy 95
   primary (field) research 65–6
   questionnaire design 68–9
   sampling methods 67–8
   secondary (desk) research 66
   target market 67
marketing mix 93
   place (channels of distribution) 87, 95–6
   price 87, 94–5
   product 93–4
   promotion *see* promotion
marketing and sales 18, 23, 170
   interdependence of functional areas 19, 137–9
   market data 85–6
   market research *see* market research
   market segmentation 72–5
   market share 84–5, 88
   mix *see* marketing mix
maternity rights 210

matrix structure 119
mean, arithmetic 90
median 91
meetings 128
memorandum of association 5
memorandums 129
mentoring 224
minimum wage 13, 28
mission statements 24
mobile phone industry 42, 45
mobile phones 128
mode 91
money-off coupons 106
moral values *see* ethics
motivation: employees 33, 218
mystery shoppers 82–3

national economy 14–15, 42, 85–6
   risk-taking in a downturn 45
National Insurance 13, 141–2
net profit 18, 159
network, computer 37
newsletters, internal 133
newspapers 66, 101–2, 108–9
non-executive directors 123
not-for-profit organisations 7–8
notice periods 210
notices, internal 132

objectives of businesses 23–4
open questions 68–9
operations *see* production department
operatives 125
organisation 119
   flat structure 117
   functions *see* functional areas
   hierarchical structure 118–19
   matrix structure 119
outsourcing and ethical operations 47–8
ownership of businesses
   advantages and disadvantages of limited companies 6
   changes in 43–4
   partnerships 3–4
   private limited companies (Ltds) 4–5, 121–2
   public limited companies (plcs) 5–6, 122
   sole traders 2–3

Index

paperless office 40
Pareto effect 74
partnerships 3–4
   incorporation 33
payment methods
   goods 153–5, 159
   wages and salaries 143–5
Paypal 39
payslips 142–3, 209
penetration pricing 94
pensions 142, 209
percentages 90
personal computers (PCs) 37
plagiarism 113
point of sale promotion 106
pollution 23
portfolio tips 62, 66, 67, 75, 89, 106, 111, 217, 221
posters 103
PowerPoint 37, 135
pre-sales service 79
premium pricing 87, 94
presentation of data 89
   graphs, tables and charts 91, 167–8
   short summaries 92
   written reports 89–91
pressure groups 28, 30
price(s)
   food 85
   quality and 78
   strategies 87, 94–5
primary (field) research 65–6
   presentation of data 89–92
primary industry 10, 11
   change in activity 44
private limited companies (Ltds) 4–5, 121–2
   advantages and disadvantages of limited companies 6
product bundle pricing 95
production department 18–19, 23, 184
   batch production 185
   cell production 186–7
   choice of production method 187–8
   flow production 185–6
   interdependence of functional areas 19–20, 137–9
   job production 184
products 93–4
profit and loss account 18, 159–61

profits
   aim of businesses 22
   companies 5
   growth versus 23
   net profit 18, 159
   partnerships and sharing of 4
promotion 18, 97–8
   Advertising Standards Agency 171–3
   assessment of effectiveness 173
   cinema 100–1, 107–8
   competitions 105
   costs 107–10
   leaflets and flyers 103–4, 109–10
   magazines 102, 108
   money-off coupons 106
   national and local press 101–2, 108–9
   outdoor advertising 102–3, 109
   point of sale 106
   public relations 105–6
   radio 100, 107
   sales promotions 104
   sponsorships 105
   staying competitive 87
   supermarkets 85
   television 98–9
promotional pricing 95
prospectus 6
psychological pricing 95
public limited companies (plcs) 5–6, 122
public relations 105–6
purchase orders 145–6, 155
purchases 159

quality control 18
quality and price 78
questionnaire design 68–9

Race Relations Act 1976 212–13
rank order scales 69
rates 13–14
record-keeping systems 178–9
recruitment process 191–2, 196
   accurate completion of documents 200–1
   application forms 196–7
   curriculum vitae 197–8
   impact of legislation
      employment rights 210–11
      equal opportunities 211–13, 214

Index

health and safety 216–17
   under-represented racial groups 212–13
letters of application 198–9
selection process 202
   informing applicants of outcome 207–8
   interview 202–7
   shortlisting 202
reflection and review 112
regional offices 119
Registrar of Companies 5
remittance advices 153, 158–9
repeat customers 83, 84
reports, written 89–91
retail price index (RPI) 52
retailers 96, 209–10
   supermarkets 42–3, 85, 96
reward schemes 35
risks
   changing business practices 43–4
   consequences of not taking 44–5
   enterprise 32–3
   health and safety: risk assessment and management 216
   uncertainty 42

Sale of Goods Act 1979 (as amended) 81–2
sales revenue 159
sampling methods 67–8
second-hand sales 82
secondary (desk) research 66
   presentation of data 89–92
secondary industry 10, 11
security systems 195
selection process *see under* recruitment process
self-employment and tax 141
services 10, 11
Sex Discrimination Act 1975 211–12
shareholders 4–5, 121–2
   stakeholders 27–8, 29, 30
short-term versus long-term 23
skimming, price 94
sleeping partners 3
small and medium sized enterprises (SMEs)
   advertising 99, 102
   automated production 188
   obstacles to success 12, 13
SMART objectives 23
social responsibility 22, 23

sole traders 2–3, 11, 43, 117
solicitors 3
sourcing work 113
specialisation 117, 118
sponsorships 105
spreadsheets 37, 38, 176
stakeholders 26–8
   conflict between different groups 29–30
   consequences of not listening to 30
start-up capital
   balance sheet 18
   partnerships 3
   private limited companies 4–5
   sole traders 2
statements of account 152–3, 158
statistical techniques 90–1
stock 161
   deficiencies 210
stock control 38
   ICT facility 39
   stationery 175
Stock Exchange members 3
student loans 142
suggestion schemes 33
summaries, short 92
Sunday working 210
supermarkets 42–3, 85, 96
supervisors 124–5, 126
suppliers 17
   ethical operations 47–8
   stakeholders 27, 29, 30
surveyors 3
surveys, customer 82, 86
suspension from work 210
sustainability 48–9, 50

target market 67
   market segmentation 72–5
taxation 13
   income tax 13, 141
   National Insurance 13, 141–2
   payslip details 143
   VAT 13, 14, 57
taxis 103, 109
technology
   production methods 187–8
   see also ICT
telephone 128–9

Index

   messages 176–7
tertiary industry 10, 11
toxic loans 14
Trade Descriptions Act 1968 80–1
trade unions 18, 28
   ethical business practices 48
   time off to carry out duties 210
training 19–20
   appraisal system 36, 193
   costs 225
   new employees 193, 194, 218–21
   timescales 224–5
   types of 193, 194, 223–4

uncertainty 42
unemployment 85
   labour turnover 193
unlimited liability
   partnerships 3
   sole traders 2

value for money 79
VAT 13, 14, 57
victimisation 212
visitors, welcoming 177–8
voluntary not-for-profit organisations 7–8

wages and salaries 140–5
   protection of wages: guaranteed payment 209–10
websites *see* Internet
wholesalers 96
women
   antenatal care 210
   discrimination 211
   maternity rights 210
wordprocessing 37, 38
working environment 36
   see also health and safety
WorldPay 39